Wet P

Stories from my Career
as a
Commercial Diver

by

sam humphrey

Illustrated by

Joel Rabe

I

WET PAY

Stories from my Career as a Commercial Diver

sam humphrey

Joel Rabe

ISBN-13: 978-1-959239-00-0
Library of Congress Control Number: 2022915406

Cover design by: samuel c humphrey
www.sidecarsam.com
Cover Photo credits to Cindy Lou Humphrey

Title Page and Chapter Illustrations by Joel Rabe
Joel Rabe retains all rights to his work.

First Edition

Published by Inspirit Alliance
Printed in the United States of America

*This book is dedicated to
my friend and cohort Tim Nordeen
and all the other divers who have died
in the performance of their jobs
May They All Rest In Peace
I hope they are all sharing a beer with Poseiden*

CONTENTS

INTRODUCTION

Let me introduce myself. I am sam humphrey. I was in the Commercial Dive Industry for over thirty years. I was forced into retirement by a catastrophic Motorcycle accident which left me a Paraplegic, but that is a different story for another time. This is not an Autobiography and will not include events in my life that don't pertain to Diving, unless they do somehow.

This book includes only my stories and accounts of events that either happened to me personally or that I viewed in real life with my own two eyes. I will not be using actual names of the other people in my stories. Except for one; that of my dive instructor - Maurice Talbot. If one or more of my stories sounds familiar and you think you recognize it, but not the people in it – that is why. Also, if you recognize parts of a story or a similar story but don't remember it the same way I tell it, just remember that there are three sides to every story; Yours, Mine, and the Truth. I will not be telling other people's stories nor stories that I have heard through the Grapevine, at the Bar, or where ever. You do know the difference between a Sea Story and a Fairytale, don't you? One starts out "Once upon a time..." and the other starts out "This is a No-Shitter!"

Commercial Divers are a Rough and Tumble bunch of Blue-Collar Workers. We work hard, long hours for weeks or months at a time. We play hard, drink hard and give each other a hard time most of the time. We are Politically Incorrect. We use Foul Language a LOT. We are generally considered Rude, Crude, Lewd, and Socially Unacceptable (when we are on the job). When we are not on the job, such as at home or with our families, etc., we can be very gentle, sweet people. Unless too many of us get together and consume too much alcohol. At that point we may devolve into our natural work selves.

This collection of stories will include foul language, politically incorrect thoughts and statements, as well as rude, crude, and lewd parts. If you are easily offended, I recommend that you quit reading right here and return this book to where it came from, or throw it in the trash if that makes you feel better. Even though I oppose banning books of any sort, you have my permission to burn this one if it bothers you that much. Otherwise, I hope you enjoy what you are about to read as a whole, or at least parts of it and find it entertaining.

Thank you,

sam humphrey

PREFACE

I was born in Moscow, Idaho in nineteen-sixty-one. I am the first-born child and only son. I have three sisters, two born in Germany and the youngest born in Japan. In nineteen-sixty-six we moved to Spokane, Washington so we could be close to the Grandparents – all of whom lived in Idaho. We had cousins in Montana, Idaho, Nevada, California, Arizona, Illinois, and Pennsylvania. So, we travelled a fair amount as I grew up.

I was partly raised by the Television. My favorite shows were Mutual of Omaha's Wild Kingdom, Wonderful World of Disney, Sea Hunt, Voyage to the Bottom of the Sea, Flipper, Twilight Zone, National Geographic Specials, any Jacques Cousteau Special, and Star Trek. I loved the Ocean and anything to do with it.

I couldn't wait to get SCUBA diving and in nineteen-seventy-eight my best friend and I took a SCUBA class in Bellevue, Washington. We dove as much as we could after that. I loved being under the water. I decided that if there was a way for me to make a living under water, that is what I wanted to do. Being raised inland in the mountains, I had no idea about Commercial Diving as a career and didn't know there were any schools specifically for Commercial Diving. Basically, I didn't know anything about it other than what I had seen in movies like The Wake of the Red Witch, Reap the Wild Wind, or Beneath the Twelve-Mile Reef.

I knew about the U.S. Navy's Man in the Sea projects and the Tektite I and Tektite II projects. I figured the best way to become a diver was to join Uncle Sam's Navy and that is just what I did right after high school graduation. I spent four years in the Navy and never became a Diver. I did, however, learn about Commercial Dive Schools and discovered that there were two of them in the Seattle area. Actually, my best friend and SCUBA buddy from high school informed me about them. As soon as I got out of the Navy, I applied to the Highline Community College program of Underseas Technology. And this is where my Commercial Dive Career really begins.

aqua omnia praebet

sine aqua

nihil habemus

A SCHOOL OF FISH
at Least We Drink Like Fish!
Chapter one

I was released from the U.S. Navy in the Spring of nineteen-eighty-three and had decided I would be a Commercial Diver. Most Commercial Dive Schools are fairly expensive. I was one of the Unfortunates who joined the U.S. Military after President Carter cut lots of VA benefits – like the G.I. Bill, so I didn't get any financial help for school from that and couldn't afford most Commercial Dive Schools. Luckily for me there were a couple Community Colleges that had Equivalent Programs. I think Florida Institute of Technology had one and Highline Community College in Midway, Washington had another. I could afford those. Since my family was in Spokane at the time, I decided to go to Highline because I qualified for Resident Status which was considerably less expensive than Out of State Tuition. I went right over to the College so I could apply for the Two Year (Seven Quarter) program called Underseas Technology and, hopefully, I would be able to start in September.

The first step in getting into the program was an interview with the Director of the program. All prospective students in the Underseas Technology program had to have an interview with him and be approved, or not, to sign up for the program. If you were accepted into the program, you would have to be SCUBA certified before the Fall classes started. Once you started the first quarter you then had to pass a physical given by a Sports Doctor and a physical exercise test based on the USN Diver's test, including swimming sixteen laps in the College pool, swimming a mile in Puget Sound, and then have a physical completed by the Highline College's Nursing program. You also had to log at least ten SCUBA dives each quarter of the first year. That worked out to a dive each week.

I set up a meeting with the Director of the program, Maurice Talbot, in June. He taught the majority of the second-year classes, starting with the Summer Quarter which was seven weeks of diving the Mark V (five - Roman numeral) Heavy Gear. Classes for that were five days a week, eight hours a day, all taking place on the Redondo Pier. I only mention Maurice because he is the father of my commercial dive career and quite an influential man in starting the careers of his students. I have a lot of respect for him and think he deserves recognition for the many good divers he sent into the industry. He is the only real person I will name in this narrative.

Anyway, I set up the appointment. June was the earliest I could get. By the time my appointment rolled around, I had been out of the Navy for three months. My hair grows fast and I had not gotten a haircut since getting out – some sort of rebellion against authority – I had a small Afro thing going on. I also had my left ear pierced, after crossing the Equator while I was in the Navy, and was wearing a silver skull in that ear. It was not a small skull. I only mention this because at that time, piercings were not a common thing. Mostly the only men with pierced ears were Sailors and Homosexuals. The message on the street

3

was that if you were Gay, you had your Right Ear pierced, and if you were straight, it was your Left Ear. But in the late seventies and early eighties so many homosexuals were getting beat up that they were getting their Left ears pierced rather than their Right. Also, there was a mentality of straight tough guys on the street who would get their Right Ear pierced just to get into fights. So, really, which Ear you had pierced didn't mean anything other than a middle finger in the face of authority, but most straight people figured a pierced ear – no matter which one – meant you were gay.

I definitely was not gay, although I am generally a very happy person. I was also tattooed, again only common with Sailors and Cons at this time in U.S. history. I wasn't thinking "Job Interview" when I showed up for my interview, although that is what it really was. I was dressed in faded jeans, purple Converse High-tops, and a t-shirt with a half-naked SCUBA diver and the phrase "Gone Down Lately?" on it. Give me a break, I was only twenty-two and headed for college! The t-shirt was a gift from my dad, he didn't realize the sexual innuendo of the phrase until a friend of his said something about it. My poor dad, I think I was pretty hard on his heart at the time.

I knocked on Mr. Talbot's office door. A gruff voice sounded "Come in" so I entered. I didn't really know what to expect, but the man I saw was a shorter, olive-skinned man. He was clean cut with silver hair and a silver-grey Van Dyke. He was wearing a black t-shirt, new blue jeans and boat shoes. His forearms each had a big shark tattoo and some other nautical stuff. On his right wrist was a heavy gold chain bracelet and on his left was a huge Rolex Dive Watch. He was also wearing a necklace of gold anchor-style chain. "Alright," I thought, "this guy looks cool." When he saw me, his eyes widened a bit, but he didn't say anything right off the bat. Did I mention that my hair is pretty curly so I was sporting a decent sized blondish Afro? I introduced myself, shook his hand, said it was nice to meet him, and stated that I was looking forward to getting into the Dive program.

"We'll see about that," he said with a firm handshake. Should I have been nervous? I don't know. I wasn't though. He looked me up and down, then asked how I planned on getting all that hair into a Dive Hat. I told him I would get it cut if need be. He smiled. Next, he asked "What does that skull in your ear mean?"

I looked him straight in the eye and responded "It means I'm a Bad-Ass Motherfucker." I tried to keep a straight face, but that only lasted a few seconds before I let out a laugh. His smile grew and he laughed a little. He had me sit down and then started asking me questions and filling out a form. He wanted to know where I was from, how old I was, what my work experience was, what some of my hobbies were, and finally, why I wanted to be a Diver. I told him that I loved being under the water and if I could, I would have gills. He asked what I thought Commercial Divers did. I responded that I didn't really know, but thought that some worked with Aquatic Animals, some maybe worked in Fish Farms, Oyster Beds, or something like that. Others might do Underwater Photography. Maybe others fixed, repaired, or replaced things that broke underwater. I suppose some salvaged ships and sunken treasure. He grimaced.

"Commercial Divers don't play with animals in the water," he stated, "maybe you should go into Marine Biology instead if you want to watch crabs fuck." I smiled and nodded my head. "What about money?" he asked.

"Money?" I questioned.

"Yes, MONEY" he responded. "Do you think you are going to get rich being a Diver? Buy fast, cool cars? Have beautiful women hanging all over you? Is that what you are after?"

"Hmm, I hadn't really thought about the pay," I answered. "I prefer Motorcycles rather than cars. I like pretty girls, but

I don't think I will ever have them hanging all over me, no matter what I do."

He laughed. "Good," he said. "You won't get rich. You'll get a girl, maybe, but you'll lose her. Shit, you probably won't even last three years in the Dive industry. We accept forty-two students at the beginning of each class. At the end of the first year, only the top twenty-six will get passed on to the Summer Quarter and second year. Of those twenty-six that graduate, only thirteen will last through the first year of work. Only six of those will last the second year. They won't be Divers; they will only be Tenders. After five years, maybe three from that class will still be in the field. After ten years, only one will be left. If he is lucky, that one will have a full Dive career. What do you think about that?"

"I will be that one." I stated matter of factly. "I don't care about the money; I want to make my living under water. I don't really care what I do. A little travel would be nice."

He looked at me, wonder in his eyes and stated "Well, the class starting in September is full. I can put you on a waiting list if you like. Many new students drop out in the first year so you might be able to fill in one of those spots if one becomes available, but that is not likely."

"Fine," I replied, "that would be great. I will enroll at the college for the Fall and take the classes required for the first year that are not Dive specific just in case I get lucky. Will you put me on the list for the class starting in the Fall of eighty-four?"

"Yes, I will. You are number thirty-one on that list right here. We will see you next year, if you are still interested."

"Oh, you'll see me before then," I stated. I stood up, thanked him for his time and told him I would see him soon. He smiled, shook my hand again and said good-bye. I walked out the door and headed straight to the registration office. I had the Underseas Technology flyer in my hand and promptly registered for all the non-Dive specific classes on the schedule for that quarter as well as a couple extra classes. I was paying for eighteen credits, I figured I might as well get my money's worth.

*   *   *

I moved to Seattle – Bellevue actually – in July. My SCUBA buddy's mom offered me a room in their house while I was going to college and I took her up on the offer. He was my best friend from high school, his two older brothers and older sister had moved out leaving a couple empty rooms, so it was a great option for me. One of his older brothers offered me a job in the Mexican restaurant he managed, so I was off to a good start.

My classes started in late September and went through mid-June of eighty-four. The guys in the first year of the Dive program were in the classes we had in common, like Math, English, Oceanography, etc. I kept hoping enough of them would drop out for me to be accepted into the program that year, but it didn't happen. I did hang out with some of the guys who had been accepted into the program though. I was pretty good at Math and English so I helped the guys who needed help with those classes. Since this program was through the college and you had earned an Associates in Applied Science (AAS) when you finished, you had to pass all of your classes. Some of the guys were more trade oriented than school oriented and had trouble with the Math or the English. They were my friends and I wanted them to succeed in school, so I helped where I could.

We went SCUBA Diving together about every other week and we drank together a *lot*. Almost every weekend we had Bar-B-Ques or went to bars after the diving. We dove up and down the Washington coast and all around Hood Canal. I had a nineteen-sixty-two Cadillac Ambulance with all the working lights and sirens at the time. It was a perfect vehicle for us. It had enough seats for five people counting me, the driver, and plenty of room for all our SCUBA gear. We were always looking for new places to dive and new bars to check out.

We did have a couple local bars that were our local hangouts and a few of us could be found at one of those bars almost every evening and sometimes even at lunch. Everybody in the class always knew where I was because of the ambulance. It was kind of hard to miss that car where ever it was parked. I had learned to drink in the Navy and was old enough to legally drink in Washington. Only about half the guys in the Dive program were old enough to drink in the bars, so we were actually a pretty small group and became fairly close knit.

Well not enough of the first-year students dropped out for me to get into that class. In fact, this was the first time in a decade that Mr. Talbot had to actually cut students himself to bring the second-year class down to twenty-six. The guys who got cut had the option to be first on the list for the next year's class and a couple of them took that option. It meant that they would have to repeat the first year, but if they really wanted to be a diver that was their choice. Their only other option would be to go to one of the other expensive dive schools. The guys who made the cut had to take the summer class, diving in Mark V gear. I didn't have to take summer school and couldn't take the Mark V class so I just did my own thing that summer. I did spend some time with a couple of the guys from that class with whom I got along really well, one from Billings, Montana became a good friend.

Late September nineteen-eighty-four I was accepted into the Underseas Technology program and finally got to take the first year Dive classes. These included introduction to Commercial Diving and the physical fitness class. If you didn't pass either of those you were automatically dropped and couldn't come back until the following year. Nobody failed. There were

8

forty-two students enrolled in my first-year class – a full group again. I had learned that was the norm. Every year was a full enrollment for the first year but more than half would drop out for one reason or another. We had one girl in our class – only the second or third time that a female had enrolled and been accepted into the Highline Dive program. Mr. Talbot was all for women in the program, there just weren't many interested in it. More than half the students were under twenty years old and were coming in right after high school, or hadn't done anything since graduating high school. Most were from somewhere in Washington. One was a welder from Kansas and another was a carpenter and pot farmer from Alaska. A few of us were older and had some sort of work history. We also liked to drink – a lot. We smoked pot once in a while too. Hell, we were in college! Isn't that what you are supposed to do at that time of your life – experiment a little?

Two of my sisters were now in the Seattle area. One was going to the U of W in the Aerospace Engineering program and the other was actually going to Highline Community College in the Airline Attendant program. We ended up renting a house together in South Seattle and had many house parties involving their friends and my Dive school buds. We also used to hit the bars together fairly often.

One Friday night my sister, who was going to Highline, a couple guys from the Dive class and I went out to one of the local bars in Midway. For some reason I had swapped out my Skull earring for a long dangly gold and ebony earring that my other sister had given me since she lost its partner. We liked this bar because it was small, had several pool tables and a small local crowd. It had a sign out front "Liquor in the front, Poker in the rear" and they really did have poker tables in the back. Anyway, we liked playing pool and drinking. My sister was good at both and could beat most guys at both so the guys really enjoyed her company. We were having a good time and feeling no pain. We were playing teams stars and stripes and my sister and I were one team, while a couple of our friends were the other team. About halfway through this game, I got up to take my shot and a little Native American guy playing pool at another table came over to me and said "You fuckin' faggot, I oughtta rip that thing right out of your ear."

"If you think you're man enough, go ahead and try," I replied with a smile on my face. He was obviously pretty drunk. His two friends came over to see what was going on. I thought "oh great, here we go." My friends got up and came over. I am not a small guy, but I am one of the smaller guys in my bunch of friends. I was about six-foot and two-hundred pounds. One friend was six-foot-four and the other was six-foot-two. The drunk and his friends were all around five-foot-six or seven and maybe a hundred-and-sixty pounds or so. I thought this wasn't going to be pretty and I didn't really want any violence. I don't like fighting and don't really see the point, but when I get to drinking I kind of get a smart mouth and don't keep it shut when maybe I should. All I can say is that it is probably a good thing that most of my friends were bigger than I was.

Okay, back to the situation. The mouthy drunk was coming towards me, his chest all puffed out and his fists closed tight. His two friends got to him and grabbed him by his shoulders. Just about then the bartender came over and asked what was going on. Before I could say anything the friends of the mouthy drunk told the bartender that everything was okay and their friend was just getting a little mouthy. The bartender told them he'd had enough of this guy for the week and that he was now officially eighty-sixed out of the bar. They said okay and took their mouthy friend out of the bar. It looked like they were used to dealing with that guy. We were all relieved and went back to our game and beer. My sister was still sitting at the table with our pitcher of beer on it. Now my sister is short, only five-foot-two. She has blond hair in a Farrah Fawcett 'do and bright blue eyes. She has a Dolly Parton figure and likes to dress nicely and slightly provocatively. She wore her blouse low-cut and form-fitting and her jeans painted on tight. She also wore Converse high-top tennies - bright yellow.

I get back to our table and pick up my glass of beer. I take a big swig and set my glass down, go to grab my pool cue when my sister stands up, grabs my earring, blurts out "I'm man enough!" and yanks the earring right out of my ear. I'm dumbfounded.

"What the Fuuu…" I don't even get to finish the question when my friends burst out laughing. My sister starts laughing and hands me the earring. I can't put it back in because my earlobe is a little torn and bleeding slightly. "What did you do that for?!" I ask.

She just looks at me and smiles. "The devil made me do it." She laughs again and says "Oh, don't be so serious."

"I'm never serious," I smile and take another swig of my beer. I pick up my pool cue and go back to our game. The rest of the night played out normally and we just had a good time drinking and playing pool. My ear healed up in a couple days and I put my Skull back in before school on Monday.

*   *   *

The first year of this Dive program is basically all community college. Only one class per quarter was Dive specific, except for the first quarter which included the Physical Fitness class. That first quarter about fifteen guys dropped out because of the physical activity required. We also had to go through a couple Hyperbaric tests. These tests were run by the second-year divers, overseen by one of the dive instructors down on the Dive Pier at Redondo. The first was breathing a hundred percent Oxygen at sixty feet in a chamber for five minutes. Two of the guys in my class went into a seizure during this event and were dropped from the program because they were more susceptible to Oxygen Toxicity.

The next test was being pressed down to one hundred and sixty-five feet on air and staying there for five minutes. This was to see how susceptible to Nitrogen Narcosis we were and also to give us an idea of what decompression in a Deck Chamber was like. We lost one guy to this event – not by a decision of the instructors, rather just because he didn't like being locked up in the chamber without being able to get out when he wanted. I think he must have been a little claustrophobic. We were also required to have a health screening done by the Highline campus Nurse's office within the first quarter. It didn't make much sense to me because we had to have an actual sports physical completed by a physician with a copy of the results given to Mr. Talbot before we were actually accepted into the program. Whatever, rules were rules, and I wanted to successfully complete the program so I was willing to do whatever was required to make that happen. The health screenings were done by the Nursing students who were enrolled in Highline College's Nursing program, overseen by the resident Nurses at the college. The students would take our blood pressures, temperatures, blood and urine samples, and measure our height and weight. The nursing students were usually cute girls just out of high school who were working towards being LPNs or RNs. They were young and inexperienced. We couldn't all go in at once to have our screenings completed, they took a little time, so we had to make appointments and would be handled two at a time.

I went to my appointment with the youngest guy in our class, he was only seventeen, fresh out of high school, but one hell of a gas welder. He could do magic with that torch. He was from Casper, Wyoming. He and I became pretty good friends. Anyway, we went to our appointment together. We got to the office and had to fill out some paperwork, then wait to be called. Casper got called first and went with the young nursing student into the examination room. He was flirting a little with her and she was flirting back. I waited in the waiting room looking at some SCUBA magazine. After a short while my friend came out all finished with his appointment. He said he was going to head back to the cafeteria if that was okay with me. I told him that was fine with me, no point in him waiting around for nothing.

The nursing student called my name and I followed her back into the examination room. She took my blood pressure and all the other measurements, filling out a form as she went along. Then she took a blood sample. I don't do very well with needles and I have always had issues giving blood from my arms. For some reason when I see a needle my arms turn completely white and all the blood vessels seem to disappear. This flustered the nursing student a little and she asked for advice. The Nurse teacher talked to me a little and decided they could get the sample from my finger tip if it would let enough blood flow. I relaxed and color returned to my arms and the blood flowed freely from my fingertip when it was pricked with the needle. Success. She gave me a hard time for being a big guy afraid of a little needle and I teased her for flirting with my friend. The nursing student ended up dating one of the guys in the second-year class along with a couple of her friends. They became regulars at our parties. All's well that ends well, I suppose.

*   *   *

This first quarter also was when Mr. Talbot would give a speech about his rules for us while we were in the program and also what to expect from Commercial Diving as a career.

His rules were that we were to be committed to the program one hundred percent. He didn't want any slackers. Being committed meant that we wouldn't miss any days without a very good reason. We would do what we were told by the Dive instructors even if we didn't fully agree with it. Safety was a major concern and he wouldn't put up with any skylarking, fighting, or any unsafe behavior. Unsafe behavior included what we did during our free time. He banned several past-times, including sky diving, car racing, motorcycle racing, snow ski racing, or anything else where we had a better than average chance of ending up in the hospital. It wasn't that he was against these things, he just wanted us committed to successfully completing the program and not wasting his time. He also said there would be no tolerance for drug abuse of any kind, of course that ended up meaning as long as you didn't get arrested for it. He was against drug abuse, but we were not tested for it. He also said alcoholism would not be tolerated, but that meant only if it noticeably interfered with your performance at school. I thought it was understandable seeing how full the classes were and how many people wanted in the program.

In his speech about the career, he repeated his talk about how many would still be diving after ten years. Then he asked questions and had us raise our hands for a positive answer. First, who is married? Two hands went up. "You won't last, stand in the back." The two got up and went to the back of the class. "Who is here only for the money?" Three hands went up. "You won't last, stand in the back." He asked a couple more questions but no more hands went up, I guess nobody else wanted to stand in the back. He talked more about the downfalls, hardships, and disappointments of the industry. He talked about how hard it would be on our relationships. He told us that we wouldn't be Divers when we graduated from the program, we would only be Tenders. It would take a minimum of two years and possibly as many as five before we actually broke out and became a Diver. While we were tenders, we would be treated badly, worked hard, and not respected. We would be used and abused and if that bothered us. we should walk out the door right now. He told us that diving was NOT a job; it was only the way one got to the actual job. The "job" was whatever task we had to do while we were under the water.

I had taken most of the first-year classes required my previous year of college, so this year I was free to take lots of electives. Even though we only had to take twelve credits to be full-time, we could take up to eighteen for the same price and I wanted to get my money's worth so I took at least eighteen credits each quarter. One quarter I paid extra to take twenty-one credits because there were a couple classes I wanted to take that were only offered once a year. I took classes in Photography, Marine Biology, Microbiology, Marine Mechanics, Marine Electronics and several others that would apply to a Bachelor's degree in case I would pursue that later on. My dad wasn't real happy that I was going into Commercial Diving. He had done some reading and found out about the dangers, risks, and health issues. He would send me articles about the issues of diving from the science and research magazines as often as he found them. One of the articles showed how dead spots formed in the brain, making it look like Swiss Cheese. He wanted me to get a regular degree and do a more normal job like teaching. He was a Math teacher at Spokane Falls Community College, so was hopeful that his children would have a more white-collar type job rather than a blue-collar job. Anyway, I was preparing myself to have a fallback in case the diving thing didn't work out for me, even though I was positive that I wanted to be a diver.

Mr. Talbot had a deal with Virginia Mason Hospital's Hyperbaric Unit where up to four of his students would work for them as Chamber Operators. To be considered for the job you had to go through another interview with Mr. Talbot explaining why you wanted the job and what made you a good candidate for the job. If you got through that okay, you would then get interviewed by the director of the Hyperbaric Unit and if you did well there you had to go through a performance test on the operation of the deck chamber and the equipment needed to make it functional – basically the compressors and the gas bottles. You had to demonstrate that you knew what each of the alarms meant and how to deal with them. You also had to show that you could fill out the documentation as required. Finally, the job was offered to all the students in the class with preference given to the second-year students.

I wanted that job, because I wanted to learn as much about the dive industry as I could and I thought it would be great experience and look good on my resume'. Luckily for me only two of the second-year students wanted the job which left two spots for my class. I did get one of the spots and it turned out to be a great job. It paid very well – about twice what minimum wage was at the time – and you could sign up for a regular schedule because the Unit was used for treating cancer, gas gangrene, smoke inhalation as well as diving accidents (which happen more often than you would think). I signed up for the on-call part as well, knowing that I could be called in at any time of day or night and was expected to be there with-in half an hour of the call. It ended up being a great experience.

I also got a work study job at the college. The Marine Biology teacher needed an assistant who would be responsible for collecting specimens for her classes and also taking care of the saltwater aquariums in her classes. It was great because it meant that I would be paid to SCUBA dive – my first job as a Commercial Diver! I was stoked. I bought a Nikonos V underwater camera and took lots of photos during my dives. I shared them with the Marine Biology teacher and she paid me for the ones she really liked. That was awesome for me.

The Marine Biology teacher had made a deal with the city of Des Moines to set up an artificial reef north of the Municipal

Fishing Pier. She had some studies going on at the reef site. My job as her assistant meant that I had to monitor her projects and give her regular assessments on the state of the reef and what kind of life was moving in. That was really fantastic for me, because SCUBA diving was not allowed there by order of the City of Des Moines. It was like my own private dive site in Puget Sound. Since SCUBA was always supposed to be done in pairs, I got to bring along a buddy every time I went. Many of my classmates wanted to dive there, so I never had any issues getting a buddy to go with me.

It was a great place to dive, because it was fairly shallow – never deeper than sixty feet. It had good water flow so the visibility was very good. The city had put in a bunch of structures, recommended by the Marine Biology teacher, like tire bundles, unused concrete septic tanks with the holes knocked out, lots of broken concrete water tanks and drain frames. The city had also dumped a bunch of porcelain toilets and sinks in the area – nothing grew on those, so they looked kind of trashy down there. The other structures attracted a huge variety of life. One of the things I had to monitor and take regular measurements of was the growth of Barnacles, Sea Anemones, Sponges and other forms of reef-building life. A huge variety of fish was attracted to the area as well as Octopi, Crabs, Nudibranchs, and the occasional Sea Lion.

My first up close and personal encounter with a Sea Lion happened there. I was diving at that spot with a classmate. Both of us were good and comfortable divers so we kind of did our own thing when we dove there. I would give him my camera so he could go practice its use and I would go collect my samples or record my data, whatever I needed to do. We both used air at about the same rate so when one of us was done, the other would be done. We usually got back to the beach within two or three minutes of each other. So, this time I was collecting hermit crabs for the teacher to use in her class and my buddy was off taking photos. Hermit crabs are fairly small so I had to skim the bottom keeping a sharp eye out and picking them up when I found them. I needed at least sixty of them. I was swimming about a foot off the bottom. It was a nice sunny day and the water was pretty clear. My depth was only about twenty feet so the light was very good. I could see my shadow on the bottom as I skimmed along.

After a while as I was moving slowly along, I saw another shadow move around mine. It was about six feet long and two feet wide. Now remember divers like to give each other a hard time whenever given the chance so I figured my friend had used all the film and was getting bored. I was thinking he is planning on swimming up behind me without me knowing and he would grab me to scare the crap out of me. I thought, ha, I'll get him instead. So as soon as the shadow was right over me, I dropped my goody-bag and rolled over quickly preparing to grab him.

To my shock and surprise, it was a Sea Lion right over me. They are not really scary animals, but when that is not what you expect it is quite startling. I think I yelled; I might have even peed my wetsuit (not that big a deal). I immediately got myself in an upright position and headed to the surface. I kept facing the Sea Lion expecting some kind of attack, but none came. The Lion just looked me up and down a couple times then swam away. Even though it gave me a fright it ended up being a very memorable experience.

To let you know why it was a scary experience was that a few months earlier one of my fellow dive students had been diving by himself off the Redondo pier on a Saturday. He was in the water alone, but he had a spotter on the tourist pier so he thought he'd be okay. The water was only fifteen feet or so where he was diving. A group of Sea Lions came swimming into the area and as they are curious animals, they swam right towards him. They were swimming all around him and scared him, I am sure. He surfaced and sank several times. His regulator had come out of his mouth and he couldn't get his weight belt off. He ended up drowning and it was a very sad situation for us all. Most of us had only known him a couple of months, but it still hits you pretty hard. It did send home the message that you always needed to be careful and prepared when you went diving and you should always have a dive buddy. It was a sobering time.

*   *   *

I was SCUBA diving quite a bit that year. I really enjoyed it and I now had access to all the dive buddies I could want. We were required to log at least ten dives per quarter our first year. I averaged more like two or three dives per week. One of the second-year students had a job at the local SCUBA shop in Midway and made a deal with the owner to give Highline dive students free air. That was great for us and really great for me because I went through three or four bottles a week.

Saturday was a common day for me to dive off the Des Moines waterfront and there were usually quite a few people on the City Fishing Pier there if the weather was half-way decent. I guess my activities were quite visible to the public. I didn't think much of it other than I thought it was awesome that I was allowed to dive in a restricted area. Little to my knowledge, a lot of the public were upset by it for several reasons. Some wanted to be allowed to dive there and called the City Manager a Nazi for not allowing them to dive there when, clearly, he allowed other people diving access. Others were fishermen who were upset because they accused the divers, me and whatever buddy I took with me, of scaring all the fish away. They did have a City Fishing Pier there, but I made it a point not to dive anywhere near it just because I really didn't want to scare the fish away and I didn't want to get caught up in any fish hooks or fishing line. Fishing line can be a real hazard for SCUBA divers.

The city manager didn't talk to me about it, although he could have. He had my phone number and could have arranged a meeting with me anytime he wanted. Instead, he took it up with the Marine Biology teacher. I guess he really made a stink about the whole site with her. She called me in for a meeting and asked me about my use of that site. She asked how often I dove there, where I dove, and whether or not I interfered with the public at the pier. I told her since we had a private access to the site about half a mile from the pier I never went anywhere near the pier. I also told her that I dove there a couple times a week. She asked if I had ever had any altercations with the public or police while diving, entering, or leaving the site. I explained how we only used the private entrance area and never had any dealings with the public, let alone the police.

She nodded and reassured me that she thought I was being respectful, but the city manager was really upset. She also said she considered him to be a petty, controlling, angry little man. He had always been a jerk to her and allowed her access to the site only because Highline college required him to. He really had no choice in the matter, however, she had to cater to his policing of the access. She said everything would be okay and I could continue what I was doing, but to make sure I was respectful to the public and city of Des Moines. I assured her I would be. I also told her I would try to be a little more discreet when I could.

About two weeks after my meeting with the Marine Biology teacher I was diving at the site, collecting samples for her class. I was collecting a few Nudibranchs. They were out a little deeper than where I usually dove and I got carried away looking at the Sea Pens, Basket Stars, and other life that was at about eighty or ninety feet. I had a buddy that was tagging along right by my side. We were having a good time and ended up using all our air out there so we had to surface and swim back to the beach on top of the water rather than up to the beach along the bottom as I usually did it.

When we reached the surface there was a City of Des Moines Police boat right there. It was like a small landing craft in that it had a ramp in the front that folded down so stuff could be slid into or out of the water from the boat. The front was flopped down and the city manager, speaking through a megaphone, told us to get up onto the ramp and into the boat. There were four police officers with him, two of which were dressed in wet suits and had all their dive gear ready to go. We complied with his request and got on the boat.

As soon as we were on board, the front was raised and we were closed in the boat. We moved our masks up to the top of our heads and removed our tanks. The city manager started yelling at us for diving in a restricted area and saying that we had to have permission to dive there granted from his office. I told him I did have permission and that I had left a message with his office letting him know that I would be diving at the site this day. He said my permission had been denied and that there would be no further diving allowed by Highline students until he had a meeting with the Marine Biology teacher. I said fine and told him I would honor his demands and asked if he would take us to the beach where we could unload. He made me empty my goody bag into the water, so I lost all the Nudibranchs I had collected for the biology class. He said he couldn't drop us back at the place where we entered, and where my ambulance was parked, because it was private property and he didn't want to disturb the owners (even though we had a very good relationship with the owners of that property). Instead, he dropped us off at the Des Moines Public Boat Launch which was about a mile south of where we had entered the water. There was no point in arguing with him and I didn't want to get the police angry with us either. We disembarked from the Police boat and walked down the dock back to the parking lot.

"Now what?" my dive buddy asked. I told him that I would take off all my gear and he could wait here with it while I walked back to the ambulance. I would drive it back here and collect him and all our gear. He said that was silly, because I would have to walk through the middle of Des Moines in my wetsuit. I could take off the top part of my wet suit, but not my farmer johns, because I was naked underneath it. It was a warm sunny day and I didn't really mind. I knew the city manager was just flexing his political muscles. I retrieved the ambulance and brought it back. We loaded all our dive gear into it and drove back to my buddy's apartment. We cleaned up, washed the dive gear and took showers, getting dressed back into our regular clothes. We called some of our friends and decided to have a Bar-B-Que and get drunk for the rest of the day. We had a good time and everybody said what a jerk the city manager had been.

On Monday I told the Marine Biology teacher what had happened. She said she had already heard from the city manager and that everything would be okay. He was just being a jerk. She said he did this about once a year, just to let her know who was in charge even though he really wasn't. She told me she had a meeting scheduled with him in two weeks and that I was not to dive at that site until after the meeting. Okay, politics is politics and I didn't want to make things any worse. I really didn't want to lose the opportunity to dive there either.

Two weeks went by, the Marine Biology teacher had the meeting with the city manager, and then she called me into her office. The new deal was that I could only diver there once every two weeks. I could not dive on Saturdays, Sundays, or any holidays. I had to have express permission from the city manager or his secretary before each dive and that meant I had to have a verbal approval from his office before each dive. I could no longer just leave a message with the office. I had to wait until I actually talked to a person and had their verbal approval. Yay, what a pain in the rear. The first couple months after that turned out to be a real pain. It was like the city manager didn't want to approve any diving. I think I only got three dives in at that site during those eight or nine weeks. After that though, the situation relaxed a little and I only had to deal with the city manager's secretary. She was much easier to deal with. She allowed me to dive once a week as long as it was on Tuesday, Wednesday, or Thursday. That was okay with me. And that is where it stood for the rest of my time as a student at Highline. I found out later on that the guy who had worked in my position for the Marine Biology teacher several years ago had recently gone diving there with a couple buddies and did some spear fishing under the Public Fishing Pier. They were stopped by the Des Moines Police when they got out of the water. The police had asked them what they were doing there and they responded that they had permission from the Marine Biology teacher at Highline to collect some samples for her. Yeah, some nice sized Ling Cod perfect for a good fish dinner. We had always known that we were not allowed to spear fish at that site and that we were not to dive anywhere near the fishing pier. Thanks guys.

*   *   *

In June we had completed the first year. Now we were ready to start the Summer quarter consisting of Mark V diving. I was really excited for this part of the course. Mark V gear is also referred to as Heavy Gear. It is the Copper and Brass dive outfit with a big leather and lead weight belt and lead bottomed boots that most people associate with Commercial Diving. Our numbers had declined considerably. Enough students had dropped the class that Mr. Talbot did not have to make any cuts. We were down to twenty-three students – three less than capacity.

The girl made it and hung in there, I thought that was great. Not everybody in the class was happy about that. I don't know why. I grew up with three sisters and knew that women could do anything they put their minds to. Our female classmate was in her early twenties. She had worked several years in road construction, as a flagger and equipment operator. She was small, five-foot-two or three, one-hundred-and-five pounds maybe. She had blonde hair in a Pixie cut, bright blue eyes and a slight frame. She exercised a lot and was in very good shape. Still the Mark V outfit was a little heavy for her.

Of course, it was heavy for everybody, but it was almost double her body weight. Just the helmet and breastplate weigh fifty-six pounds. The weight belt is at least eighty-four pounds but can be added to. Each boot weighs seventeen-and-a-half pounds – that's thirty-five pounds for the pair. The canvas suit that you wear to round out the gear weighs about twenty pounds making the combined weight of the complete outfit right at one-hundred-and-ninety-five pounds. You can make it float though. It is work for anybody to walk around on deck while wearing that outfit. Our dive pier was on Puget Sound at Redondo just south of the Highline campus, so we had to deal with the tidal changes of water depth off the end of the pier. There was no crane to get you in and out of the water, only a ladder.

If you were lucky your dive would be over at high tide and you would only have to climb about eight feet to get back on the pier. However, you might have to climb as much as twenty feet or more if your dive was over at low tide. I think three more guys dropped out of the program because they thought that was too much. Personally, I thought it was great – a good workout. I love diving the Mark V gear. It is my favorite dive gear of all time. Call me crazy.

We dove Mark V gear Monday through Thursday. Every

Friday we had a class on small engine repair and compressor maintenance. Mr. Talbot had a minimum number of dives we had to make in the heavy gear, honestly, I can't remember what it was. All I knew is that I wanted to dive it as often as I could. I ended up doing at least one dive every day, in fact I think I averaged six dives a week. Some of the students dove as little as possible.

Our female dove the suit almost every day also. She was a real trooper. I do remember one time her dive ended on a low tide and she had a long climb to make. About half-way up she stopped. I was on the radio and asked her if she was alright. She said she was seeing spots and feeling dizzy. Carbon Dioxide poisoning I told her. I advised her to hang on to the ladder, open her air supply and exhaust valves wide to flush the helmet with fresh air. I put someone else on the radio, then I and one other guy climbed down the outside of the ladder. We took off the weight belt and removed the lead-soled boots. The guy tending her hose kept a good strain on it and we assisted her the rest of the way up.

A couple of the guys in the class thought she should be dropped from the class for that. I didn't, nor did most guys in the class. Mr. Talbot didn't think so either. In fact, he told a couple of the guys that they were neither as good at diving nor had the drive she had, so if he were to cut someone that day, it would be one of them. She wasn't the only one who had issues climbing the ladder in full gear. The guy from Kansas was a big guy – I think he was at least six foot four and well-built. One time when he had to make the long climb, he made it within five steps of the top when he fell backwards and landed in the water.

At first, we thought he was just messing around, but he was unresponsive for a little bit. Finally, he responded to our questions and said he didn't know what had happened. Everything just turned blue then black and the next thing he knew he was floating in the water with a couple of us swimming next to him. Obviously, he had not vented enough on his climb out and had passed out from Hypercapnia – too much carbon dioxide in the circulatory system. He had chipped his front teeth when he landed on his back in the water – probably hit is mouth on the breastplate – and his mouth was a little bloody. Other than that, he was okay.

Mr. Talbot didn't require us to enter the water by climbing down the ladder. We could jump off the end of the pier if we preferred. He taught us the proper technique for doing that so we wouldn't break our teeth or get hurt some other way. Some of us thought that was great fun and the greater the distance to the water the better! I learned to control my buoyancy well. By the end of the quarter, I could swim in the gear, I could turn myself upside down and right myself. I could pop my feet out of the water with my head hanging down in the water and get myself back into an upright position. I could use the suit as an elevator stopping at any depth I wanted and hold myself there. It was just a matter of valve control. I really loved that outfit.

At the end of that quarter, it was tradition to get a photo of each of us dressed in heavy gear with a Mermaid sitting on our lap. The second dive instructor had a friend who had a Tugboat moored in Lake Union that we could use as a setting for the photos so they would look very nautical. In the past classes, one of the students usually had a girlfriend who was happy to pose as the mermaid for the photos. In our case, no one did. Well, one guy did. His girlfriend was a stripper and she said she would do it but wanted five hundred dollars to pose! That was way too expensive for our measly student budget. The girl in our class said she would do it; she could even get a couple of her friends to help out so we could have three or four mermaids in the photos. That sounded good until she said she and her friends wouldn't go topless. All the past classes had topless mermaids, that was part of the tradition.

Our female classmate stood her ground, but not enough of the guys wanted a mermaid with a bra to make it financially viable. In the end we hired a woman from a singing telegram company to do it. She was small, cute, but old enough to be our grandmother. She was a good sport though and, in the end, we had a lot of fun photos to show for it. The girl wanted a topless male mermaid for her photos, but no one else would help with the fees so that didn't work out. A couple of the guys said they would pose with her, but she didn't go for that, the one or two she wanted to pose with didn't want to pose with her - spoilsports. I always thought we should have let our female classmate get her friends together for a group of mermaids. Mermaids don't have to be topless to be sexy. Besides, everybody knows the more the merrier!

We had a six-week gap between the end of the summer quarter and the start of the fall quarter. Mr. Talbot allowed the students who wanted to, and who he thought were responsible enough, to use the Mark V gear for Pile Cleaning work around the south sound. I and two other guys were the only ones who wanted to do it. I think we ended up only doing that about three times, but it was fun. Plus, it was my second paid commercial dive job!

*   *   *

The first quarter of our second year started in late September. We were now officially second-year students, yay! There was a whole new class of first-year students. We didn't see much of them, though and didn't get too friendly with any of them, although I did work with a couple of them in later years out in the field.

All our classes during the second year were held at the Redondo Pier. We didn't have to go up to the Highline campus except to take care of paperwork stuff – registration, financial aid, etc. We were pretty much isolated from the rest of the college so it seemed more like a trade school. The next pier over had a really good seafood restaurant on it. We did lunch there sometimes and happy hour many, many times. They offered a bottomless bowl of steamed shrimp and clams as an appetizer during their happy hour and I am sure they lost money on a few of us. We were always welcome there though. We probably helped keep them afloat with our alcohol purchases. The only time any of us got in trouble there was one sunny afternoon; a couple of the guys had started squabbling with each other. We were all seated at one of the tables outside toward the end of the pier. The two weren't getting too loud, but they were getting a little pushy. We told them to calm down, but instead they stood up and started shoving one another.

Like I said we were close to the end of the pier, so when one pushed the other a little hard, he started going over the railing. At the last moment, he had grabbed the other guy and their momentum was such that they both flipped over the railing landing in the drink with a big splash. We all got a good laugh at that. The bartenders said they weren't welcome back for the rest of the day. They didn't mind anyway because they wanted to get back home and change into clean, dry clothes. Some of us met up later at one of the local bars and continued our drinking. Their row wasn't very serious and they had finished arguing and were back to being the best of buds.

One of the purposes of the second year was to familiarize us with the different dive gear that we might use out in the field. I think the department had nine or ten different types of dive helmets. The newest was the Superlite Seventeen. That was the industry standard at the time and most of the people in the class wanted to dive that hat. I liked trying them all. Another favorite was the Miller. I liked it better – mostly because it was all brass – but my head didn't fit in it real well, so it wasn't very comfortable for me. I ended up doing most of my dives in a hat called the Savoie. It looked like it had used a motorcycle helmet for its base, but it had a bigger face-port so you had a bigger field of vision in the water.

Mr. Talbot ran a pretty tight ship. We had to keep everything very clean and keep up on the maintenance of all the equipment. The program had a lot of great equipment that not many of the other schools had. At the end of the pier was a Bell-Bounce system with a small, perfectly spherical bell – barely big enough for two divers. It could connect to the Deck Chamber so we could practice Bell transfers and dive from the Bell on an umbilical just like SAT divers did. It was great experience. There was also a huge tank on the pier that was set up for underwater welding and burning. It gave us a working depth of about twelve feet. It had portholes so the instructors could watch what was happening in the tank. Though Mr. Talbot liked to let the water get dirty enough so visibility was not very good. He said that was more like the real world. We did have to do black-out dives where the face-plate would be covered over so the diver couldn't see anything. We had to learn to do stuff by feel. That ended up being a great experience because more than half of the commercial diving done is done in black-out conditions. Overall, this school did a pretty good job of preparing us for work in the field.

Mr. Talbot did not tolerate tardiness either. The first class in the morning started at eight o'clock sharp. If you were late, the rule was ten pushups required for every minute of tardiness. We did our best to be on time. Most of us usually showed up by seven-thirty and used that time to clean and get ready for the day. A couple guys, of course, showed up as close to eight as possible. One day one of the guys came in about three minutes late. Mr. Talbot just looked at him and told him he knew what to do. The guy said no, he wasn't going to do any pushups. Mr. Talbot told him he would or he could leave the class. The guy started arguing. This was the first and only time I saw Mr. Talbot lose his temper. He had gotten angry before and had stern words with us, but he had never lost his temper. This time he got all red in the face and started yelling quite loudly. The student wouldn't give in, he just kept arguing and yelling at Mr. Talbot. After a bit, Mr. Talbot told him to just leave, get all his gear together and leave, he was out of the program. The guy left the class, packed his personal gear and left. We never saw him again. Personally, I thought that was silly to quit the class because of thirty pushups. Later one of the other guys in the class, who was friendly with the tardy student, said the tardy student was suffering from diarrhea that day and didn't want to take the chance of soiling his pants in front of the class. I thought that was stupid too. He could have just explained the situation to Mr. Talbot – he was a reasonable man. No matter, the student quit the class and let his pride keep him from finishing the dive program. Stupid, but he probably wouldn't have made it in the industry anyway, so it was probably for the best.

*   *   *

The final quarter ended in early June. The dive instructors helped us get jobs in the field at the end of the program. Basically, what that meant was that dive companies would call Mr. Talbot when they had job openings and ask him for graduating students to fill those positions. The majority of the positions were for tending, but once in a while there would be an opening for something else, like ROV assistant, or Life Support Tech assistant. We were all hopeful and excited to start our careers. By this time our class size had dropped to fourteen. The only student who had been cut was the tardy guy, the rest had just dropped out for one reason or another.

At the end of May a company called SubSea called Mr. Talbot and needed five guys ASAP. The guys chosen would leave right away and not be required to finish the last week of school. Mr. Talbot picked his top five and offered them the jobs. I was not one of them. A few days later, a company called Can-Dive, out of Vancouver, BC called and needed a handful of guys to help with their display at the nineteen-eighty-six World's Fair and Exhibition. I was asked to fill one of those positions. I was happy with that even though it wasn't a real job. I thought it would be a good foot in the door and it did turn out to be just that.

I finished up the class with the final nine remaining students, everybody passed. I was happy to see that our female classmate had completed the program also. Earlier in the year, I had sold my ambulance. Shortly after the movie Ghostbusters had been released, I painted the Ghostbusters logo on the back door of the ambulance. That attracted a lot of attention and when I decided to sell, it sold quickly. A fraternity house from the U of W ended up with it. I replaced the ambulance with a nineteen-sixty-seven Volkswagen window bus to haul all my dive gear around in. I painted it red, white, and blue. I painted a facsimile of the American flag on the roof, blue in the front with thirteen white stars along the rain guard. That vehicle gave me a little grief crossing the border into Canada. I had to convince the border guards that I wasn't some kind of hippie smuggling pot or coke across the border. Luckily for me, Can-Dive had sent a letter of introduction to Mr. Talbot requesting seven students, which I had with me, and we were travelling in a three-car caravan. We were allowed to cross the border and enter Canada after a short delay and a search of only my bus. The border patrol didn't bother searching the two other cars in our group.

One of the Can-Dive employees had a large house in Vancouver with his family. His house had a large, unfinished basement with a family room, a couple bedrooms and a bathroom, that he had offered up for us to stay in while we were working at the exposition. He had talked it over with his wife and she was happy to let us stay. She even offered to fix breakfast for us every morning, as long as we didn't mind having breakfast with their two children. We didn't want to intrude and took her up on her offer only once. On the first day when we showed up, I had bought a bouquet of flowers and presented it to the wife as a thank you in advance.

We spent a week working for Can-Dive. What we did was help keep their exhibition clean and dive in their exhibition tank using different types of diving gear. Usually, we would have three divers in the tank at any one time. One would be in SCUBA gear, another in Mark V gear, and a third in the newer "lightweight" gear. Lightweight gear was any commercial gear that wasn't Mark V. Most common was the Kirby-Morgan Superlite Seventeen, but also included the many different dive hats like Miller, Savoie, or Desco Pot.

There were also band masks, which were like the front part of a dive helmet with a neoprene back rather than a full helmet. There were a couple different makers of the masks. Can-Dive had been part of Oceaneering so had a bunch of Oceaneering's own hat called the Rat Hat – named after the main guy involved in its production. I rather liked it, but most of the other guys didn't. So, I mostly dove the Mark V or the Rat Hat in the tank. I think I did SCUBA only once. It was fun, but we weren't paid for it. We got passes to the park and all our meals paid for. Can-Dive also bought us beer at the beer tent at the end of the day. It was great fun for a bunch of guys who had just graduated from college. At the end of the week, I got the guys to chip in for a thank you card and a hundred-dollar gift certificate at one of the nicer restaurants in Vancouver. We presented it to the Can-Dive guy and his wife for letting us stay at their house. I had no issues with my bus getting back into the U.S. of A.

*   *   *

GONE DOWN LATELY?
Chapter two

At the time of my graduation, I was seeing a woman who lived in Spokane Valley. She was the little sister of the younger woman my dad was dating at the time. We had been introduced by my father who had volunteered my help with the building of her horse fence without talking to me about it first. One weekend when I had returned to Spokane to visit my dad, he announced that we would be doing some work for his girlfriend's little sister. What the heck? They offered a free Bar-B-Que and all the beer I could drink. Okay, I guess that's better than a poke in the eye with a sharp stick. Anyway, the little sister and I hit it off pretty well and we started seeing each other. She lived alone in a small, two-bedroom, single bath house on an acre with a pregnant horse, a dog and a cat.

When I returned from Canada, I needed a place to stay and my girlfriend said I could move in with her. I thought that was a fine idea, as I would probably have ended up spending most of my spare time with her anyway. I moved all my stuff, which wasn't much, just clothes, dive gear, some tools, my motorcycle and my sixty-seven VW bus, to her house.

About a week after that – the last weekend in June – I got a call from a guy in Redmond, Washington. He said he represented the American interests of Can-Dive. He said there was a small job coming up in Cody, Wyoming and wanted to know if I would be willing to go on it. I was ecstatic – a real dive job! I told him that I was available and if he would give me the details, I would be happy to fill the position. He said to not get too excited, it was only a two- or three-day job and was not a permanent hire. I told him I was okay with that. Then he asked if I knew of anybody else that might be willing to go on the job. I said I could make some calls and see if I could find someone. One of the guys I had graduated with was working the summer at his uncle's resort on Priest Lake in northern Idaho. I was sure he would be happy to go. I called him up and, as I thought, he was very happy to accept the job.

I called the guy in Redmond back and told him I had found a guy to fill in the position. He gave me the details of the position. He gave me the name of the motel in Cody where I would be meeting the Diver and the Supervisor. He said I needed to bring my own dive gear and that I would be the Standby Diver and the other guy would be the Tender. We would get a straight day-rate and all our expenses would be paid. He said that Standby was to be SCUBA because we would be working out of a small boat. That sounded good to me. I wasn't real familiar with how things really worked or should work in the field. We were to show up on Sunday. The job would start Monday morning. The motel would be covered the Saturday night before, also, if we wanted to show up a little early. The Diver and Supervisor would be there Saturday.

I called the guy in Idaho back and told him it was a go and we were to leave on Saturday. I told him he would be the tender and his pay rate was to be one hundred dollars per day plus expenses. He thought that was fantastic. I loaded my bus with my equipment, tools, and diver reference books – I wanted to make sure I was prepared. I drove to Nordman, Idaho and picked up my friend. We loaded his stuff into my bus and headed down to Wyoming. I don't really remember the drive down until we got to the Buffalo Bill dam on the Shoshone river. That was the dive site of the job. We just looked at it as we drove by on our way into Cody. We got to the motel and checked in – our rooms were already paid for and we each had our own room.

This was already more than we had hoped for. We got the front desk to ring the room our Diver was staying in – he was our contact for the job – so we could let him know we had arrived. It was just about seven p.m. A woman answered the phone and I thought I had the wrong room at first. I told her who I was and who I was looking for. She said that was great and introduced herself as the wife of the Diver, and the Supervisor of the job. Hmm, that was interesting I thought. I heard her tell her husband who was on the phone, and then a muffled conversation. She came back on and asked if we had eaten dinner yet. We hadn't and I let her know. She asked if we would like to have dinner with them in a half-hour or so. I replied that we would be delighted to join them for dinner. We got ready and met them in the lobby.

We had dinner at a pretty nice steak house in Cody, it had previously been a brothel and was named after the madam of the brothel. The food was excellent. We had a couple beers with dinner. During the meal we talked about everything. I learned that they were husband and wife. They had their own dive company down in Texas, where they were from. They did contract work for Oceaneering and now Can-Dive since it had separated from Oceaneering. They laid out the main plan of the job. It seems that we were there to look for a D-nine Caterpillar bulldozer that had slipped down the bank into the river with the operator and his dog on board. The dog had made it back to the beach, but the operator's body had not been found. The construction company wanted the dozer back, but for the publicity we were hired to find the body of the operator. They figured it would only take a day or two to complete the job – that is locate the D-nine and mark it with a buoy. They also said that we would all be working out of the boat.

The Supervisor would be operating the radio and filling out the dive log. The Diver would stay in the boat and oversee the operation. I, as the Standby, would do the actual diving. My friend would do the tending, which meant handling lines and doing whatever he was asked to do. So even though the Diver was being paid three hundred dollars per day to dive, he would not be diving. I would be doing the diving for the Standby rate. The Diver wanted to know if I had a problem with that. I told him of course I did not.

I was happy to be working in the dive industry and would do whatever it took, besides, one hundred and fifty dollars a day was way more than I had ever made anywhere before. I was ecstatic. One more thing they said, we were to meet out front of the motel at seven in the morning every morning. We would go to breakfast from there and be on the jobsite at eight o'clock. There would be no lunch break and we would work until four in the afternoon, at which time we would pull the boat out of the water and secure all the equipment, about an hour's worth of work, then head back to the hotel. So basically, I had a ten-hour work day for one hundred and fifty bucks plus meals. Awesome. The Diver took care of the dinner bill, beers and all.

In the morning we met out front and we went to a pancake house for breakfast. The Diver took care of that bill too. We went to the jobsite, loaded up the boat, set everything up and went to work. The dive rig consisted of a bank of four K-bottles filled with air, rack box- which is the valves and gauges used to deliver the air from the source to the dive hose, radio, three-hundred-and-fifty-foot dive hose, and a KMB-nine band mask. My SCUBA rig was set up in the back of the boat out of the way.

We dropped an anchor in the general vicinity of where the construction crew thought the D-nine might be. I put on the band mask, splashed, and followed the line down to the bottom. The anchor had landed on a forty-five-degree slope of rip-rap – large broken rock that was used to stabilize river banks. I was about ninety-five feet deep. I had taken a search line with me – a rope that I would tie off to the anchor that I could use to make circle searches with. The water was pitch black – I could see nothing. I stretched out the search line and made my circle searches. We moved the anchor once, about forty more feet towards the middle of the river and I continued my search. The bank sloped at forty-five degrees all the way to the bottom of the river bed which happened to be one hundred and forty-three feet. I found nothing.

I returned to the surface doing my decompression on the anchor line, which was referred to as the downline. That was our first day. The diver had decided this wasn't going to work and called the head office to have them get a Magnetometer sent to us. It was to arrive early the next day. It did and we used it to search for the D-nine. We ran a grid pattern search of the whole area. After six days of searching, we got a ping on the magnetometer. We dropped an anchor at the spot to establish a downline.

I dressed in and splashed for the second time. I followed the line down to the bottom; it was at one hundred and thirty-eight feet. No dozer. I reattached my search line and started my search. I found the dozer about ten feet away from the anchor. It was completely buried with rip-rap except for the tubular steel cab cage. I felt inside for the body, but to my surprise and relief, no body was in there. I felt for the seat belt, found it and confirmed that it was not closed – either the operator hadn't been using it like he was supposed to, or he had released it to get out of the cab as the machine slid down the embankment. I got a buoy on the D-nine and left the bottom. The next day we packed everything up, signed the required documents, said our good-byes, and headed home.

That was my very first actual commercial dive job. It ended up being an eight-day job with only two dives. Two days of driving rounded out the whole thing to a ten-day experience. I earned twelve hundred dollars for the week and had no out-of-pocket expenses, not even gas. Can-Dive paid for that too. It was an awesome experience and I could hardly wait for the next job to come up. Yeehaw! I was off to a good start.

*   *   *

About a week after returning home from Wyoming, I got another call from Redmond. There was a job in Post Falls, Idaho where a tender was needed. I was happy to be considered and gladly accepted the job. I was to meet the Supervisor at the lumber mill just west of the bridge that went across the Spokane River there on Monday morning at seven. I would be told about the job there and then. I just needed to bring my SCUBA gear.

I got to the lumber mill about six-thirty in the morning on Monday. Nobody was around. I went over my notes to ensure I was in the right place, it appeared that I was. About ten to seven a guy in a pickup drove up. I met with him and he turned out to be the Supervisor. He said we would wait for the third guy to show up, then he would explain the job. Right at seven another truck arrived. Driving the truck was the guy from Vancouver whose house we had stayed at while working the World's Fair. It was good to see him.

This job was to be the installation of a Cathodic Protection System for the bridge. We were to install an array of electric cables from the beach across the river bottom with legs going on both sides of the bridge support pilings. The cables were to be buried approximately eighteen inches below the mud level. What that meant was that we would have to dig a system of trenches, lay the cables in the trenches, then cover the cables with bags of concrete restoring the river bottom so the cables wouldn't snag debris flowing down the river. The dive company was hired by the Idaho Department of Transportation, who would supply a crane to assist us as well as have a representative on site to monitor our progress and answer questions.

The Idaho DOT representative showed up at eight a.m. He had blueprints of the bridge showing what the layout should look like. He said the crane, with operator, would be on site the next day and available to us as needed. The system parts would be delivered as we needed. The state supplied a couple sections of dock that we could use as a dive platform.

There were two dock sections. They were small, about ten feet by eight feet and didn't have any railing, just a two-by-four toe board running around the outside edge. With the help of the crane, we set up the dive station on one section. The dive station consisted of a tiny Quincy Three-twenty-five air compressor powered by a small Yanmar diesel engine, an Oceaneering Rack Box, a Helle dive radio, a three-hundred-fifty-foot dive umbilical, and a Rat hat. Standby was my SCUBA rig stored on one corner of the dock, which we were calling a barge by this time. The other dock - or barge, Ha! - had a P-two-fifty water pump on board along with three-hundred feet of two-and-a-half-inch canvas fire hose, and a Hand Jet.

The hand jet was a weird Tee-looking thing made up of plumbing fittings. The fire hose was attached to the base of the tee and the top of the tee was tapered down to one-inch pipe that was open at both ends so water would flow out each end of the tee. By the time we got our dive gear and hand-jetting equipment set up on the "barges," the decking was only about four inches off the water. Every time a small wave came up, water washed over the deck. Also, if any two of us stood on the same end of the dock it would tip and sink below the surface. Yay. The plan was that one guy would be on the "Jetting Barge," one guy would be on the "Dive Barge," and the third would be in the water doing the diving work.

In case of emergency, the radio operator, the Dive Barge guy, would don the SCUBA gear and aid the diver. Hmm. Oh well, I guess this is how it's done in the real world. This job was a day-rate job also. The Supervisor and Diver would each be getting three hundred dollars per day and I, as the Standby Diver/Tender, would be getting one-hundred-and-fifty dollars per day. The days were to be eight hours, but really were ten hours long. The official work day was eight a.m. to four p.m., but that didn't include set-up in the morning and breakdown in the afternoon. All three of us would be doing the diving, which was to be done in four-hour shifts – a morning dive followed by an afternoon dive.

The depth averaged eighteen feet with the deepest dives in the middle of the river only about twenty-four feet, so we could easily spend four hours in the water without worrying about decompression. The plan was to have a regular rotation of all three of us, so each of us would make two dives every three days. What ended up happening was that I dove every day, usually in the morning, followed by one of the other guys diving in the afternoon. The pay rates did not change, but I didn't care. I was just ecstatic to be working as a diver and getting paid. It was still more money than I had ever made before and the work environment was fun.

The first dive was made by the Supervisor so he could assess the river bottom and devise a plan of action. He finished the dive after about an hour-and-a-half. He said there were quite a few water-logged timbers in the way and some rock that couldn't be moved by the hand-jet, but could be moved by the hand of the diver. Other than that, the bottom consisted of fairly stiff mud. He said the job was very doable, but might take longer than the week originally slated for the task. The Idaho representative said that the logs could be hooked up to the crane and removed, that would help out quite a bit. I learned that up here, for this company anyway, job titles didn't mean much other than what your payrate was going to be. That pretty much sums up the first and second day. We would meet back at the mill the next morning at seven.

This jobsite was about a half-hour drive from where I was living so I just drove back and forth every day. The Supervisor was from western Washington and was staying at a campground, at the end of the bridge on the other side of the river from the mill, sleeping in the back of his truck. The guy from Vancouver, the Diver, was staying at the same campground in a small camper trailer he had towed from home. While working this job, I learned that the Redmond guy actually lived in Spokane and was the little brother of the Diver from Vancouver, BC. The Diver had gotten the Redmond job for his little brother, but they didn't get along well enough for the Diver to stay at his brother's house, even though it was only forty-five minutes from the job site.

The next day went pretty well, the sun was out and it was warm. Our work outfit consisted of shorts, tennis shoes, optional t-shirt, sunglasses, and gloves when we were handling the crane line. I dove first. My dive outfit was a quarter-inch wetsuit, fifteen-pound weight belt, three-pound ankle weights made up of commercial fishing net weights (they looked like large lead bead anklets), gloves, booties, a fifty cubic foot Bailout Bottle, and the Rat Hat. The river water was pretty cold, so the wetsuit was comfortable to work in. I removed a couple logs and did a little hand-jetting. It took a little bit of experimenting to figure out how to get the best use of the hand-jet, but it ended up working pretty well. There were big rocks that had to be moved out of the way about every two feet. All this made the actual trenching move along rather slowly. It was kind of fun work though. At noon we swapped divers. That is how the work went for the rest of the week.

The following Monday, the Redmond guy met us at the job site. He told us that the state guy had informed him that the state of Idaho would pay one thousand dollars for every log we had to pull out of the water. The Redmond guy said he would pay each of us one hundred dollars for every log we pulled out, so, of course, there were many more logs found that were in the way of our trench digging. In fact, we pulled out so many logs, that after a week and a half, the state guy told the Redmond guy that the state wouldn't pay for anymore. That was okay, because we were only a day away from finishing the trenching anyway. In the end we only pulled up twenty-three logs, really not that many, but probably twice what we actually needed to remove to get the job done.

The second part of the job was to lay the cable in the trench. We started that on a Monday and finished it early Tuesday afternoon. Then we had to wait a day for the state to hook up the array to the power system and check that it was working the way it was supposed to. We got paid to hang out and watch, because they wanted us on site just in case they needed us to make a dive for some reason or another. The tests were all successful and we didn't have to make any dives. The next day we started the third, and final part of the job; covering the cable with concrete bags.

The Diver and the Supervisor didn't want to dive for that part. I guess moving eighty-pound bags of pre-mix concrete was too much physical labor for them. Anyway, the Redmond guy came to work for the next several days for that part of the job. I dove in the morning and he dove in the afternoon.

This is when I learned that he and his brother had gone to the same dive program at Highline under Mr. Talbot that I had completed, only they had graduated in the early seventies. They both had gone down to the Gulf of Mexico to work for some dive company, but the Redmond guy quit after a couple months. He went into Real Estate after that. In nineteen-eighty-five his brother got him hired on to Can-Dive as an office manager in Redmond because Can-Dive couldn't work in Alaska anymore since cutting their ties with Oceaneering. They needed a presence in the U.S. so they would be allowed to work anywhere in America.

That was the purpose of the Redmond office – to allow Can-Dive to continue working their contracts in Alaska. The Redmond guy got bored there and asked permission to look for work in the lower forty-eight. Can-Dive didn't care as long as it didn't interfere with their Alaska operations. They told him they wouldn't send any crew members, and he would have to make do with the equipment they sent him – which happened to be the stuff they wouldn't send on their jobs and usually needed some kind of repair.

Anyway, the Redmond guy worked out all the time and was in pretty good physical shape. He tried to outdo me in the water, by placing more bags in a dive than I did. But he just didn't have the experience of working under water that I did, it is quite different from working on land, so he just couldn't outdo me. He tried hard though, and had a tough time admitting that I was placing more bags than he.

We finished that part of the job on a Wednesday afternoon. The state came back and tested everything. They were happy with the results and signed off on the completion of the job. We spent the next day taking everything apart, loading it up and completing the demobilization. All in all, it was a three-

and-a-half-week job close to home. I was extremely happy. So far, I was having a great start to my career in commercial diving.

*　　*　　*

I got called for a few more little jobs in the next couple months. There was less work than time off and I was wondering when I might get another good job. I talked to some of the guys in the Can-Dive office, and they said I probably wouldn't work much until the following spring. They advised me to get some other job to get through the winter. The Redmond guy didn't have anything for me to go on, so I started looking for another job. Then I got a call from Mr. Talbot. He said that American Oilfield Divers, based in New Iberia, Louisiana, was looking for tenders. He said all I had to do was show up and they would put me to work. He gave me the contact information and wished me good luck. I called the office of AOD and they said yes, they had lots of work and could send me offshore as soon as I got there. Yeehaw! A real commercial dive job! I told my family and my girlfriend that I would be goin' South for work. They were not happy, but I was.

I got a call from my friend in north Idaho, who had gone on the Wyoming job with me, and he said that Mr. Talbot had called him also. He was heading South and wanted to know if we could go together. I told him that would be great, I would rather make a trip like that with a friend than alone. I told him I would pack up my bus and head his way the next day.

I loaded all my gear and some clothes into my bus. The

following morning, I drove to the resort on Priest Lake and collected my friend. We loaded all his stuff then hit the road. We drove down to Interstate Ninety and headed East. We almost made it to the top of Lookout Pass, on the Idaho-Montana border when the engine in my bus seized up. Well, this sucks. What are we going to do now, my friend wondered. I thought a bit and remembered that I had a spare VW engine in my dad's garage, so I told him we would get towed back to Spokane and put a newly rebuilt engine in my bus. My friend didn't look too happy and figured that would put us weeks behind schedule. We turned the bus around and coasted down the mountain and into Mullan, Idaho. I called my dad to let him know what had happened. He agreed to retrieve us with his truck. A couple hours later we were on the way back to Spokane.

We got to my dad's house in the late afternoon. My friend asked if we should unload the bus. I said no, I'll swap this engine and we'll be back on the road tomorrow morning. Yeah right, my friend said. I kept my mouth shut and went to work. All in all, it only took me two hours to get the engines swapped, after all, there are only four bolts, two flexible hoses, two wires and the throttle cable to disconnect and reconnect. I rebuilt Volkswagen bugs as a hobby, so I had all the tools and jacks needed. The Bus was really easy to swap engines on, because you could remove the rear bumper and the rear engine deck piece which allowed you to pull the engine straight out without having to lift the body like you had to on the Bug or Karman Ghia.

Anyway, I was all done and ready to go in time for a late dinner. My friend couldn't believe it. My dad knew I could do it, because he had seen me do it several times before. Before you ask, yes, I was still living with my girlfriend in Spokane Valley, but she didn't have a garage at her house – it had been converted into a Horse Barn. Because of that, I kept all my automotive tools and engine parts in my dad's garage.

He let me keep stuff in his garage in trade for doing small maintenance on his Bug, and plumbing stuff around his house.

In the morning, my dad treated us to a great breakfast. He asked if we were sure we knew what we were doing. We said no, but it was what we wanted to do. We headed East on Interstate Ninety to Interstate Fifteen, in Butte, where we headed South to Interstate Ten, in Phoenix. From there we headed East to Louisiana and down to New Iberia. I think we only took a couple days to make the trip, maybe three, I don't really remember.

We got to the office of AOD and introduced ourselves. We filled out all the paperwork and got our employee files set up. They told us we needed to get a pager and wait for a call. I said I was ready to go to work right away, and they said, yes, they were aware of that. They would give me a call as soon as they had something. The head guy in the office said if I really wanted to work right away, I could start the next day in the warehouse out back for four dollars an hour. We were only going to get paid four-and-a-quarter per hour offshore, so I said I would do it. I went out back and met with the warehouse manager. He was a big, black guy with half a fat cigar protruding from his mouth. He said he was called "Bubba" and I could start in the morning. Alright, I thought, I am employed. Yeehaw. I contacted one of the guys, the kid from Wyoming, who had come down the previous spring as part of the group that left a week before the end of our dive program. He and a couple other guys had rented a house in Broussard and said I could crash there for a share of the rent. That sounded great to me. I now had a job and a place to stay, things were moving in the right direction.

I spent the next several days working in the yard loading equipment for jobs onto flatbed trucks. I drove those trucks to the docks where the equipment was loaded on to boats that would take it out to dive jobs. Some of the gear was loaded on dive boats that were owned by AOD and were going out to do jobs. After about a week-and-a-half of this, seeing several jobs get loaded out without me going on them, I talked to the head office guy. He was the main guy who decided who went where. He said that Bubba was happy with my work and I was doing well in the yard, but if I really wanted to go offshore, he would send me on the next job that came up. That happened to be the next day. Yay, finally, I get to go offshore.

*　　*　　*

I was to meet the boat at the dock in Morgan City, Monday morning. The boat would be leaving at eight a.m. sharp no matter who was on board, so you better not miss the boat; if you did, you were out of a job. I was just a tender and was expected to help load food stores and stuff, so I showed up around six a.m. The captain met me and showed me to my cabin. It was a small room, about eight feet, by sixteen feet. There were four sets of bunk beds, two on each side of the cabin with about a four-foot space between them. Eight tenders would bunk in this cabin. I threw my gear in there, I was first on the boat so I had my choice of bunks. I took the top one on the left as you entered the cabin. There was one head on board for the use of the dive crew. It had four toilet stalls, two urinals and four shower stalls, all stainless steel and not super clean. I would definitely be wearing flip-flops while showering.

Eight tenders, five divers, and a dive supervisor were on board by a quarter to eight. One diver had not shown up yet. When the divers showed up, they just dumped their gear on the dock then jumped on the boat. They expected the tenders to load their gear onto the boat and put it in their respective cabins. The supervisor told me "Divers don't haul gear, and tenders don't buy beer." I didn't know what that really meant until we had come back to the beach at the end of the job. Right at eight o'clock a sixth diver showed up just as we were undoing the lines securing the boat to the dock. He got his gear on board just in time and had to jump across a small gap between the dock and the boat to get on board as the boat was just pulling away from the dock. I see the boat really doesn't wait for anyone. Eight o'clock departure means departure at eight o'clock! The supervisor was on deck and started yelling at the diver for being late. The only thing I remember him saying is "If you're not ten minutes early, you are ten minutes late!" That phrase stuck with me my whole career.

It took us about six hours to get to the dive site. Once there, the anchors had to be set and that took about two hours. A four-point anchor pattern was set, which meant two anchors off the bow, one port and one starboard, and two off the stern, port and starboard. While all this was going on, we, the tenders, got to work setting up the dive station. The supervisor and the divers were all in the galley watching T.V. and eating. One of us was called the LT or Lead Tender. He told us what to do and what to put where. This dive station was made up of two Lister-Quincy Fifty-one-twenty compressors, a dive shack (where the supervisor would be) that had the dive rack and a bunch of other controls in it, four six-hundred-foot dive umbilical's, a Deck Decompression Chamber (DDC), a bank of eight K-bottles filled with air, two banks of sixteen K-bottles each, filled with Oxygen, a bunch of deck whips (air and gas hoses), and gauges. There were also two big three-stage diesel-powered water pumps and hundreds of feet of canvas fire hose, and a couple tee hand jets similar to what I had used in Idaho. In addition, there were two Industrial Tool-Air compressors with several hundred feet of faded red CP hose. CP hose is inch-and-a-half, red, rubber hose with CP fittings on each end. CP stands for Chicago Pneumatic, the company that supplies the pneumatic hoses and fittings used. Piled on top of the CP hose was a fifteen-foot-long section of sixteen-inch diameter plastic pipe. It had some plumbing on one end that included a quarter turn valve and a CP fitting that matched those on the CP hose. That was an Airlift, I learned. But wait, we're not done! There were also two big diesel-powered DC welders, hundreds of feet of welding leads, ground leads, and the necessary welding heads and ground clamps needed to get the job done. Some of the welding leads had an Oxygen hose married to them, these attached to a whip that had a Broco head on it that was used for underwater burning. These were called "burning leads." We completed the set up by six p.m., eighteen hundred hours as it was called offshore; just in time for dinner.

At nineteen hundred hours, seven p.m., the supervisor called a meeting where he would go over the job details and line out who was doing what. Often, offshore jobs run twenty-four hours a day with a twelve-hour dayshift and a twelve-hour nightshift. This job would not run that way. We would only work daylight hours. Our shift would start at six in the morning and would go until six in the evening. If we needed to spend more time to complete a task we would work until we reached a good stopping point. We would get paid our hourly rate for the hours we worked, but were guaranteed twelve hours every day whether we worked them or not. After forty hours, we would be paid time-and-a-half. All the tenders were required to be on deck and working the full shift. The divers were to report fifteen minutes before their scheduled dive time. We would start the actual work the next morning. The first dive would be to determine if we were at the correct site, establish a downline, and survey the area so the supervisor would know what conditions we were actually dealing with and how to proceed with the work. Dress code for work was basically whatever we wanted to wear with the minimum being shorts and shoes, no open-toed footwear. When working with the Davit (small crane) we would have to wear a hard hat.

Most of us wore shorts, a t-shirt, tennis shoes or boat shoes, and sunglasses. Our supervisor wore khaki shorts, a khaki button-up, short-sleeve shirt, white calf-high socks, boat shoes, and aviator-style sunglasses. The divers came out on deck in shorts and flip-flops. They would change into their dive gear at the DDC and leave a little bag with a shirt, shorts, and a towel there. The divers mostly stayed out of the dive work area unless they were diving or sitting as the standby diver. Usually, the standby diver would sit in the dive shack with the supervisor. In dive rotation, the diver would get dressed-in mostly and sit as standby diver first, while the diver in front of him was diving. Next, he would be the diver. At the end of his dive, he would get in the chamber (DDC) if he needed surface decompression, and after that head back inside the boat. If it was sunny out, most of the divers would hang out on the bow and catch some sun.

When the divers needed surface decompression, one of the tenders would be designated to operate the chamber. That was a coveted spot, because the operator got to sit in the shade and didn't have to handle the hose and lines. We lowered and raised all the dive hose, welding lead, water hose, and equipment lines by hand. It could be quite a work-out, especially if we were working in deep water. Some guys wanted to do as little of that as possible, I rather enjoyed it. I ran the chamber a few times but mostly worked the deck. Three of the tenders were hired right off the street, answering a classified ad that AOD had placed in a newspaper. They had no dive experience, hadn't been to any dive school, and basically had no idea what they were doing. The LT and the four of us who had gone through dive school had to teach those guys everything. Their failure was our failure, which ultimately was the LT's failure, so we made sure everybody worked together to get the job done correctly. You know about shit, right? How it rolls downhill? Well in the dive industry it rolls downhill in a BIG way and none of it lands on the divers – at that time and in the Gulf anyway. If a tender failed, or a task didn't get completed, or a diver had a hard time, it was the LT's fault and none of us wanted that. We wanted to work and it was the supervisors who got to pick their crews for the most part. The supervisor usually had an LT that would work with him on all his jobs and would take the LT's recommendations for tenders. You wanted to keep your LT happy if you wanted to work with him.

The task on this job was to swap out a bad valve on a twenty-two-inch gas line. To get the job done, the divers would have to dig out the valve assembly with the hand jet, swap out the fitting, which consisted of removing twenty bolts (more or less) on both flanges, cleaning the flanges if necessary, replacing the bad valve with a good valve, putting new gaskets between the flanges, and re-installing the bolts on both sides of the valve. After that was done and the oil company pressure tested the line, the divers would then cover the valve with sandbags. That would complete the task and we would head back to the beach or on to the next job, depending on what the supervisor heard from the office.

The first dive of the job was made first thing the next morning. We tied an Odom weight to a half-inch poly line and threw it overboard to use as a temporary downline. About one-hundred-and-fifty feet of line went overboard before the weight landed on the sea floor. The deck of the boat was about eight feet above the surface, so we had a ladder in place for the divers to climb out of the water and get back on the boat. They were allowed to jump in without using the ladder if they wanted. None of them used the ladder to enter the water. The first diver splashed and followed the line to the bottom. He told the supervisor that visibility was about a hundred feet. He said he saw a small pit about twenty feet off the downline and went to investigate. He found the valve handle protruding from the bottom of the pit. The valve had been leaking which created the pit, making it easy for the diver to locate. The diver tied a line from the valve handle to the Odom weight. He called it a "travel line." His dive lasted about half-an-hour. His maximum depth reached was one-hundred-thirty-two feet. He wasn't required to do any in-water decompression, but he had to do twenty minutes in the chamber. We had five minutes to get him out of the water, undressed, into the chamber, and pressed back down to forty feet where he would spend twenty minutes breathing pure Oxygen.

When the diver came out of the DDC, he and the supervisor had a consultation. They decided the best tool to use for the excavation of the valve would be the airlift since the bottom consisted of "sugar sand." Sugar sand is loose sand that flows and doesn't pack. When you dig a pit in it, the sides end up having about a forty-five-degree slope so the top of the hole is twice as wide as the hole is deep. If the hole isn't initially dug deep enough, the sand will slowly fill back in before the task is completed. A hand jet wouldn't do any good here, because, for a hole the size needed, sand would just be blown all over and fall right back in the excavation area. The airlift would lift the sand up and away, and, hopefully, the ocean current would carry it away from the excavation. I listened to this conversation because I wanted to learn all I could about how things were done down here in the "real world" of commercial diving.

We, the tenders, got the airlift set up and ready to go. We attached a running line from it to the down line, then lowered it into the water. There were some weights attached to the bottom of the lift to help it sink, and help keep it in the proper upright position. We lowered it to the bottom, then the next diver splashed and went to work exposing the valve assembly. He was in the water about an hour, but didn't get the task completed. He had to spend about ten minutes of in-water decompression at thirty feet and then breathe pure oxygen for about forty-five minutes in the chamber at forty feet.

Breathing pure oxygen in the chamber was done in twenty-minute intervals with a five-minute break breathing air in between each oxygen period. This put the diver's time in the chamber at just under an hour. This was the dive pattern kept up for the remainder of the job. It took all day and into the next before the valve was exposed enough to swap it out. One of the divers was a real crybaby and complained about everything when he was in the water – everything going wrong was the tender's fault (of course). When he surfaced, he complained to the supervisor about how we were doing everything wrong. Whatever.

The actual valve swap started out okay. One diver removed the majority of the bolts, leaving two loosely in place so the next diver could hook the valve up to the davit line, remove the remaining bolts then have us pull the old one up and send the new one down. The diver doing this was the crybaby. It took him half an hour to hook the line to the valve and remove two bolts. He dropped one of the bolts and lost it in the sand. Somehow, all that was the tender's fault. We sent the new valve down and he bolted it up to one side of the flange, but he forgot to insert the gasket, so he had to unbolt it and start all over. He was having trouble getting the gasket to line up and stay lined up as he tried to bolt the valve to the pipe.

Finally, after about thirty minutes of whining and failure, the supervisor had that diver leave the bottom. His bottom time was almost seventy minutes, so he had in water decompression stops at fifty feet, forty feet, and thirty feet. It took him twenty-five minutes to get into the chamber at forty feet from the time he left bottom. He also had to spend fifty-two minutes breathing oxygen. The supervisor rounded his oxygen time up to sixty minutes so he would have three equal O_2 (oxygen) periods at forty feet. The diver was not happy and I think the supervisor extended the O_2 period as a little punishment for the diver's behavior. For some reason, divers seemed to consider chamber time as punishment. The supervisor knew that the diver's failures were not the fault of the tenders although nobody actually said anything. Remember, supervisor's failures and diver's failures were *always* the fault of the tenders even if they weren't.

The next diver went down and told the supervisor that the flange surfaces needed to be cleaned, which he did. Then he got the gasket and valve loosely bolted to one side of the pipe. That completed his dive. The following diver got the other side of the valve flanges lined up with the other pipe and got a couple bolts loosely in place. That was his dive completed. He was the last diver of the day, so we secured for the day and would continue the following day.

The first diver of the day got all the bolts put in and torqued to the gas company's specifications. It took a little less than the normal dive time, but he still decompressed on the original schedule. As he was decompressing, the supervisor contacted the home office, who, in turn contacted the gas company to let them know the valve was ready to be pressure tested. While all that was going on, we were basically on standby. That meant that after we had all the gear secured and prepped for the next dive, we could do our own thing.

It was sunny and hot. The seas were pretty calm and the supervisor asked if we wanted a swim call. I didn't know what that was. The LT told me it was when we were allowed to swim off the boat. The davit would be swung out over the water and we had a line attached to it so we could use it as a swing rope to jump into the water. All the tenders were happy to have a swim call. It was fun, the water was warm and we got to burn a little energy in a fun way. It lasted about six hours, or until dinner time. What a great way to spend our down time. In the late evening, our supervisor got word from the office that the gas company said the pressure tests were positive and we could go ahead and cover the valve back up. We would start that first thing in the morning.

There were ten pallets of sandbags stored at the middle of the boat. The plan was to use a piece of bailing wire to fasten a pair of sand bags to the down line and drop them. The diver would remove the bags from the down line and place them under and around the valve, repeating this procedure until the valve was covered. We sent the first pair down and would wait for word from the diver to send the following pair and so on. The first diver to start placing sandbags was the crybaby. Great. But what could go wrong, really?

The crybaby splashed and got to the bottom, almost immediately he called for the next pair, so we sent them down. About a minute later, we heard screaming and swearing coming over the dive radio. What the heck? The diver said the sandbags had landed on his leg and he thinks his leg is broken. Fan-fucking-tastic. We jumped the standby diver, because the diver said he couldn't get himself untangled and back to the surface, all the while screaming in pain like a little girl. The standby got to the diver and removed the bags from over his legs. They were not tangled at all. They left the bottom together and the standby got the diver over to the ladder. Two tenders were on the ladder at the water so they could help the diver out of the water. We got the diver on deck and laid down on some blankets.

We got the standby up and out of the water. Two of the other divers and the supervisor removed the wetsuit pants from the injured diver and looked him over. There was no break, and very minimal bruising. There was a very small puncture where it looked like the bailing wire might have pierced his wetsuit and skin, but it wasn't even bleeding so it was hard to tell if it was a fresh wound or not. The crybaby was still whining and saying it must be fractured and he couldn't dive anymore. Fine. He was taken out of dive rotation. He then asked when the helicopter would arrive to take him back to the beach. The supervisor busted out laughing and the rest of the divers just stared blankly at the crybaby. The supervisor told the crybaby that he wouldn't dive anymore on this job, but that he would go back to the beach with the rest of us when the job was over. Also, he would be on standby pay rather than dive pay for the rest of his time out here. Then the crybaby really started making noise. He was complaining that he already wasn't going to be getting depth pay anymore since he wouldn't be diving, but he had come on the job as a diver and expected dive pay. The divers really liked depth pay because it was a dollar per foot from fifty feet to one hundred feet and a dollar-fifty per foot from one hundred feet to one hundred and fifty feet, paid daily. Finally, the supervisor agreed to dive pay, but said it would be dropped from class two diver down to class three diver. I don't know how the pay thing really worked out. I tend to think the supervisor was just badgering the crybaby. I am sure the supervisor was tired of the crybaby's shit.

The rest of us got back to work. I was wondering why we didn't use the davit to lower a whole pallet of sandbags to the bottom all at once. I figured the diver could remove the sandbags from the pallet easier than untying them from the downline. It wasn't my place to say anything though, so I kept my thoughts to myself. While we were getting the next diver ready to go, he asked the supervisor why didn't we just lower a whole pallet into the water with the davit. The supervisor looked at him and smiled, asking "What would the tenders do then?" We spent the rest of that day and most of the next day lowering sandbags down the down line, two at a time. That's how we finished the job.

That afternoon, after the completion of the job, the boat crew began picking up anchors. We started breaking down the dive station, by "we" I mean the tenders. The supervisor told us we had about a six-hour boat ride back to the beach and the sooner we got the gear ready to offload, the sooner we could rest. That was a pretty good motivator, it only took us about three hours to have the gear ready to off load. On our boat ride back, it came to light that the crybaby and a couple of the other divers, along with some of the boat crew and a tender or two were smoking pot. I learned that was a fairly common practice offshore. I asked about the piss tests that might be required by the dive company and was told that employees were only requested to submit to a piss test when the company wanted to fire that employee. It was the assumption of the company that most of the divers and tenders were pot smokers so that was an easy way to rid themselves of unwanted employees. The other way they got rid of you was to just never call you for any jobs and hope that you would find work elsewhere.

We hit the beach in Morgan City about twenty-three hundred hours, eleven p.m. for you landlubbers. There was a crew from the company yard to unload the boat, so none of us were required to help with that. The divers did expect the tenders to load their gear from the boat into their respective vehicles though. Remember, "divers don't haul gear, and tenders don't buy beer." So, we helped the divers get their gear into their rigs. It only took a couple minutes. There was a company van at the dock to take all of us tenders back to the company yard. Two of the divers went in the company van with us. We loaded all our personal gear into the van and were ready to go. Nobody helped the crybaby with his gear and he whined about that the whole time we were unloading. When the van was loaded up, we all got in and the van driver took off. We made it to the nearest bar, I think it was called the "Wheel In." This is where I found out what "tenders don't buy beer" meant. We closed the bar down, I don't know what time that was, and I have no idea how much beer we drank other than it was a lot! So ends my first offshore dive job in the Gulf of Mexico. Fun stuff.

*   *   *

I had the next couple days off. One of the guys I shared the house with wasn't working either, so we decided to jump in my bus (the sixty-seven VW painted red, white, and blue, with stars and stripes on the roof) and drive to Lafayette, Louisiana. That's where the University of Louisiana is, and we heard there were some good bars there with lots of good live music. We figured we could party with some girls and have a good time. We headed to the University district.

Somewhere close to Lafayette, we took a wrong turn and ended up in a predominantly black neighborhood. We are both white, raised in the Northwest and definitely not racist. In fact, we didn't have much experience with the type of racism seen in the south. To us people are people no matter what color, race, or religion they were. Anyway, being lost in the wrong neighborhood became obvious when my bus started getting pelted with rocks, bottles, and other debris. We were being yelled at, but couldn't really understand what was being said other than we were the wrong color to be in that part of town.

I asked several times how to get to where we wanted to be, but was answered only with foul language. After about fifteen minutes of trying to escape, we crossed some railroad tracks, and finally made it closer to the college area that was populated with more accepting people. We found several good bars with great music and had a lot of fun drinking and dancing with all different kinds of people the rest of the evening. Most of them had never met anyone from the northwest and told us we had a funny accent. It ended up being a good time with good food and good drink.

Heading back to Broussard the next day, not so much. I don't remember the name of the parish we were driving through, but we got pulled over by the local police. They were quite rude and aggressive. My hair was fairly big as I hadn't gotten it cut in a while and my friend's hair was well over his ears, close to his collar. Plus, we were in my colorful bus. We were arrested and thrown in the klink. The guy guarding the cell, kept talking about getting the razor and making us more presentable. I asked what we were arrested for and they said "Vagrancy." I told them we weren't vagrants, homeless or anything like that. The deputy asked if we were employed then. I told him we were currently employed by American Oilfield Divers in New Iberia.

They did know of AOD. They asked for proof of employment. I showed them my pager as proof. They laughed and said anybody could get one of those. We didn't have any other proof. In fact, the only ID we had was from Washington state. We had no proof of residency in Louisiana. It was looking a little grim and becoming more likely that we were about to get an unwanted haircut with a rusty razor. I kept trying to convince them that we were responsible, upstanding citizens. That made them laugh and remark that there was no such thing as an upstanding diver. I finally convinced them to call the AOD office to confirm our employment status. The call was made, employment was confirmed, and we were released with hair intact. Whew. Before returning my keys to my bus, though, we were told that we needed to get our proof of employment cards from AOD and make sure we had them on us at all times. Lesson learned.

We drove back to our place in Broussard then walked to a local bar. It wasn't much and not very crowded, but it was close to home and we felt pretty safe drinking there. Some other divers and tenders showed up and we ended up getting pretty drunk. The next day I got called out for another job.

I went into the office and told the personnel manager that I didn't like working with guys that smoked pot on the job and asked if I could get on a crew that didn't put up with drug abuse at work, that would be better for me. I didn't want to be held responsible for the actions of divers or tenders that were stoned on the job. The manager said that was no problem and he could get me on a crew that was drug-free on the worksite. I'm not against recreational drug use in general, as long as it doesn't interfere with your life. I didn't care what guys did on their time off, but when working, especially in the diving field, I think people should be on top of their game. The office put me on a crew that was drug-free as I requested. The supervisor of that crew had a reputation of getting jobs done well, and on time. He had a very good rapport with the office and tended to work more than most of the other supervisors employed by AOD. I went to work for him the following day. After getting on his crew, I didn't have much time off anymore. Fine with me, I was there to work offshore, not hang out on the beach.

*   *   *

The jobs all ran together. I don't remember where one ended and the next started. I worked with a core group of two or three divers and three or four tenders that were consistently requested by that supervisor. We would work with different divers and tenders as the size of the crews needed to be changed. The smallest crew I worked on consisted of four divers and six tenders, the largest had sixteen divers and twenty tenders, most jobs had crew sizes somewhere in between.

The large crew was for an oilrig inspection job. We were to clean all the legs, horizontals and cross members with a water-blaster then inspect all of that visually and with a non-destructive magnetic tester looking for cracks and corrosion.

The crew didn't need to be that large to get the job done, but the company got paid for the number of personnel on the job – the more workers on the job, the more money the company was paid. That was weird to me. It was a twenty-four-hour work schedule. Dayshift ran from noon to midnight and nightshift ran from midnight to noon. That was for the tenders only though. The supervisors' shifts were eight in the morning to eight at night and eight at night to eight in the morning. The divers had a rotation and only had to be on deck for their dive time. Like the other jobs, dive time consisted of standby dive, actual dive, and chamber time if required. There were two LSTs (Life Support Technicians) and two assistant LSTs whose only job was to run the decompression chamber. They had started out as regular tenders but ended up doing nothing but working on chambers. They would go from working the DDCs to working on SAT systems which is a whole other part of commercial diving that I wasn't involved in yet. Normally on a Sur-D-O2 (Surface Decompression using Oxygen) the divers would run the decompression if there were no LSTs on the job. I was assigned to the dayshift and would be working the deck, not operating or assisting with the DDC. That was fine with me.

The first step in completing this job was to clean the areas to be inspected. To do this we utilized a ten-thousand psi water blaster. The divers would use the wand (nozzle with handgrip and trigger) to blast the encrusted life and debris from the framework down to the coated surface, or bare steel if the coating or paint was coming off too. All kinds of barnacles, anemones, rock oysters, and other sea life had attached itself to the rig. As the diver blasted this stuff off the rig, huge clouds of pulverized debris would linger. This attracted all kinds of fish. It was like a fantastic seafood buffet for hundreds of fish.

The oilrig created an artificial reef that already attracted all kinds of sea life. It was a whole, thriving little ecosystem out there. The artificial reefs created by the oilrig supported so much sea life that both commercial and sport fisherman would visit the area and catch all kinds of fish. SCUBA divers would come out to the rigs for spearfishing, shrimp collecting, and taking photographs of the sea life. In fact, one of the perks for us was that we could SCUBA dive or free dive during our free time. It was incredible. The visibility around the rigs that were way offshore was usually very good. It made for awesome diving and several of us took full advantage. All we had to do was stay out of the way of the working divers, not interfere with any progress, and be ready to work when our shift started.

The water blaster was a pretty dangerous tool. A ten-thousand psi stream of water coming out of a pencil-lead sized hole has a lot of destructive force. It removes scale and encrusted material better and faster than any scraper you could imagine. It can cut through flesh and wetsuits like a hot knife through warm butter. The divers needed to be hyper aware of the danger and be sure to be very careful when using this tool. They were told to never tie the trigger in the on position. Many divers wanted to tie the trigger because squeezing the trigger tired out your hand after a while. If you weren't used to it, even ten minutes of squeezing could tire your hand. So, of course divers would want to tie the trigger.

We had one diver on the job who showed the other divers just why you shouldn't tie the trigger in the on position. A couple years earlier, he had been doing the same job we were now doing, more or less, with a ten-thousand psi water blaster. He had tied the trigger. The wand got away from him. Now when you have a hose that has anything blasting out the open end, the hose will whip around like an angry, insane monster snake. It is really hard to get a hold of and it has a mind of its own, whipping around trying to blast anything and everything around it. And that is just what happened. This loose wand had started at the right foot of this diver and cut its path all the way up his right leg, barely missing his groin as it continued up the right side of his torso and neck. He was wearing a KMB ten band mask at the time, and the jet stream from the blaster cut the band mask off his head. It gouged a bloody trench right up the side of his face, missing his right eye by a mere half an inch.

The stream from the blaster had cut his wetsuit off his body leaving a nasty body-long open wound. He was lucky he didn't die, let alone lose his balls and cock or his eye. Even though this had happened several years ago, he had this huge, nasty scar to remind him, and other divers, of the dangers of the ten-thousand-pound water blaster. It was also a good warning for the new and younger divers who refused to believe or heed the warnings of more experienced divers and supervisors. The funny thing about the diver with the scar is that he was so frugal with his dive gear that he was still using the same wetsuit he had been wearing during the incident. He had just glued and sewn it back together. He figured it was a perfectly good wetsuit, so why not continue using it.

One of the ways a supervisor could tell if a diver had tied the trigger was that the water blaster would never shut off. When you released the trigger, the machine would idle down. Because of this, everybody on deck could gauge how the diver was doing. Normally there would be some sort of pattern where the trigger would be squeezed for ten to fifteen minutes then released for a couple, then squeezed again. The supervisor knew something was not quite right if either the trigger was squeezed for an excessively long time, or if it hadn't been squeezed for quite a while. Once, during my free time, the supervisor saw me on the deck and asked me to put on my SCUBA gear and go check on the diver. The trigger had been squeezed continuously for over half an hour. I obliged. I donned my gear, splashed and followed the diver's umbilical down to the diver. The diver was at about eighty feet, sitting on a horizontal leaning back on a riser. His head was slumped down. He had the wand stuffed under one leg, with his hand on the trigger assembly. I saw a zip tie squeezing the trigger in the on position. I looked in the faceplate of the diver and his eyes were closed. He appeared to be sleeping. I didn't touch him or anything, I just returned to the surface and told the supervisor what I had observed. The supervisor just shook his head and remarked that he had figured as much.

I went in to clean up and prepare for my shift. On my way in, I heard the supervisor start yelling at the diver over the dive radio. The supervisor had turned the volume to the diver all the way up and started screaming at him to wake up and return to the surface as quickly as he could. The diver was trying to say he hadn't been sleeping and hadn't tied the trigger, although everybody knew he had. After the diver was back on deck, the supervisor yelled at him some more. The supervisor took the diver out of rotation for several days, until we were done with the first round of deeper dives. This was quite upsetting for the diver because even though he would still get his diver day rate, he wouldn't be getting depth pay. I figured he was lucky he didn't get sent back to the beach and replaced. We were getting deeper every couple of dives and the deepest depth we would be diving to was around one-hundred-and-sixty feet. This diver was about to lose out on a fair amount of depth pay.

The LT (Lead Tender) on this job got put into the dive rotation in the spot of the diver who was being reprimanded. He didn't get a daily dive rate, but he did get the depth pay. He was pretty happy, even though it was only for a few days. I took over the tasks of the LT while he was in dive rotation. It didn't come with a pay increase for me, just more responsibility. The nice thing about it was, that the next job I went out on, I went out as the LT and that came with a new day rate. I got a raise of fifty cents an hour, up to four-seventy-five from four-and-a-quarter. Not much, but it was nice to move up a little. Plus, it was one step closer to breaking out as a real diver. I was pretty stoked. Anyway, I continued on with the present job, no extra pay, just more responsibility and more getting yelled at – both by the supervisor and the divers, but mostly the divers.

I did my job pretty well, so the supervisor didn't have much reason to yell at me for my own personal performance, but now I was responsible for the running of the deck and all the tenders under me. Great. All kinds of people become tenders and this is where the weeding out process of the dive industry begins. Also, remember, at this time one didn't have to go to any sort of dive school to become a tender in the Gulf of Mexico. If you were a good tender, you could work your way up through the ranks and become a diver, and even a supervisor without ever having gone to dive school. I knew some of those guys and even worked with some who were still diving in the late nineties and early two-thousands.

It has started to become hard to be a "certified" diver now without a certificate of graduation from an accredited dive school, even if you are an exceptional diver. Anyway, now when any tender didn't do his job, messed up or whatever, I got yelled at for it. The idea was that I would get yelled at and then I would yell at the employee who wasn't performing up to snuff. Remember about rolling shit? The thing is, I am not very good at yelling. Besides, I don't think people perform better under stress or with negative reinforcement. I believe in positive reinforcement, an idea not popular in the Gulf diving arena at the time. So, when guys were doing things wrong, I would let them know then take the time to show them how to do it correctly. Most of the divers just shook their heads.

One of the tenders, who was hired off the street, couldn't read or write. He hadn't told anyone, so none of us knew. If the office knew, they hadn't told anyone on the job. This may not seem like a big deal. I mean does a diver or tender really need to read or write to do the job? After all we are basically just laborers – "jack-of-all-trades, masters of none." Well, truth of the matter is that everything on the dive station is labeled – all the valves, hoses, etc. That way anyone could look at the valve and read "Inner Lock Exhaust," or "Diver One Supply," or whatever the case might be. As it happened, a diver was in the water at about one-hundred-twenty feet, halfway through his dive, when the compressor supplying his breathing air died. Of course, the supervisor started yelling right away about the loss of air supply.

Those of us working the deck heard the compressor quit and the guy who couldn't read, ran over to see what the issue might be. The compressor wouldn't restart. Another tender got the second compressor running. Now the valves needed to be re-aligned. The tender, who couldn't read, was at the valve manifold on the volume tank which was the junction of all the airlines coming in and going out. He needed to shut the valve for the line coming in from the dead compressor and open the valve for the line coming in from the running compressor. This sounds fairly simple, but it really wasn't. There are many air hoses on the deck and they are usually all bundled up so they aren't just laying all over the deck. We don't need tripping hazards all over the work deck. Because of this, you can't just look at a hose and see where it is coming from – that is one reason valves and lines are labeled. Anyway, this guy was just looking at the valves. I kept telling him, "Close compressor one, and open compressor two." He just looked at me like a deer in the headlights.

The supervisor was yelling "Where's my air?! The diver's suffocating here!" I replied that we were on it and getting it to him. I looked back at the tender, who couldn't read. What the fuck is he doing, I was wondering after telling him - I don't know how many times - to open one valve and close the other. After a time, it seemed like five or ten minutes, but was probably more like one or two, I just ran over to the valve manifold and closed compressor one's valve and opened compressor two's. Then I asked him what the deal was. He looked at me like he was about to cry and told me he didn't know what valve was which. I asked him why not, since they were clearly labeled and all he had to do was look at the label.

That is when he told me he couldn't read. Normally he helped set up the dive station and would memorize what all the valves did as he hooked them up so, even though he had been working as a tender for several months, no one had discovered that he couldn't read or write. He hadn't been involved in the setup of this dive station, therefore didn't know what valves controlled what. I told him I would teach him to read and write if he wanted. Sadly, I never worked with him after that job, so didn't have much of an opportunity to help him out. I don't know what ever happened to him after that job.

The loss of compressor one wasn't that big of a deal. The dive station was set up so there was a bank of K-bottles filled with air that served as our Standby air. All the supervisor had to do was open the standby air valve on his Air Supply Rack and the diver would have air. There was never a time the diver would have lost his air, unless the supervisor was asleep. Also, divers were supposed to wear a Bailout Bottle so they had their own emergency supply of air that they could use to get back to the surface. Typically, a commercial diver has, at a minimum, three supplies of breathing air – Main Air, Standby Air, and the Bailout Bottle. I think some of the supervisors liked to yell at the crew just to get the guys riled up and running around like chickens with their heads cut off. Some form of entertainment for them, I suppose.

Funny thing about Bailout Bottles though, was that at this time in the Gulf of Mexico, divers weren't required to wear one. It was left up to the diver whether or not to wear the back-up air supply. Most divers didn't, when they were surface diving. Those that did were often ridiculed by other divers for being scaredy-cats. I mean, you don't really need a Bailout Bottle to do the job, do you? Not until you need it to get back to the surface anyway. Many divers figured you could just remove your dive hat and disconnect from the umbilical if you lost air or the umbilical got fouled or whatever. I guess that is what it takes to be a manly man. I was one of the weenies who always wore a Bailout when I dove. Mr. Talbot always used to say "There are old divers and there are bold divers, but there are no old bold divers."

This job finished up after a couple weeks. We completed it to the satisfaction of the client. A crew boat came out to pick up the extra divers and tenders and return them to the beach. We, the core dive team, were on our way to the next job. We were met by a supply boat that brought out food, full air and gas bottles, and whatever supplies and equipment we would need on the next job. Our dead compressor was traded for another working one from the yard. We, the tenders, cleaned up the dive area and made sure it was ready for the next project.

That is how work went for me for the next several months. Some of the jobs were good, some were not so good. I worked with some really good people and worked with some whom I hoped I never had to work with again. I was offshore for Thanksgiving, Christmas, and New Year's Eve. I tried to keep in touch with my family and my girlfriend, but that was rather difficult. I could call when I was on the beach, but since I started working offshore, I was rarely on the beach. In fact, in the next few months, I was on the beach less than six days.

Often while we were working near oilrigs, other dive boats would show up. It was fairly common for the oil companies to hire more than one dive company to do different jobs on the same oil rig. That was fun because we would yell across to the other boat to see who was working on it. Divers and tenders often worked with more than one company so it was common for us to know members of the dive crews on other boats. Several times I saw some of the guys I went to school with.

The boats and oilrigs in the Gulf had communication with the beach by marine radio. The marine radio could hook up to the telephone lines utilizing some sort of satellite connection. It was expensive and not super reliable. When we were off shore we were allowed one five-minute call per week. To make the call, we would have to go to the bridge and wait in line. When your turn came, you would walk up to the radio and give the offshore operator the number you wanted to call. The operator would make the connection and you would wait for it to go through. If no-one at the other end answered, that was it, no second try. You were done for the week. If you did get through and someone answered, you got to talk. The connection could be good or bad, depending on the state of the weather between the boat you were on and the beach where the marine operator was. Then, after five minutes, your call was terminated whether or not you had said what you wanted to say.

Since it was over the radio, everyone on the bridge (including all the people in line behind you) could hear both sides of the conversation. If you were talking mushy talk with your girlfriend, everybody heard and would give you a hard time about it all week. If you were heading towards divorce, everybody heard. If your wife found out about your girlfriend, everybody heard. There was very little privacy off shore. Towards the end of January nineteen-eighty-seven, work off shore was slowing down. I was told that I probably wouldn't go offshore until sometime in the spring, like April or May. If I wanted, I could work forty hours per week in the yard, with Bubba, for four-and-a-quarter per hour. Yay, a pay cut and a cut in hours, just what I wanted.

I called the Redmond guy from Can-Dive to see if he knew of any work coming up. He said yes, in fact, there was a small job at a dam in Spokane that would be starting up in March and there was a spot for me there if I wanted it. I told him I would be there and be ready. I went into the office of AOD and told them that I appreciated the work, but had been offered a job up in the Northwest. They told me that was fine and that I would always have a place to work at AOD whenever I wanted it. I thanked them again for the opportunity to work and left on good terms. I packed up my bus and drove the two thousand three hundred miles back to my girlfriend's house in Spokane

Valley. So ended my first stint as a worker in the commercial dive industry in the Gulf of Mexico. I was really hoping I would have enough work in the Northwest that I would never have to return to the Gulf of Mexico. Hah!

*   *   *

GULF DIVER VERSUS INLAND DIVER
Are you a Real Diver?
Chapter Three

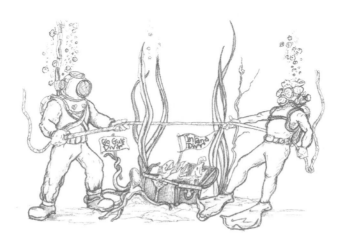

After getting back to the Northwest and getting settled in, I called the guy from Redmond to let him know I was back and available for work. He said nothing was going on at the moment, but the job at the dam was still on track for March. My girlfriend, now my first wife, convinced me to trade my sixty-seven bus in for a new Mazda pickup. It was much more comfortable to drive and worked well carrying my dive gear around, plus it got better gas mileage than my motorcycle. I messed around a bit waiting for a call, any call. A couple weeks later, the guy from Redmond called and asked if I was available to do a little job in Seattle. I told him of course I was available. I was to meet him at the Seattle ferry terminal with all my dive gear, which was basically a SCUBA set up, at eight in the morning on Monday.

I drove to Seattle the Sunday afternoon and stayed with my

sister, who was living in Seattle and working for Boeing at the time. Monday morning, I drove my new little truck down to the ferry docks. It was easy for the Redmond guy to spot me in my new truck. He had a whole dive system in the back of his pickup; Quincy three-twenty-five compressor, forty-gallon volume tank, Oceaneering rack box, three-hundred-fifty-foot dive umbilical, Helle dive radio, deck whips, and a Rat hat. I was to be the diver, the Redmond guy would run the radio, and some random kid who just finished dive school, would be the tender.

It was a simple job, just dive under one of the ferries and remove a fishing net that had become entangled in the propeller. The Redmond guy didn't know how to set up the dive gear, so I did that with the help of the tender. We would get paid sixteen-seventy-five for working topside. My wet pay would be double that; thirty-three-fifty, paid hourly for the time I was in the water. Our pay would also go up to time-and-a-half after eight hours. Wow, what a change from pay in the Gulf. We only got paid for time worked though, and that didn't include travel time. Travel time was ten dollars per hour. Travel time also didn't count for overtime, it was a completely separate pay. Our actual pay wasn't quite as good as it sounds. I was really happy with it though.

It took us about an hour to get set up and meet with the contact at the ferry dock. I jumped in the drink off the dock and swam under the ferry to locate the tangled-up screw. I found it in short order and my depth was only about fifteen feet. I had no worries about decompression at that depth. It was a nylon and poly mesh commercial fishing net wound all around the screw and pinched in some of the rudder bearings. It was tough to cut that stuff out. Part of the net that was around the propeller shaft had melted from the friction and was more like a plastic casing than like fishing net. I had to saw that stuff off with the knife.

All said and done I was in the water about two-and-a-half

hours. I brought most of the net back up with me. The client was happy to see that stuff. He said it was fishnet from the Indians. I learned that the Native Americans were allowed to fish with nets whenever and where ever they wanted. Nets getting caught in propellers was fairly common. I got out of my dive gear, got dressed in my work clothes, then the tender and I broke down the dive station and loaded it into the Redmond guy's truck. Job completed. Seven hours of work with three of those done in the water, according to the pay check. That was pretty nice for me at the time. I wasn't in any union and the paycheck came from a Canadian bank, to be paid in U.S. funds, so there were no deductions. It is amazing how much bigger a paycheck is when no deductions are taken out of it.

Work was spotty for me the following summer. The Redmond guy told me that American companies weren't real happy having a Canadian company do the work. He thought we needed to be able to use a name that didn't sound Canadian. That was most likely one of the reasons he was having trouble getting much work. Another reason I think is that we were a new entity and it just takes time to get going. I think I worked about four or five days a month through October. I enjoyed the work, it was usually just me and one other guy, several times it was the guy from Redmond on the job with me. He would do the paperwork and I would do the diving. We worked in irrigation ditches, small earthen dams and small-town water systems. We even did a couple jobs for the Spokane City Water Department. There was no work from November through April. I got a job at Mount Spokane as a chairlift operator to make it through the winter.

In the spring of nineteen-eighty-eight, work was still slow and spotty. I took a job as a Domino's Pizza delivery guy. The manager let me have time off for the occasional dive job. Work in May and June was very slow because the rivers would run high from snowmelt run-off. That made the river currents too high for divers to get any work done. In July there was more work, in fact it got busy enough that I had to quit Domino's. Over the winter, the Redmond guy had convinced the Vancouver office to let him register a new name. He also talked them into moving the office to Spokane so he wouldn't have to drive to Redmond every week. He found a real office in a building of a construction company. They had an unused office on the second floor of their building that they rented to him. They also allowed him to store equipment in their fenced yard. In Redmond he only had a desk with a phone in some marine company's office. The place in Spokane was a huge upgrade. The construction company even let him put the name of the dive company on their sign so we had a presence. The new name was United Marine Divers. We got t-shirts printed up and everything. That was pretty cool.

The work that summer and fall was mostly small stuff. Our dive team was mostly just me and one other guy. Many times, the other guy was the guy who got the office moved from Redmond to Spokane. If we got a bigger job, we would have a three-man dive team. One of the three-man jobs that summer took place in a small town in Oregon. It was at an earthen dam that created a reservoir used for irrigation and the city water supply. A huge stream of water at the bottom of the dam was flowing out of the access tunnel. They needed someone to go into the tunnel access to see what the problem was and how it could be stopped.

The day before the job, the Redmond guy and I drove down to the job site together in his truck. We had the dive package and my SCUBA set up in the back of his truck. The third guy was from Western Washington and was supposed to meet us at the job site the following day. At eight in the morning the Redmond guy and I got to the job site and met with the client. He showed us the access tunnel.

The tunnel was a concrete, rectangular tube going into the bottom of the earthen dam. It was about eight feet high and six feet wide. The entrance to the tunnel was a regular-sized, steel man-door. It was open and a stream of water as wide as the door and about four feet high was pouring out through it. The "diver" was supposed to go through the door and find where the flow was coming from. Ha ha! The other guy hadn't shown up yet. We talked about the best way to do it. About ten a.m. the other guy showed up. We had worked together several times. He was going to be the "diver" on this job.

He got his wet suit on with weight belt and ankle weights. We decided the best way to start was for him to enter the access tunnel by walking, if he could, and go from there. He walked to the door from the side and kind of rolled himself around the door jamb. The water came up to his chest and was trying to push him out the door. He was struggling and flailing around a little. I couldn't do anything to help him, other than keep an eye on him and help him if he got into trouble. He inched his way over to the side of the tunnel and found some piping. There were several different sized pipelines attached to both sides of the tunnel. One side had a thirty-six-inch diameter pipe close to the floor and a couple other pipes up the side. The other side of the tunnel had four different pipes that were three to six inches in diameter attached to the wall.

The water flow seemed to be a little less on that side of the tunnel also. The diver could grab onto one of the pipes and pull himself up the tunnel. We decided that is what he would do. He had a KMB band mask. He put that on (so we could have communication and in case he had to go under water) and headed into the tunnel. He got about twenty feet inside the tunnel and said he had located the source of the water. One of the flanged joints of the thirty-six-inch pipe had become separated. Upstream of the break, there was about two feet of water on the floor, no current. He kept walking into the tunnel.

Close to one-hundred-twenty feet in, he found a valve on the thirty-six-inch pipe. He wanted to know if he could close the valve. The client said he was welcome to try. He got the valve closed in about fifteen minutes. The water flow had started slowing down as soon as he started closing the valve and it had completely stopped when he got the valve all the way closed. Another fine job completed. All said and done that job was just about five hours. It took us eight or nine hours to drive down to the job site and the same to return home. The pay was pretty good for the amount of actual work we did. I was still enjoying the commercial dive work and enjoyed travelling around to different parts of the country.

*   *   *

One of the two-man jobs I did with the guy from the office was in Spokane. A local construction company was hired to replace some water mains that went across the Spokane River. Our job was to inspect the trench after it was dug, to make sure it was ready to lay the pipe. After the pipe was laid, we were to inspect the pipe to make sure it was laying in the trench like it was supposed to. Then, after the construction company buried the pipe, we would do a final inspection to ensure everything was good. The office guy had also made a deal with the construction company for me to work as a sub-contracted laborer. That was great for me, because I would get to work more and at my tender rate, which was double what the laborers were getting. When I dove, I would get my wet pay, which was double my tender rate. I couldn't beat that with a stick!

The office guy only came out to the job site when the diving was going on. The rest of the time, I worked as an employee of the construction company. They were using a conventional crawler crane with a drag-line bucket to dig the trench. I helped the crane operator spot the bucket and line up his drags. I also checked the spoils for debris that might hinder the laying of the pipe. I worked for two weeks on that job, but only dove three times. When we dove, the office guy would bring the dive package to the job site in his pickup. I would set up the dive station and make the dive. The office guy would operate the radio, fill out the dive log, and be the standby diver. The standby dive set up was my SCUBA gear. If something happened to me, the idea was that he would don the SCUBA gear and jump in to help me out. That meant that if he was in the water, nobody was on the radio. I didn't think much about it at the time, that was kind of the norm in the Northwest at that time. Later on, I came to realize that was a pretty stupid way to do a job. We were lucky that we never had any issues.

*　　*　　*

We started doing more dam work that summer. We did small jobs for Washington Water Power. They owned six or seven dams on the Spokane River and a couple on the Clark Fork River. Whenever we did those jobs, we had a minimum of a three-man crew. We also did a couple jobs for the Grant County Public Utilities Department (PUD). We were also doing ROV (Remotely Operated Vehicle) work all over the place. Our name, and reputation as a company that got the job done, was getting around. Another change we were making is that SCUBA wouldn't be used for standby as often.When we worked on dams, we were required to have a standby that was on an umbilical and had communication with the topside. That was much safer and only made sense, if you really thought about it. Because of this, we needed more dive equipment; dive hoses, deck whips, and dive hats. The Vancouver office sent us several Rat hats and a couple KMB band masks. Since these were coming from Canada, they required a paper trail of importation, even though they were manufactured in the U.S.

Our office had received some of this gear without documentation. It just so happened that some of the newly received equipment was needed on a job. It needed the documentation to be allowed on the job. The job was starting on the following Tuesday, it was Friday afternoon when the office guy discovered the issue. Paperwork for the equipment needed to be registered at an office in Olympia, Washington, then it would need to go up to Vancouver, where the equipment came from so the office there could verify the numbers and certify the documentation. After that, the paperwork needed to get back to the office in Olympia to be filed, and finally back to Spokane so it could be shown to the client before the equipment was allowed on the job site. It couldn't be faxed, because they had to be originals, not copies, not even certified copies.

Next day air wasn't very common then, besides, it had to go to a couple different offices, one of them being a government office. Even with next day air, it would take at least four or five working days to get the documentation registered and filed. What to do, what to do? The office guy knew I rode a motorcycle and asked if I might be interested in running the paperwork all over on my bike. I told him I would gladly do it for ten dollars an hour, plus meals and snacks. He thought about if for a while. We haggled over the deal for a few minutes.

I agreed to eight hours of tender pay, gas paid, and meals and snacks paid. If I used a hotel that would be on me, but he really needed the paperwork by eight o'clock in the morning Tuesday. Okay. Give me the documentation and I will get it done. I drove to my sister's house in Seattle that Sunday. Early Monday morning, like four a.m., I hit the road heading to Olympia, two hours south. I was at the government office in time to have a McDonald's breakfast before the office actually opened at seven. I got all the papers signed and certified. Then

I rode up to the office in Vancouver, BC. It took over an hour to get across the border because of the traffic. When I got to the Can-Dive office, they were waiting for me. I got in and out of the office there in less than an hour.

Next. I had to get back to the office in Olympia so the documents could be filed with the state. It only took a few minutes to cross the border back in to Washington. I made it to the Olympia office about an hour before they closed, basically just enough time to take care of what we needed. With all the documentation signed, certified, and filed, I took our copies back to Spokane. I arrived in Spokane about eleven p.m. and called the office guy, telling him of my success. He said I could just bring the documents to the office when he opened it the next morning at eight. I got to the office and gave him all my receipts. We figured I had just run about one-thousand-two-hundred miles in less than thirty-six hours. Mother Nature had been good to me. I didn't get rained on at all. It was sunny most of the day I was riding. I had fun doing it and got paid to boot! What could be better than getting paid to ride your motorcycle?

Still, there was no work after the end of October. Work wouldn't start until the following Spring, mid-June before it really got going. That winter I worked at Mount Spokane ski area again and also took a few classes at Spokane Falls Community College. I was thinking that if dive work was going to be so seasonal, I could do something else in the winter months. Teaching, I thought, might work well as an opposite to diving. I started working towards a degree in Biology and a Teaching Certification.

*　　*　　*

The following spring, in late March, the Exxon Valdez wrecked off the coast of Alaska, resulting in a huge oil spill. The head office, Can-Dive, was getting all kinds of calls for people and equipment to be used on the clean-up of that mess. They called our office looking for people that could go up there. Our office had a fair bit of work scheduled to start in May, so we needed to keep enough people around to crew our jobs. It seemed like everybody and their brother wanted to work in Alaska. I wanted to work in Alaska too, but I also wanted to dive more than anything. The Valdez spill didn't create any dive work, instead there was lots of ROV work. The EPA wanted the whole sea bottom, in the area of the spill, surveyed with underwater cameras. The best way to do that was with cameras on ROVs.

All kinds of boats and their crews were hired to support the ROV teams and the clean-up crews. Some of the guys who dove with us also operated ROVs. Those guys went to Alaska. A few guys that tended with us thought they would make more money working on the boats up there. They left for Alaska too. What that meant for me was that I would be running jobs. Can-Dive had sent us several Rat Hats. I had been trained by the techs at Can-Dive to service them. The office told me to take one of the Rat Hats and use it as my own. I could consider it my own hat rather than a shared company hat. That was better for me, since I didn't have to share it with anybody else anymore. Very few divers in the Northwest had their own dive hats back then.

We were a small company. Realistically, there were only three guys, including me, that regularly worked out of the Spokane office. On almost every job we would have at least one and sometimes two temporary hires. Again, our busy time didn't start until mid-June, but the oil spill kept people working all through the summer and into the fall. That summer we had somewhat of a personnel change. Many of our semi-regulars didn't come back after the oil spill work. On top of that, many divers from the Gulf of Mexico came up to the Northwest looking for work, hoping to get to Alaska.

None of these divers had experience working on dams. I, on the other hand, had two seasons worth of dam experience. Because of that, I ended up running quite a few jobs. Lots of the Gulf divers think they are "real divers" and inland divers are just half a step above sport SCUBA divers. In other words, they had very little respect, if any, for inland divers. In reality, dam diving can be some of the most dangerous and definitely the scariest commercial diving there is.

We worked fairly regularly at Wanapum dam on the Columbia River. I had been going on jobs there for the past two years. I was familiar with most of the guys that worked at the dam. They were very helpful in getting our work completed. When we were diving in front of a turbine intake, we would have the dam personnel lock out that unit so no water would flow there. The dam guys would also shut down both units on either side of the one we were working on. Wanapum dam has ten turbine-generator units so there were always several units running. They were quite noisy, even in the water. Also, if the units were running above seventy percent, a lot of water would be flowing which made for a lot of turbulence both upstream and downstream.

We were called out to Wanapum to place stop logs in front of a unit so the dam personnel could do some maintenance. We had done this several times before. It was a very easy job and one I was very familiar with. To place the stop logs, the dam had a gantry crane that would lower the stop log, a sixty-ton block of concrete and steel, into the stop log slot. When the stop log had bottomed out, we would dive down and undo the two shackles, one on each end of the log, and return to the surface. It took several stop logs to block off the unit. The top of the bottom stop log was about seventy feet deep.

The actual dive took less than fifteen minutes to complete, and could be done in five. One guy would usually do all the logs in each slot. The water was pitch black, there was no visibility, but you were in a rectangular slot, following a crane wire down, so really no way to get lost. Plus, there wasn't anything to get fouled on. Like I said before, with other units running it was quite loud, making communication a little difficult. I suppose it could be kind of scary if you thought about it too much. Or didn't think about it enough!

Anyway, this particular time, we were working with a guy who hadn't worked for us before. He had been in my dive class at Highline, but I hadn't heard nor seen hide nor hair of him since graduation. He told the office that he had worked continuously since finishing dive school and had broken out as a diver in the Gulf. I don't know if that was really true or not. He didn't have his own dive hat. Not a big deal in the Northwest at the time, but kind of strange for a diver coming up from the Gulf. Gulf companies used to have company hats, and most SAT diving is done with company hats. But sometime in the seventies, some diver with more money than brains, bought his own hat. In the spirit of keeping up with the Joneses, other divers started buying their own hats. Then the companies stopped supplying company hats and a diver had to have his own hat, or a borrowed one, in order to dive in the Gulf. So, I thought it strange that a guy who broke out in the Gulf as a diver didn't have his own hat. That's okay though, I had two Rat Hats and a KMB Ten band mask, usually used for standby, available for his use. He opted for one of the Rat Hats.

He got suited up and I made sure he knew how the Rat Hat worked. We put him into a man-basket and lowered him into the stop log slot. When he got to the water, he climbed out of the man-basket and swam over to one of the gantry crane wires. Over the radio, I asked if he was okay. He said he was, but didn't really like the Rat Hat. He said he was fine though. His task was simple; follow the wire down to the top of the stop log and remove the shackle from the log, then swim along the log to the other side and undo that shackle. When both shackles were released, he was to let topside know so the crane could come up a little, ensuring that the load had been released. At that point the diver would come back to the surface, exit the water, and wait for the crane to come up the rest of the way. Then the dam crew would hook the crane on to another stop log and send it down until it rested on the previous log. At this point the diver would jump back in and repeat the process.

When the diver got down to about twenty feet, he said it was really dark, pitch black in fact, and he couldn't see anything. He said he had forgotten his light and needed to come back for it. We had never used lights before for this task and I told him that a light wasn't required. I noticed he was breathing really hard. He sounded a little stressed over the radio. I asked if all was okay other than that, and he assured me all was well. I told him we always did it by feel and never had any issues. He said he could do that. Ten feet deeper and he nervously asked if I was sure that the turbine unit had been shut down. I told him I was positive since it was I who had walked the Lock-Out Tag-Out procedure with the dam operator, ensuring it was done. He told me that he thought maybe we tagged out the wrong unit. I assured him again that the correct unit had been shut down, as well as the units on either side of the one we were diving on. Okay he said, and continued down.

Another ten feet, now he is only at forty feet. It has already been about fifteen minutes since he left the surface. Oh, My Gawd! What is taking this guy so long? He tells me he can feel water rushing past him and he thinks the dam is trying to suck him in. I tell him that is not the case, it is just the turbulence he was feeling. I could hear over the radio how the water was moving him around a bit. Then he said the hat was flooding. He thought the neck dam had come off and he needed to surface. Hmm, I had never had that issue with the Rat Hat and

I had been diving it for over two years. But if the diver wants to come up, we let him come up. So, I told the guy to open the free flow valve and surface. We would check out the hat when he was back on deck.

He sounded a little relieved and returned to the man-basket and we got him back on deck. The neck dam had **not** come off the hat. In fact, everything with the hat was fine. He did have a little water in the hat, but that could have been purged through the duck bill flapper on the right side of the hat. It worked more or less like the spit-valve on the Mark V, so he shouldn't have had any issues with that. He had spent seven weeks with me diving the Mark V in our dive school. Of course, I don't remember how many times he actually dove in the heavy gear. Anyway, he was all shaken and looked scared. He said he wasn't feeling well and didn't think he could finish the dive. Finish the Dive!?! He hadn't even started it! Oh well, he was a Gulf diver, a "real diver," and I wasn't. Ha!

I put him tending hose, and had the other guy run the radio. I got dressed in and completed the job. I used the same Rat Hat that he had used, so I could see if it was actually having any issues. I did the maintenance on all the Rat Hats we used, so I was fairly sure there weren't any issues, but you never know. My first dive to seventy-some feet went fine, no issues with the hat what so ever. I used that hat for the remainder of the day and had no issues with it. Yeah, that was what I figured. This guy had been a little full of himself and full of cow dung in dive school too. I told the office guy that we didn't need to work that guy anymore. I never did work with him again.

A few weeks later, I heard through the grapevine that this guy was telling everybody who would listen that we were a horrible company to work for. He said we used inferior equipment, old dive hats that didn't work, and personnel who didn't know what they were doing. He was telling all his buds not to work with us. Whatever. It was no skin off my nose. Our equipment was well maintained, serviced and documented. I knew, because I was involved in the process. On top of that, we had been using the equipment for several years without issues. We had a good reputation with clients for being professional, and completing the work properly and on time.

*   *   *

We started working fairly regularly for Washington Water Power also. It was nice for me to work on those jobs, because most of their dams were either in Spokane, or within a one or two-hour drive from my house. One of the most common jobs to get called out on was to inspect the trash racks for blockage that would result in reduced water flow through the turbine, thereby causing reduced output of said turbine-generator unit. WWP had told us that Little Falls Dam, just west of Spokane, was suffering reduced flow through the turbines resulting in a thirty percent reduction in power production. They needed us to inspect the trash racks for blockage and remove whatever was blocking the water flow.

I went out to the dam with one of our regular guys and met another guy, an old guy, who had done a few jobs with us, at the dam. The "old guy," who was in his early fifties, had brought his dog and his son on the job with him. He was divorced and had his son for the summer. His son was a young teenager and couldn't be left home alone. Back then it wasn't a big deal to bring someone on a project as long as they didn't get in the way of the job being done. Several guys would bring their dogs with them on jobs also. Neither the kid nor the dog interfered with our work. That guy only did a few jobs with us that summer because he was caring for his son.

Anyway, Little Falls Dam had a funny forebay. Well, maybe

not funny, but it was different than most dams we worked on. Basically, it was a water canal built above the ground. It was an open top channel that had embankments on either side restricting access to the upstream side of the dam. The dam itself was too small to dive off of, so we had to get a barge in the channel just upstream of the dam. We put the dive package on the barge and floated it down to the trash racks. The channel was about sixty feet wide and thirty feet deep. The trash racks went most of the way across the upstream side of the dam. That was a fairly big area to be blocked enough to reduce the productivity of the dam that much. Well, there was only one way to find out what the issue was, and that was to dive in and assess the situation. Oh well, I suppose we could have used an ROV with a camera on it to inspect the trash racks, but we needed to dive to remove the blockage anyway. The diver might be able to start removing the blockage as soon as he discovered what it was. An ROV wouldn't be able to do that. So, we sent a diver down. It wasn't me, and it wasn't the old guy because he wore glasses and his vision was too bad to see much when he was diving. Remember, we did a lot of work by feel anyway, so you didn't need good vision to perform a lot of jobs under the water.

The diver jumped into the pond and followed the trash racks down to see what the problem was. He got down to about seven feet when he said he was on bottom. No Way! The forebay was supposed to be thirty feet deep here. The diver surveyed the bottom and discovered that he was on the top of a hill made up of Pinecones and mud. Pinecones and mud! Picture that if you will, a huge mound of Pinecones mixed with mud twenty-five feet high. The top of the hill went upstream about five feet before it sloped down to the natural bottom of the forebay channel at a forty-five-degree angle. That is a Lot of Pinecones. We weren't prepared for that. We had thought that it was most likely blocked by branches, animal carcasses, plastic bags or some other such trash. We had a water blaster with us. That would do no good here. We had an airlift with us, but that wouldn't do any good either, it would just move the pinecones upstream a little bit and they would just move right back in and block the racks again. We needed to remove them from the forebay altogether.

Because of the high embankments on either side of the channel, it wasn't cost-effective to get a crane with a clamshell to do the work. Instead, we came up with the idea of floating a small boom truck on a barge down to the trash racks. The boom truck would lower a rectangular, expanded metal basket down and the diver would fill the basket with pinecones. When the basket was full, the boom truck would raise it out of the water and swing it over to the downhill side of the channel embankment and dump it. After emptying the basket, it would be lowered back down to the diver and the process would start all over again. This turned into a very labor-intensive process, but there wasn't any other good, cost-effective way to get it done.

To fill the basket with pinecones, we tried several different tools. We tried grain shovels, snow shovels, regular spade shovels, and a potato fork. What we found that worked best, however, was a four-tong pitchfork. The diver would go down and pitchfork pinecones into the basket until it was full. It took a good fifteen to twenty minutes to fill the basket which was about eight feet long, six feet wide and four feet deep. Since the depth was less than thirty-five feet, the diver could stay in the water all day without having to worry about decompression. The work was physically tiring though, so we dove two four-hour blocks. One diver would work in the morning, and the other would go in the afternoon. All three of us dove, tended, and ran the radio, so each guy would get at least two dives every three days. We worked an eight-hour day of diving, with about an hour of set-up and an hour of breakdown. With an hour drive each way, we were looking at twelve-hour days for ten hours of pay. It was still good for me.

It took us eight days to get the job done. With mobilization and demobilization, it was a ten-day job. We didn't work weekends, so it was kind of like a regular job; for two weeks anyway.

*   *   *

Sometime in mid-July, I went on a job with two guys who had come up from the Gulf, and one from the Can-Dive office. The guy from Can-Dive was going to run the job. One of the guys from the gulf had been working with us for the past year or so. He grew up in Blanchard, a small town in north Idaho just a few miles from where I grew up. He was a couple years older than I, and had graduated from DIT (Diver's Institute of Technology) in the spring of nineteen-eighty-three. He had reddish-blond hair and got teased once in a while about it. The other guy from the gulf was a friend of his. They had worked for the same company in the Gulf; Cal-Dive. The other guy was from California but had decided to move to the Northwest if he could find enough work in the dive industry here. He was in excellent shape. He also came from a Greek family and most women thought he was pretty good looking, your typical tall, dark, and handsome guy you always hear about. He never had any trouble meeting women. The guy from Canada was the oldest. He had been with Can-Dive for a while and supposedly knew what he was doing. He was also very full of himself. He thought he was a great diver and God's gift to women. Even though he was married with a son, he would pick up girls in the bars we went to after work. I didn't like him much and I don't think he liked me much either. We had to share a hotel room for this job, so we got along.

We had been called out by the company that owned a pulp mill in Newport, Oregon. They had a grey-water outfall that extended about four-thousand feet out into the Pacific Ocean. It appeared that the pipe had sprung a leak about twenty-five-hundred feet from the beach. We were told that the outfall had developed a leak in the same place a couple years earlier. The client rep said the leak had been repaired by encasing the pipe in concrete. The pipe wasn't pressurized, so there should not have been a problem. Our job was to locate the leak, inspect it, and report our findings. It was supposed to be a two-day job at most.

It can get quite stormy off the Oregon coast and the waves can get pretty big. This would make it nearly impossible to dive with the set-up we had. If we couldn't dive because of weather, we would get paid a standby rate to sit at the motel and wait for a good dive day. Our dive package was set up on a very small, flat-bottomed, all steel tugboat sort of thing. It was about thirty feet long and ten feet wide. The deck was about two feet above the water level. There was a small pilot house in the middle of the boat that could barely hold three people. There were five of us on the boat, probably a bit overloaded, but we did all have life jackets. The engines were below deck in a space that was only five feet high. It was dirty, greasy, and smelled like burnt oil. That is where we stowed all our dive gear as we motored out to the work site. It wasn't really a tugboat, and it looked like it had been hand-built in someone's garage. It bobbed around really badly in the waves. We called it the "Cork." I don't remember what its real name was.

We were lucky with weather the first two days. The first day we went out to the area where the leak was. We found it quite easily, because there was a huge plume of orange-brown water flowing to the surface. We dropped anchor and used the anchor line as a down line. The guy from Canada informed us that he would not be diving. He would be the non-diving supervisor. Fine with me, fine with the other two guys also. The depth varied between thirty and forty feet, depending on the tide, so we had at least three hours and twenty minutes of dive time each. Blanchard dove first. He reported back that he had found the pipe and the leak area. There was a huge mushroom head of concrete resting on top of the pipe. He said it looked like the concrete had been poured on top of the pipe without any kind of form.

The blob was about twelve feet in diameter and two to four feet thick. He also said that the wave action had scoured out a cavern under the pipe, so the concrete blob was resting on the top of the pipe in mid-water. The pipe was bent down a little which stressed the pipe and enlarged the original crack. Effluent was pouring out of the leak on the bottom of the pipe. The hollow under the concrete was about four feet deep. It extended under eighty-percent of the concrete mushroom head. It was dark in the hollow, and the diver couldn't see what was under there. He did reach in and wave his hand around but didn't feel anything. The diver returned to the surface and we headed back to the beach. The client would have to decide the next step.

The next day we were told that we were to break up the concrete with jackhammers. The rubble would have to be removed from around the pipe so it could be properly repaired. After the repair was complete, we were to fill the cavity with sandbags to support the pipe. We spent that day getting the equipment to do the work loaded on the "Cork." We planned to go out the next day and start the concrete demolition. Unfortunately, a storm came in and the seas were too rough for us to go out. We spent the third day in Newport, waiting for the weather to clear. We couldn't hang out on the beach because it was rainy all day.

The sun was shining on the morning of the fourth day. There wasn't a cloud in the sky. It would be a great day for diving. We motored back out to the work site, dropped anchor and started diving. The first step was jackhammering. We used ninety-pound pneumatic jackhammers with a five-gallon bucket tied on to it to float some of the weight. Even set up like that, it was very physical work and after two-and-a-half hours the diver would be worn out, at least Blanchard, the redhead, and I were. It seemed like the Greek could do it all day. All three of us dove that day. We continued doing this for the next several days. The rubble started building up enough to hinder our progress the second day of demolition. We took a five-gallon bucket down to move the rubble away from the work area.

I was pulling rubble out of the hollow when I saw a Wolf Eel hiding there. I told the guys that there was a Wolf Eel there, but they didn't believe me. In fact, they laughed and gave me a hard time about it. I didn't really care; it was in fun. I did work carefully though, making sure not to bother the Wolf Eel and keep from getting bit. Their bites could be really bad because they had lots of nasty bacteria on their teeth. They also had a pretty strong bite and could rip flesh. I was diving a dry-suit and didn't want the eel to puncture it. The Greek went down next and ran the jackhammer his whole dive. That finished out the day.

The following day, Blanchard dove first. He went down and had to remove rubble. He was huffing and puffing moving the rubble away. About half-way through his dive, we heard a scream over the radio, followed by all kinds of foul language. Then he started yelling "Something bit me, something bit my hand! I've been bit!" We got him back to the surface and up on the boat. A couple fingers on his right glove were shredded. Luckily, he had pulled his hand away before the eel got a good bite. His fingers were fine, not a scratch on them. We all laughed about it. I told them again, that I really had seen a Wolf Eel hiding in the hollow. This time they believed me. After we made sure his hand was okay, he put on a new glove and jumped back in to finish his dive.

After several days of good weather, we finished removing all the concrete and prepped it for repair. On one of the days, it was sunny and calm. We were all feeling good and enjoying splashing around in the water. I dove my turn in rotation as normal. When it was time for me to return to the boat, I came up feet first. I was just playing around and thought the guys would get a laugh out of it. We always talked about how comfortable we were in the water, who could stand on their head, who could whistle (after a certain depth whistling becomes impossible), and things like that. I thought I'd show them I could surface feet first and right myself on the surface. Well, the goofball from Canada freaked out. He thought I was having a problem and without listening to me on the radio he started yanking on my dive umbilical, pulling me back to the boat. I righted myself at the boat and got up on deck. I pulled my hat off and asked the Canadian what his problem was. He replied that he thought I was out of control and needed help. I told him that was what a radio was good for, to ask the diver whether or not he is okay.

The next day we used a Plitco clamp to repair the leaking pipe. The client had never heard of it, neither had the guy from Can-Dive. The two divers from the Gulf had suggested the clamp. They said they were very commonly used in the Gulf. It was very easy to put on and seal the leak. We got that done in one day and were ready to start placing sandbags the next. Sadly, a storm blew in overnight and we spent the next couple days on standby.

The third day of standby, our office manager called me. He said that he had bought me a bus ticket to return home to Spokane. I told him the job wasn't done yet and he said they only needed two divers from here on out. Fine. Whatever. I knew I had the least experience, even though I had the most seniority. When I got back to Spokane, I went into the office to talk to the manager. He told me that the guy from Can-Dive had told him I wasn't a very good diver. So many guys were coming up from the Gulf that summer, that I was easily replaced. The office manager told me that I should probably go back to the Gulf and break out as a diver there before working in the Northwest again. Fuck him. I told him that too. I also told him not to bother calling me for work, because I wouldn't work for a guy who didn't appreciate the guys who got the jobs done for him.

A couple weeks before that job, I had moved out of my wife's house. We had filed for divorce. She took all our trucks, we had two, but she let me take my motorcycle. I also took my tools and my dive gear. She got everything else. Most of it was hers anyway. We just wanted different things out of life. She didn't like me being a diver and working out of town all the time. She didn't like that there wasn't a regular schedule for my work. After you finished a job, you weren't sure when the next job would start. I was running around with a bunch of bikers at the time too (I was a member of ABATE). She didn't like that either. Anyway, because of that, I had moved in with my dad. It was very kind of him to welcome me back into his home. But after a couple weeks, I really needed to be on my own. The job in Oregon that I had just finished up had given me a very good paycheck. I was thinking of buying a new motorcycle with it, but upon further reflection, decided I should buy a house instead. I found a nice little house a couple days later, bought it and moved in. I also bought a nineteen-fifty-six Willy's station wagon, Santa Claus red.

There were other dive companies in the Northwest, so I started making calls. In the dive industry, you have a better chance of getting a job if you ask for one face to face with the owners or managers of the companies. I jumped on my bike and made the rounds. There were really only five other companies of any substance at the time in the Northwest. None of them had work for me, they were all crewed up. One of my biker friends worked for the Coors distributer in Spokane. He got me a job working in the warehouse, running a forklift, unloading train cars, loading trucks, and repacking damaged cases of beer. It was a pretty fun job and paid pretty well. It was on par with what I was making as a diver, but I didn't want to do that for the rest of my life. Since I didn't have any diving prospects through the fall and knew there wouldn't be any work until late spring, I entered the Teacher Certification program at Whitworth College.

That fall, I actually did get calls from a dive company based in Portland, Oregon. The jobs were short and I went as a tender. Both my warehouse employer and my professors at Whitworth let me have the time off to do the diving jobs. I think they thought it was cool to be involved with a commercial diver.

*   *   *

ROVS ARE GOING TO TAKE
ALL OUR WORK!
Chapter Four

In May, the spring of nineteen-ninety, I had finished my first year at Whitworth College. I had gotten a job at Grant Elementary in Spokane for the winter. I was a Teacher's Assistant, helping kids with math and reading. That was fun and rewarding work. I had also worked several small jobs with a couple other dive companies on the west side of the Cascade mountains. The office guy from UMD in Spokane called me and asked me if I was available to go on a job. I told him I was. I guess enough time had passed that we both had cooled down and could work together again. Upon reflection, though, I think he was getting more work and just needed bodies to go out on jobs. Realistically, there weren't many divers in the Northwest, especially the Inland Empire – Eastern Washington, Idaho, and Montana. He was getting a lot of work with Washington Water Power and Grant County PUD. He was also getting a little work with Montana Power Company, Spokane City Water, and a few irrigation districts. He was getting a lot of calls for ROV inspections too.

This job was for WWP on a small dam in Waterfront Park,

downtown Spokane. The trash racks were blocked enough to reduce the output of the turbine-generator units. This dam is in the center of the park, so it could be clogged with anything like leaves, pinecones, trash, dead ducks, and other debris. Blanchard, the redhead from Northern Idaho, was running the job and the third guy was a rancher's son from the Tri-cities. He was kind of a grump or sourpuss, but he worked okay. I had worked with him a couple times at Wanapum dam and got along with him fine. He was diving a Superlite Seventeen now. Last time I worked with him, he had been using a band mask. I guess he upgraded. I was still using a Rat Hat. Blanchard was diving his Superlite Seventeen. It was becoming the norm to wear a helmet rather than a band mask when doing dam work. It was better protection for the diver's head. We still drug a KMB band mask around with us to put on the standby hose.

Our supervisor, Blanchard, made the first dive. He said there was a pile of debris about ten feet high, forty feet wide and five to eight feet long blocking the trash racks. The depth of the forebay here was about eighteen feet, so that big a pile of debris was substantial. He and the client had thought something like that was most likely, so we had a dump truck and a boom truck with a trash basket on site. The trash basket was the same expanded metal basket we had previously used at Little Falls dam. The boom truck would lower the trash basket to the bottom and the diver would fill it up. We used both a pitchfork and a shovel to fill the basket. There were some fairly large rocks in the debris, which we lifted into the basket by hand. When the basket was full, the boom truck would lift the basket out of the water and dump it in the dump truck. At the end of the day, the dump truck would unload the debris somewhere offsite.

This job was fun, because it was in the middle of the city park. The weather was great for the duration of the job. Visitors to the park would stop and watch what we were doing. We had to be very professional on this job, since we were in such a public place. That wasn't really a problem for us though, we were pretty respectful people. The job lasted about a week. When it ended, I went back to the elementary school. The second week of June was the end of the elementary school year and I was out of a job. I was also working part time at the Spokane Falls Community College Math Lab as a tutor, so I wasn't out of work.

Dive work picked up for me that summer though. It was a fairly busy summer for UMD. We were diving all over the Inland Northwest.

We did lots of trash rack cleaning. We cleaned sand from forebays with an airlift. We sealed leaky spill gates. We did lots of video inspections of dams and bridge piers. There was quite a bit of ROV work also. Most video inspections could be done better, faster, and less expensively with ROVs. We didn't have any ROVs, operators, or tenders that worked out of the Spokane office. Can-Dive had to supply all of that. I had worked a little bit with the ROV guys in Vancouver.

In the summer of nineteen-eighty-eight, I had worked with Can-Dive's main ROV pilot on several jobs. One of the more interesting ones was a preliminary ROV inspection of Crater Lake, Oregon in preparation for Sylvia Earle's Deep Rover dive in the lake that summer. I had also helped him prepare the ROVs that Can-Dive had rented to James Cameron for the making of his movie The Abyss. I had worked with the Can-Dive ROVs more than any other American employee of theirs. That made me the best candidate for being an ROV tender in the Spokane office. Yay. Sarcastic yay. Plus, none of the other guys really wanted to have anything to do with ROVs. They were afraid ROVs might one day replace divers and the less they had to do with that, the better.

My thought on that, really, was that if the work could be done without the aid of a diver, then it should be. The only time you should use a diver was when there was no other way to do the job. Don't get me wrong here. I loved diving, and I wanted to be a diver. I just figured that if there was a safer way to do the work, then by all means, do it safer. That usually meant without a diver. If a diver wasn't in the water, he couldn't get hurt or die.

Well work was work. ROV tender paid the same as dive tender at the time, so financially, it wasn't that much different. Of course, I didn't get to dive as often. I did get to travel all over the Northwest, though, and that was awesome. Part of the reason I wanted to be a diver was so I could work in all parts of the world. ROVs could go places divers couldn't, or shouldn't, so I did get to work on some dams and bridges that most divers never saw.

The past couple summers, like I said, I had worked with Can-Dive's main ROV guy. He taught me a lot. He was also involved in the Newt-Suit operations and Can-Dive's other One-Atmosphere Diving Equipment, like the Wasp and the Deep Rover. I tended on some of those jobs for Can-Dive when they couldn't get enough Canadians to fill the positions. I learned a lot about those systems too, but those are stories for later.

By this time, the summer of nineteen-ninety, the Spokane office guy was trying to do more without Can-Dive. Probably because Can-Dive had their own stuff going on and couldn't loan as much equipment and personnel as they had in the past. I had worked with an ROV called the Phantom Five Hundred a fair amount. It was a small ROV with three thrusters; one in the center of the body for going up and down and two at the back of the body for going forward and backward. The body was yellow fiberglass about eighteen inches wide, three feet long and a foot-and-a-half tall. It was surrounded by a three-quarter-inch aluminum tube crash frame for protection. It only had a camera mounted on it, but it also had attachments for sonar, magnetometer, and a small grasping arm. It could only deal with currents up to one knot. It was usually accompanied by a five-hundred-foot umbilical, but if needed, a one-thousand-foot umbilical was available. There was a place in Seattle that had one of these for rent.

This summer, the Spokane office guy rented that ROV. He hired a couple different American guys who said they were proficient ROV pilots. Hah! What a laugh. The Can-Dive pilot was good. I never saw him get the ROV fouled, and he always, or almost always, knew where the ROV was in the water. He had very good spatial awareness of the ROV's position. The pilots we used this summer, and for the next several years, were not anywhere near as capable or aware.

Regardless, I went out on these jobs when asked. The first one I remember was a trash rack inspection. The depth was only fifty feet at the deepest. It was a two-man crew, as normal for small ROV jobs, just me and the pilot. This pilot was from Poulsbo, Washington. I was assured that he had extensive experience as an ROV pilot and I should follow his lead. Okay. He told the dam operator that we didn't need him to reduce the flow through the dam because the ROV would be able to overcome the small amount of current produced by the dam. Hmm. Also, of course, we didn't need to worry about the ROV getting sucked into the dam because that's what trash racks were for – to keep debris, and ROVs, from going through the turbine. True enough.

We set up the control station on top of the dam and lowered the ROV into the forebay on one side of the dam. The pilot started the inspection going up and down the trash racks, slowly moving across the dam. All was going well until he got towards the center of the dam. We saw a bunch of tree branches on the video screen. Suddenly the ROV wasn't responding to commands. It was stationary and wouldn't move. I tried helping by pulling on the umbilical, to no avail. It was stuck. The pilot didn't know what to do. He was going to call the office. I told him to wait and let me talk to the dam operator.

When I asked, the dam operator told me that the dam was running at ninety-five percent capacity and he figured that the water was going through the dam at about three knots. I asked him if he could temporarily slow it down. He responded that he would have to get permission from the head office and it would take about an hour to reduce the flow if it was okayed by the company. I told him that would be fine. After about an hour-and-a-half, we were informed that the dam production had been reduced to thirty percent, slowing the water flow to just under one knot. I thanked him and informed the pilot.

The ROV was still unresponsive. I tugged on the umbilical and finally felt it give. We still had a picture on the screen, so I knew the umbilical was still attached to the ROV. I pulled the ROV to the surface and up onto the deck of the dam. There was all kinds of debris; branches, plastic bags, and fishing line entangled all over the front of the ROV cage. All three of the thrusters had plastic bags twisted up in them, so the propellers couldn't turn. We cleared all that stuff and ensured that the ROV was in good shape and operable. It was. I talked the dam operator into keeping the output at thirty percent. He said he could give us two more hours at that rate. I ensured him we would be done by then. We were. We ended up getting a pretty good video of the trash racks. After it was viewed by the dam company, they called up our office and scheduled a trash rack cleaning. Good for us.

The next inspection we went on was on bridge pier footings for a railroad bridge in north Idaho. I went out with the same pilot. The deepest depth was only ten feet. It should have been a simple and quick job. There were only two footings to inspect. One of the footings was only in five feet of water. We set up on the river bank and launched the ROV. Not fifteen minutes into the job, the pilot got the ROV stuck. The water wasn't even over my head. Luckily for me, it was a sunny day. I put on a pair of shorts I had with me and jumped into the water. I followed the umbilical to where the ROV was fouled and saw that it was tangled in the tree branches of a tree that was up against the pier footing. I freed the ROV and made sure there was no debris trapped in the thrusters. We did a quick performance test of all the functions and got back to work. The pilot finished that pier inspection without any other incidents. On to the second and final footing.

The pilot started on the downstream side of the second footing. The mud level here was about ten feet deep. Over my head. I was hoping there wouldn't be any issues. We got the two sides and the downstream face inspected without any issues. The pilot moved the ROV to the upstream face of the pier and low and behold, he got fouled. Great. The pilot struggled with the controls for a while before I told him to forget it. I would swim over to the footing and do what I could to free the ROV. It was fouled in tree branches about seven feet under the water. Luckily, I had enough leverage standing on the pier footing that I could pull on the umbilical and free the ROV. Again, I made sure the thrusters were free of any debris. I put the ROV back in the water and the pilot finished the inspection. I saw a bad trend forming here. But who was I? This pilot had lots of experience and knew what he was doing. Yeah, whatever you say.

A few weeks later, and after a couple regular diving jobs, I was called to go on another ROV inspection. Okay. It would be with the same pilot as the previous two jobs. Yeehaw. This job was on Boundary dam in northeast Washington. The inspection depth was figured to be forty to fifty feet. Oh boy. I reminded the office guy of our previous issues and suggested he allow us to take a dive package with us. He said we weren't inspecting trash racks, we would be looking for a crack, so there shouldn't be any debris where we would be inspecting. Besides, he already had a dive crew up there doing some other work, so we didn't need to bring a second dive package with us. That worked for me. I took my dive gear with me just in case I might need it.

We set up the control station on top of the dam, off to one side. The dive team was working from the center of the dam. There was about a thirty-foot air gap from the top of the dam to the surface of the water. The divers were using a crane with a man-basket attached to raise and lower the diver into the water. We would just raise and lower the ROV by hand. It wasn't that heavy. We ran through all the pre-dive function tests on the ROV with positive results. We put the ROV in the water and started the inspection. All was going well. The actual depth of the inspection ended up being closer to eighty feet.

We were more than half-way finished with the inspection and still no issues. So far so good. A few minutes later, the ROV quit responding. Shit. I must have jinxed it. We still had a picture on the screen. The machine wasn't stuck, I could move it around by pulling on the umbilical. The thrusters just weren't responding to the control input. Maybe it was a loose connection, I was thinking. I mentioned this to the pilot, but he told me that wasn't possible. He had made all the connections and ensured me that they were all snug as a bug in a rug. Okay, he was in charge and it wasn't my job to set it up. I was just a tender, and just there to assist as needed and tend the umbilical. Sure thing.

The pilot decided we should get the ROV back on deck and check it out. I concurred. After getting the ROV back on top of the dam, we ran through all the checks. The light worked, the camera worked and one of the thrusters worked. Two of the thrusters were not working. Let's check all the connections, I suggested, again. The pilot assured me that he had and they were all fine. Next, he opened up the body of the ROV. Uh oh. This was something the owners of the ROV said not to do. If the ROV required that kind of maintenance or repair, they were adamant that they would do it at their warehouse. The pilot didn't care. He said he knew all there was to know about how ROVs were wired.

He continued to disassemble the ROV. He pulled out the control wires for the thrusters and inspected them. They looked good. There didn't appear to be any reason for the malfunction. I told him we should just put it back together and take it back to the place we rented it from. They would take care of it. He told me he knew what he was doing and could fix it here in the field. The next thing I saw, he had pulled out a pair of wire clippers and started clipping wires from inside the ROV housing. You have got to be kidding me! What the **FUCK** are you doing? Again, he assured me that he knew what he was doing. At this point I was positive that he *didn't* know what he was doing, but what could I do? I was just the tender. I took some pictures so I would have some evidence to back up my story when we got back to the office. I knew somebody was going to be in trouble, and it had better not be me. You might not think that this was such a big deal, but this particular ROV cost about fifty-thousand dollars at the time.

The pilot finished clipping and re-attaching wires without any success. This time I didn't listen to him, I just checked the connections and found that the main connection from the control unit to the umbilical was loose – about an eighth of an inch out. I pushed it back in and tightened the connection. The thrusters worked again, but he had rewired them wrong and they functioned backwards from the markings on the control box. He wanted to take them apart and put it back to normal. I told him we should just finish the inspection and take the unit back to the shop. He wouldn't do that. He rewired it and closed it up, hoping that nobody would be any wiser. Yeah, no. I helped him get it all back together and finish the inspection, but when we got back to our shop in Spokane, I told the office guy what a fiasco that day was. The office guy was not happy. Did he fire the pilot? No. The pilot convinced him that he knew what he was doing and, in fact, had saved the day because he got the ROV working again. Holy guacamole. I would have been fired if I had done that.

*   *   *

Later on that summer, I got another call about an ROV job. This one was different, though. A company that owned a dam in the north Cascades had their own ROV, operated by one of their own employees. That employee had actually been trained by the Can-Dive pilot over the past couple summers. That company figured they would save money if they had their own ROV and pilot, rather than call Can-Dive (or whoever) to do the inspections for them. Their pilot was having some issues with their ROV. They had requested me on the job because they had worked with me before and figured I would be more help than someone less familiar with ROVs. They said a dive team was needed also. That was good for us, because I was also part of a dive team. Three of us went up to the dam to see what the issue was and what we could do to help out.

Well, here was the issue. The pilot had been doing and inspection of an intake screen at a depth of about one-hundred-seventy feet, when the ROV had become unresponsive. No matter how much they had pulled on the umbilical, the submersible would not respond or get free. It was stuck on something. The light and the camera still worked, but the visibility wasn't very good. The ROV had been in the water for two days by the time we got there.

There was only one thing to do, and that was to jump in the water and follow the umbilical down to the ROV to see what the problem was. Since I had the ROV experience, I got to make the dive. I put on my gear and splashed. We had the pilot turn the light on to help me locate the machine. I didn't really need that to find the ROV because it was obviously at the end of the umbilical. It took me two minutes to get down one-hundred-seventy-three feet to where the ROV was. I did a quick survey and saw that the umbilical had about four-and-a-half wraps around a branchy tree trunk that was stuck in the screen. The umbilical had been pulled so tight that I couldn't just unwind it from the tree. I needed to disconnect the umbilical from the ROV, free it from the tree, then recover the whole mess to the surface.

The pilot started yelling over the dive radio. He said definitely DO NOT unplug the ROV. I told him it couldn't be done without unplugging it. He reiterated that I was not to unplug it, but should free the ROV by unwinding it from around the tree trunk. I tried. It wouldn't come undone. I told him so. I also told him that if he powered down the ROV, there shouldn't be any issues caused by unplugging it. Finally, I convinced him to power it down, by telling him I would tie the ROV to the tree before I unplugged it so I wouldn't lose it. The forebay depth at this dam was over three-hundred feet – a little beyond our dive capability with our shallow water dive package, which had a depth limit of two hundred feet.

He powered it down. I unplugged the umbilical, unwound it from the tree trunk, then plugged it back in and secured it to the ROV. I untied the ROV from the tree and followed the unpowered ROV unit back to the surface as the tenders came up on the umbilical and my dive hose. My total bottom time was less than ten minutes, but I did a ten-minute decompression stop at ten feet just to be safe. I didn't need to get the bends. Besides, the nearest Decompression Chamber was several hours away in Seattle. I didn't need to be making a trip there either.

I was back on the surface and out of the water with a total dive time of less than twenty minutes. By this time, we were getting paid in four-hour blocks, so with depth pay, I had just made a fair chunk of change. Good weather, easy job, great crew, what more could you ask for? For the next few years, that is about how ROV jobs went.

The submersibles would get fouled enough, that we would always be sure to have a dive package with us, or at least very nearby. Also, a lot of the companies that owned dams started buying their own ROVs and employing their own pilots. That way, they weren't so dependent on companies like us.

*   *   *

My very first experience with ROVs was actually at Highline Community College during my third year there; my second year of the Dive program. It was in late spring. Some guy from Can-Dive brought it - a Phantom Five Hundred - to the dive pier and showed us how it worked. He spent the day with us, letting everyone in the class operate it. He showed us how to set it up, making sure all the umbilical connections were snug and secure. He went over how to do the pre-dive checks and the function checks once the machine was in the water. Then he went over the video monitor. There was a depth reading and a compass heading. The video quality was impressive and the lights were very bright. We had to do our regular dive class also, so there was a diver in the water at the same time the ROV was deployed.

We were at the stage of our dive class where we were doing a final pipe assembly project. The pipe project was made up of a bunch of different twelve-inch pipe fittings; elbows, valves, tees, and straight pipe sections all with flanges and gaskets. We were graded on how fast and how correctly we finished the assembly. All said and done, I think it was around ten feet wide and six feet high. We used the davit on the end of the dock to lower the pieces into the water, to give us a little experience working with crane wire underwater.

It was my turn to work on the project the day the guy with the ROV showed up. So, I was in the water when the first group of classmates were playing with the submersible. It is a better ROV experience if the operator, or pilot, has something to look at besides the bottom of the sea. That "something different" happened to be me working on my project. As far as I knew, I would be working on my project off the North side of our diving pier and they would be flying the ROV off the South side of the pier. Never the twain shall meet.

I was putting bolts in a flange that I had just lined up at the top of the project. I had it nearly completed. My focus was on flanges, a gasket and bolts. I was not paying attention to anything else going on in the water. I was straddling the pipe, leaning over the flanges so my butt was sticking up above the pipe a bit. I guess that was too irresistible of a target for my fellow students. I felt something hit me in the butt. It wasn't hard, but it was a little startling. It didn't scare me, really, but I did turn around quickly to see what it was; the ROV of course. I waved at the camera and went back to work. I was being timed on the project completion, so didn't want to waste time playing with the ROV. My classmates, however, didn't have the same concerns. As soon as I turned around and went back to work, they butted me again, and again. It was sort of like having a baby goat around that wanted to play and wouldn't take no for an answer. I kept working and trying to ignore the interference. After a little bit, they must have become bored with the harassment and left me alone. I completed the project and surfaced.

After I got out of my dive gear, it was my turn to play with the ROV. The monitor set-up included a VHS recorder, and of course, everything was being recorded. We played the tape and everybody got a good laugh seeing my butt get bigger and smaller as the ROV rammed me and backed off. Even I had to admit it was funny. College students. Sometimes you wonder if they will ever grow up. It was interesting to see how an ROV could aid a diver. All in all, it was an interesting experience. The guy from Can-Dive who brought the ROV for us to try out, was the same guy manning their office in Redmond who would give me a call later to go on the job to Cody, Wyoming.

Even though most of the divers didn't like ROVs, because they were afraid the ROVs were taking dive work, I kind of liked the ROV work. It was easy, usually pretty clean, and about three out of five times would result in the need of a diver to rescue the ROV, like the job in the north Cascades. Those jobs made for travel to out of the way places that were fun to see and easy money diving when required. The way I saw it, there was no way divers would become obsolete because of ROVs. Even though Oceaneering, and several other large companies, were building all different types of submersible machines, there were just some things divers were needed for. Some of the large working class ROVs were even the size of Volkswagen Bugs. They could do some pretty incredible stuff. They could work way deeper than humans could dive to. There was some stuff they could and would do, that a diver just couldn't. But, at the same time, there were things that only a diver could do. Even with the invention and improvement of the one-atmosphere dive systems, there were just lots of things they couldn't do. There would always be work for human divers.

*   *   *

BETWEEN DESPAIR AND DIVORCE
Where you Find Diver in the Dictionary
Chapter Five

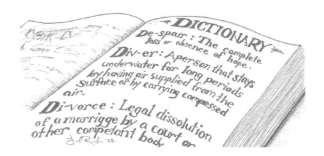

In the Fall of nineteen-ninety, I went back to Whitworth College. I wasn't working at the Coors distributer anymore. I'd had a pretty busy summer with the dive and ROV work. At the start of the school year, I returned to Grant Elementary to continue helping kids there with math and reading. I made the same deal again with the teachers to allow me to do the occasional dive job as they came up. The diving in the Northwest was still really seasonal. Perfect for me.

I only did a couple dive jobs that school year. Dive work didn't pick up for me until mid-June of nineteen-ninety-one. I did go to Madison dam in Montana for the annual trash rack cleaning in May, but it had only been a two-day job this year. For me the summer work was a little slow.   I did some work at several dams around Spokane and in Montana, but I was nowhere near the top of the list of divers working for UMD. Fortunately for me, the list was fairly short. That also meant that every job I went out on usually included a new guy. At least I wasn't at the *bottom* of the dive roster!

One of the types of job UMD secured was screw inspection and clearing on the tugs that pushed barges up and down the Columbia River. We did several of those that summer. A two-man crew was all that was ever sent out on those at that time. The work was usually completed in one dive that lasted less than four hours. Typically, it would be completed in less than an hour, but sometimes might take two. We also did these on SCUBA. I know, dumb, but we still did it. The worksite where the tugs were moored was in Wilma, Washington, about a two-and-a-half-hour drive from Spokane. We didn't get paid travel, but at least the company supplied the vehicle and paid for the fuel. We were getting paid dive pay in four-hour blocks. If you dove in the morning and then dove in the afternoon, you would get eight hours dive (wet) pay. If you dove only once in the eight-hour day, you would get four hours wet pay and four hours tender (dry) pay. If you didn't dive, you were the tender and would get paid dry pay for eight. Fine and dandy, and what you would expect, unless you only worked half a day. In that case, whoever dove would get wet pay for the four hours, but the tender would get his dry pay for eight hours (a deal we got through the union). Since wet pay was double what dry pay was, it meant that both the diver and the tender got paid the same whether they dove or not. So, guess what? Now nobody wants to be the diver. I mean why dive if you weren't going to get paid any more for it than the guy who stayed topside and dry?

It just so happened that Blanchard and I were the two who went on most of these jobs. At first, he took the dive every time. But that was before we had figured out how the pay thing really worked. We had run several ideas by the office manager, to no avail, so we were left with both being paid the same, no matter what part of the job we did. So, of course, we started arguing about who had to do the diving. Finally, we came to an agreement to take turns. He would dive on it the first time, but the next I would dive and so on. Naturally we still tried to get away with not diving by claiming it was the other guys turn. Well, that was one reason to keep our dive logs up to date. Ha!

We'd show up on site and find the captain of the tug. He would take us down to the engine room and show us that he had secured the engines and locked the shaft so the propeller couldn't turn while we were in the water. He would also lock the rudders so they couldn't move either. Next, we would set up the dive station on the back of the tug, which meant we would get two sets of SCUBA gear set up. We would have a two-hundred-foot line with a clip on one end to clip to the diver for use as a tending line. The chosen one would dress into his dive gear and don the SCUBA, splash, and complete the inspection and clearing of the propeller and rudder. Usually, it was commercial fishnet caught in the screw. Along the Columbia, the natives were allowed to set up their fishnets anywhere and anytime they wanted. It irritated the tug companies, but it made for fairly steady work for us.

Anyway, it usually only took one SCUBA tank to do the job, every once-in-a-while it would take two. The pay didn't change, however, because dive time was counted from when you first got into the water until you last got out. It would only take one diver to do the work. Plus, it was the diver who would have to write the report for the captain, as he was the one who had eyes on the situation. The only paperwork the tender was responsible for was the dive log. It was a good thing we got along with each other. We usually had a beer on the way home. Fun times.

*   *   *

In October of nineteen-ninety-one, I was back in school at Whitworth and back as a teacher's aide at Grant Elementary. Again, I had the same deal about work. This time I got called out to do a one-day job at Long Lake dam on the Spokane river. Blanchard would be running the job. The third guy was an older guy, who only dove heavy gear – you know, the Mark V set up that weighed two-hundred pounds. He was a true old school diver. He had never been in the lightweight gear – what we were all using these days – and he didn't even want to try it out. It was heavy gear or nothing, so he only tended. After a few jobs, he started complaining about only being a tender. He did have a lot of dive experience all around the northwest, but it was all in heavy gear. He said he would bring his gear and use it, but the Quincy three-twenty-five air compressors we used wouldn't supply enough air for the heavy gear.

Anyway, this job was to seal the sides of the spill gate. The spill gate was made of a bunch of square timbers, like railroad ties, stacked on top of each other. They always leaked on the sides, because the timbers had to have enough clearance to put in place and remove. Typically, we would use two-by-twos or two-by-fours in six-foot lengths to seal the majority of the leak. Then we would stuff rags in the crevices to make the seal better. We would finish off by stuffing wood pellets on top of the rags. Those would swell and seal the leak close to one hundred percent. On a small job like this we would set up our dive station on top of the dam, where the radio/rack operator would be, right over the gate we were working on. The diver and tender would be in a small boat or skiff right in front of the gate to be worked on.

This dam only had one spill gate to be sealed. The bottom of the gate was only twenty feet down, so it would take only one dive. Blanchard was supervising – meaning he did all the paperwork – and would run the radio and dive rack. I would dive and the heavy gear guy would tend. I got my dive suit on and loaded the rest of my gear into the skiff. Then the tender and I motored over to the spill gate and tied off to a steel beam there. My dive helmet was lowered from the top of the dam – about ten feet above us in the boat. I got completely dressed-in and hooked up to the umbilical. I noticed that the pneumo hose was a little longer than normal. The pneumo hose is a small, quarter-inch, rubber air hose that we used to measure the depth of the diver. It is called "pneumo" which is short for Pneumofathometer. I tucked the extra pneumo hose into my bailout harness. I put on my Rat Hat, checked comms (radio communication), checked air flow, and splashed.

I went to the right side of the gate and started sealing the leaks with a two-by-two. Even though the leaks are fairly small, less than a half-inch wide, a lot of water flows through and it is more forceful than you would think if you weren't aware of it. When you get the board close to the leak, the water sucks it into the crack so hard and fast that the board is grabbed right out of your hands. You don't want your fingers or toes to get in the way, because they would get stuck between the board and the gate or side of the gate slot which is made of metal or concrete. Any loose part of your dive gear is just as likely to get sucked in and stuck also. Well, I had been doing this gate sealing for quite a while on lots of different dams. I was well aware of the danger and very keen on keeping my appendages clear of the sucking gaps. I got the right side sealed up with the boards and rags.

Then I moved along the bottom, stuffing rags as needed.

With the bottom finished up, I moved to the left side of the gate. The gap on this side was substantially bigger than the other side. I needed a two-by-four here to start sealing. A two-by-two would have gotten sucked right through the gap. I could see light through the gap and the water was rushing so fast, it was making a whooshing noise. Blanchard came over the radio and asked if everything was okay. He could hear the water rushing through the gap. I assured him I was fine, but would need a two-by-four here. He gave it to the tender, who passed it on to me. I took it down to the gap and got the board into position, ready for the water to suck it into place.

Unbeknownst to me, the pnuemo had freed itself from my harness. I was watching the board and my fingers and toes. No thought of the pneumo. When the board was close to position, I let the force of the water grab it out of my hands and suck it into the gap. The board was jammed in its proper place securely. I went to go back to the surface to get some rags from the tender, but could only come up about a foot. What?! Oh, Shit! My pneumo was pinched in between the board and the gate. I pulled on it to no avail. I pulled on it really hard. No movement, no chance of relief. Okay, no problem. I'll just get my knife, that is always clipped to my bailout harness. Where's my knife? Oh, my *gawd!* There is no knife clipped to my bailout harness. I'm not SCUBA diving, so I don't have a knife strapped to my leg.

"Uh, Topside? I have an issue." I reported.

"What's the issue? Are you alright?" Blanchard asked.

"Yeah, I'm fine," I replied, "I'm just stuck. My pneumo got sucked through the gap and pinched between the board and the gate."

"So, just cut it with your knife," he stated.

"Uh, yeah, there-in lies the issue. I have no knife with me," I said in shame. "Could you send one down to me, please?"

"Why don't you have a knife with you?" he interrogated, "You should **ALWAYS** have a knife with you."

"Yeah, I know. I usually do. I keep one clipped on my bailout, but I didn't check to make sure it was in place before I splashed." I sheepishly stated. The tender sent me a knife and I cut the pneumo hose close to where it was pinched, leaving it as long as I could. I tucked it back into my harness and finished the job.

Both guys gave me a hard time about that the whole time we broke down the dive station. On the drive back to the yard, they were still giving me a hard time. Yeah, yeah, I know. We went to a bar, after we had unloaded the gear at the yard, and I bought them a couple beers. We got the job done and nobody got hurt, so it was a good day. Years later, Blanchard still teases me about it once in a while.

* * *

This was my final year at Whitworth. I had already earned my B.S. in Biology the previous spring, so was working on my teaching certification. One of the parts of that program at Whitworth was to work with children from different cultures. That was usually done during the Jan-Term, a four-week period that counted as a one class semester credit. I was hoping to go to Jamaica and work with an orphanage tied to Whitworth there. The school had received a request from an orphanage in Brasil, but had never sent any students there before. I was an older student, and had travelled the world a little, so the school asked if I would go there rather than Jamaica. They didn't want to send a younger, inexperienced student to a place they knew nothing about. I guess I was expendable. Ha. Anyway, I told them I would go, if I could go for more than just four weeks. I always wanted to visit Brasil and this would be a good way to do it. They said I could go for more than four weeks, but would have to return the first week of February for the start of Spring semester, when I was scheduled to do my student teaching. I headed to Brasil the day after Christmas and returned the first week of February. It was a fantastic experience. I met my second wife there. She came to the states the following June, and we married in July. But that is another story for a different time.

I did my student teaching at Libby Middle School on the east side of Spokane. I finished it in mid-June, and earned my Washington state teaching certification. It was a good experience. I had the same deal for diving that I had from the beginning of my study at Whitworth. In May of nineteen-ninety-two, I was called out on a short dive job in Spokane. It was to be a one or two-day job removing stanchions that had supported a temporary bridge under the Stevens Street bridge across the Spokane River. The job was to be done on Saturday, so it wouldn't interfere with my student teaching. Perfect. It was only going to be a two-man crew, with the support of the construction crew who was doing restorative work on the bridge. I would be working with a new guy from Lewiston. He had been on a couple other jobs for UMD with the other guys, who said he was okay. Not so perfect. Oh well, the river was only twenty-four feet deep at its deepest. There was very little current because a dam was just a couple thousand feet down stream. The river was split in two here also, because of an island in the river and the main flow of the river was the channel on the other side of the island. It would be like diving in a lake. The visibility was also very good. It should be no problem.

The actual work for us was to burn bolts that secured giant H-beams to large concrete blocks. There were about twenty beams to release, four bolts securing each beam to its block. This might only be a half-day job. The construction crew would have a couple guys in a boat who would hook a crane wire to the top of the H-beam. The crane operator would take a slight strain on the wire so the beam wouldn't fall over after we had cut the bolts off. The crane wasn't really a crane, it was a carry deck. A carry deck is kind of like a mini boom truck. It is small and pretty maneuverable, but has limited capabilities. We would use a Broco set up to burn the bolts. Broco is a system that uses a copper tube with steel rods packed inside and oxygen flowing through to make a ten-thousand-degree exothermic fire that will burn through steel and many other things. It was fun, because playing with fire is always a little fun, but playing with fire under water was *really* fun.

Lewiston had loaded the truck with the dive package, welder, oxygen bottles, and Broco gear Friday afternoon. I met him at the shop Saturday morning and loaded my dive gear into the truck. Then we drove down to the site and set up all our gear on the walkway under the north side of the bridge. We had short hoses, one-hundred feet, for this job. That should be fine. It was less than sixty feet to the furthest beam and deepest depth of twenty-five feet. I would dive first, and if I didn't finish in four hours, Lewiston would dive in the afternoon.

I got dressed in and we did all the checks; air, comms, Broco spark, burning oxygen flow. I carried the Broco torch with me as I walked down the bank into the river. We had made the plan to remove the

H-beams starting from the downstream north corner, working our way upstream. After the first row was removed, we would move to the next row towards the center of the river. There were four rows of five beams to be removed. I reached the first beam to cut. I was at about fifteen feet of depth. I could see the bottom of the boat above me. They were using oars to move the boat so I wouldn't have to worry about a spinning propeller. Lewiston told me the first beam was attached to the crane and ready to be cut. I burned the four bolts. At the finish of the last bolt, the H-beam jumped three or four inches up. That was pretty good and controllable. I informed topside the beam was free and I was clear so they could come up on the load and swing the beam away. First beam gone, easy-peasy. I moved to the next beam.

After about ten minutes, I was informed that the next beam was hooked up and ready to go. I burned those four bolts with the same result as the first beam. So far so good. Of course, it shouldn't be any other way. It wasn't like this was the first time I had done any of this type of work. We finished the first row in about an hour. Okay, it was looking like it might take two divers, but we should definitely be finished today. The next row took just about an hour also. All was going well. On to the third row.

Now I was at about twenty-four feet of water. The conditions were all the same; clear, calm water. I could still see the bottom of the boat. After getting confirmation that the first H-beam was hooked up, I burned the bolts. Same result as all the others. I moved on to the second beam in that row. Same deal, after confirmation, I burned the bolts and the crane operator took it away. On to the third H-beam. I got confirmation that it was hooked up and ready to go. Okay, here I go, burning it free. At the finish of the fourth bolt being burned, the beam did not jump. Okay, it didn't fall over either. I hid behind one of the beams on the fourth row and informed topside that the beam was free and clear and they could take it away.

I saw the fourth H-beam wiggle a little, then the third beam fell over and trapped my hose between itself and the river bottom. Then Lewiston started screaming over the radio, asking if I was alright. Our communications are two-way, hardwire radio where topside can always hear what the diver is saying. But for the diver to hear topside, there is a switch on the radio that cuts off the diver so the diver can hear what topside is saying. When topside is talking, the diver cannot be heard. You have to release the talk switch to hear the diver. Well, Lewiston wouldn't release the button, so he couldn't hear me.

The longer he kept asking me how I was, the longer he was getting no response. I was yelling at him, telling him he needed to release the switch, but, of course, he couldn't hear me. He was getting more and more excited, because he couldn't hear me. I heard him screaming to the construction crew that they needed to get me off the bottom, because I wasn't responding. I was, but he couldn't hear me. I couldn't get back to the beach, because my hose was too short to double back, since it was trapped by the fallen beam. Luckily for me, there was a few inches between the beam and the rocky river bottom, so I was still getting air. I couldn't tell topside I was okay, because Lewiston wouldn't take his finger off the talk switch.

I decided to climb the next H-beam to get to the surface so the guys could see me. The boat was still above me. I made it to the surface, but my dive hose wasn't long enough for me to climb into the boat with my hat still on. I needed to disconnect from the umbilical to get into the boat. I was hanging on to the side of the boat trying to tell them what the deal was, but they couldn't hear me through the helmet with Lewiston still yelling over the comms. I gave them a thumb's up, so they knew I was okay. They waved and yelled to my guy on the beach and got him to calm down a little.

Finally, I could tell him I was okay and what the situation was. I needed a wrench so I could disconnect my hat from the umbilical. A guy in the boat had a crescent wrench in his pocket. Yay. I turned on my bailout and one of the guys in the boat undid my air hose. I unclipped from the umbilical and climbed into the boat where I removed my hat. Lewiston got the umbilical all the way back to the beach. The guys in the boat took me back to the beach. We talked about what had happened.

It seems that the top of the third beam in that row was under the surface and the boat guys hadn't seen it. They assumed that the fourth beam was the third beam, and the one I was going to burn so had hooked up to that one. When the crane operator came up on the load it caused the boat to move and bump the H-beam I had released, knocking it over. Okay. Accidents happen and nobody got hurt, so we were okay and good to finish the job. The construction company guys had called their office and told them what was happening as it was happening. The office told them to shut the operations down for the day and file the necessary accident reports. Also, I found out that the carry deck didn't have enough wire on it to reach the H-beam now located on the bottom of the river. They didn't have enough slings to reach either. They would have to come back later with enough rigging to reach that beam. Lewiston was pretty shook up and said he needed a break before we went diving on that project again anyway. We broke down the dive station, loaded everything into our truck, and headed back to our yard.

When we got back to the yard, I called our office guy at home to let him know what had happened. Our secretary was in the office, getting some extra work done and also to be there in case we needed anything on the job. After we told her what had happened, she started crying and couldn't understand why we weren't more shook up. I told her that nobody had been hurt and no equipment had been damaged, so it was a pretty good day. She told me I needed to take things more seriously and asked if I didn't realize I had almost died. I told her she didn't need to be so dramatic and I had not nearly died. I explained that I had protected myself by hiding behind a stanchion in a row that we weren't working on. I had my bailout, so if the umbilical had been severed, I would still have had air. I had not been close to dying by any means. She just shook her head and made some remark under her breath about divers. I didn't hear it. I gave her my report of the accident and all was well. On Monday I went back to the student teaching, and a different crew went back to the bridge to finish the job. Lewiston didn't go with them, but he did continue working with us for the next couple years.

*　　*　　*

After I finished my student teaching, I was more available for dive work. I contacted some of my friends in Vancouver, BC who were working for Can-Dive to see if anything was going on up there. I was told there wasn't much going on at that time. A crew was doing some work with the Newt-suit. Another crew was out doing something with the Deep Rover. Some were working in the straits of Vancouver. One guy who had gone overseas to work out of Singapore for the early spring had just come back home. I hadn't talked to him in almost a year. Last time we had talked, he told me how he and his girlfriend were madly in love and wanted to spend the rest of their lives together. He was saving money for a new house in Vancouver.

They were currently living in a small apartment to save on bills. He had found some SAT work in Asia. His plan had been to do the hitch in Asia, return home and get married. I was looking forward to having a beer with him and catch up on all that was new in his life. I also wanted to hear about his stint in SAT. The guy who told me my friend had returned said my friend wasn't doing so well upon his return and it might be good for me to come up and visit. He also told me my friend was back at his parent's place, so that was where he could be contacted.

I called my friend at his parent's place. He said things were not so good for him at the moment, but, yeah, a visit and a night at the bars and strip clubs in Vancouver would be just what he needed. Sounds good, but weird, because he wasn't really into the strip clubs, especially since he had been with his girlfriend. Anyway, he invited me up for the weekend, I could crash at his parent's place, they had a spare room, and I got along with them well.

Friday morning, I left for Vancouver on my scooter. My scooter was a nineteen-eighty Yamaha Eight-Fifty Special. Anyway, I got to his parent's place in the mid-afternoon. He was there and was kind of mopey. His parents told me he was okay; just needed some emotional support. They were happy I had come to visit and cheer him up some. They made an excellent dinner for us, then wished us fun at the bars, but make sure we were safe and wouldn't drive drunk. We took a taxi to the Orange Number Five, my favorite bar in Vancouver at the time.

We sat at one of the booths in the back, but with a good view of the stage. A slender beautiful blond was writhing around on stage like a cat in heat. She was wearing frilly laced, lavender, bikini style lingerie which she would slowly and seductively remove later on. We were there to drink beer and catch up on how things were going for us since we last talked. Our gaps in conversation, of which there were many, we filled by watching what was going on in the middle of the bar on stage.

I talked to him about finishing college. I described how much I had enjoyed the student teaching but how hard it was for someone in my particular demographic to find a teaching job. Besides, I could earn twice as much money diving in half the time as I could teaching. On top of that, I really enjoyed that my work place and job changed all the time with diving. Teaching might become somewhat repetitive. Maybe I could substitute teach during the school year. I explained to him that we were getting about one new guy on every job we were doing lately. I recounted my experience with the H-beam falling over and we laughed about that, but both said how lucky I was that nothing seriously bad had happened.

He talked all about his SAT experience in Asia. He had loved it and wanted to go back for more. He said the people he worked with were great. Divers from all over the world worked there and got along well with each other. Well, except for the Dutch, he said. Most of the Dutch were capable, but they were all full of themselves. They were always saying things like "If you ain't Dutch, you ain't much!" We laughed. He said the companies paid very well and treated their dive crews better than the American companies did. He liked it a lot. In fact, he was going to head back as soon as he could secure another spot on a SAT team. He had several offers already.

Whoa, wait a minute, I said, what about your fiancé? I thought you were planning a big wedding and were buying a house and all that stuff. I thought she didn't want you working away from home so much anymore. What's the deal? He looked at me, then looked down at the table. He wrapped both his hands around the pint glass in front of him and stared at its contents, about eight ounces of a dark bubbly liquid with a beige foam covering. I looked at the blond on stage. She was on her back waving her legs in the air, showing her deepest self to all who would look.

I finished my beer in one large gulp and ordered two more, one for each of us. My friend said he needed a shot of something, whiskey or tequila. Now, while I like a good tequila, rum is my favorite. My friend wouldn't drink rum unless there was nothing else around or it was free. He really preferred a good whiskey. A good Irish whiskey. Well, **now** you're talkin'! How about a couple of Irish Car Bombs? He laughed, and agreed. So Irish Car Bombs it was. And keep 'em comin', please! Oh boy.

After the second car bomb, he started talking and wouldn't stop except to drink another bomb. Yes, he and his fiancé had been planning to buy a house. That was what he had been saving for the past year, and why he had taken the SAT job. It would supply enough money in one job, when adding it to their savings, to buy a house outright. No rent, no monthly payment, a great way to start out their new life together. I asked him what was different now. He looked at me square in the eyes. I stared back at him and thought I saw tears welling up. Then he turned his head and looked at the girl on stage. I followed his gaze and beheld a dark-skinned beauty with an athletic build, dressed like Barbara Eden in "I dream of Jeannie" and covered in veils. She was swirling around the stage like Salomé dancing for King Herod.

"She's gone," he stated. "She's gone, disappeared, and took *everything* with her."

"Everything? What do you mean by 'everything'?" I asked.

"All of it! Everything. All our furniture, her car, my truck. Money! Ev-Er-Ree-Thing! Everything. Every last penny," he revealed.

"Every last penny?" I questioned. "Aren't you being a little overly dramatic? It can't be that bad." I smiled and shook my head.

"No," he replied, "all I have left is my dive gear and my tools I took with me to Singapore."

Then he told me all the sad, sad details. He had called her when he first arrived in Singapore to let her know he had made it safe and would be back in a month or so. She had reassured him all was well and she was anxiously awaiting his return. He had no contact with anyone while he was in SAT, that was the norm at the time. After getting out of SAT and back to the beach, he had called her, but she didn't answer. In fact, the call didn't go through, not that alarming with all the international call issues in Asia then. He had called his parents, and though they hadn't talked with her in a while, they had no reason to be concerned. He overnighted in Japan on his way home and had issues with his debit card there. Again, not alarming with the international dealings. He just used his credit card instead.

When he landed in Vancouver, BC, he called his fiancé again. This time the operator informed him that number was no longer in service. He thought that was weird because that was his number as well as hers. He tried again. Same message from the phone service. So, he called his parents, apologizing, but could they pick him up from the airport and take him to his apartment. He told them he couldn't get ahold of his fiancé. They said they could. After retrieving him from the airport, his parents took him to his apartment. He didn't see his truck in the parking lot. He didn't see her car either, but it was usually parked in the garage that came with the apartment. He went up to his apartment door and stuck the key in, but it wouldn't turn.

He took the key out and looked at it to make sure it was the correct key. He saw that it was, so he put the key back in the door lock and tried again. Again, it wouldn't turn. He knocked on the door, but no one answered. Then he banged on the door, still no answer. By this time, he was getting a little perturbed. He went down to the manager's apartment and knocked on the door. The manager opened the door, looked at him, and asked what he could do for him. My friend asked the manager to let him into his apartment.

That's when the manager told him that he didn't have an apartment at that complex anymore. The manager informed him that his fiancé had moved out a couple weeks earlier. She had told the manager that she and my friend had purchased a house and were getting married soon. The manager had inspected the apartment after she left and had then returned their deposit to her. My friend was flabbergasted. He asked the manager if she had left a forwarding address, but the manager only replied that yes, she was moving into my friend's new house. My friend did not have a new house. Oh boy. After some more questions, my friend learned nothing more than he no longer knew where his furniture, belongings, or truck were to be found. He told his parents of the situation and they took him back to their home.

When he got back to his parents, he called some friends. Nobody had heard anything from his fiancé in more than a couple weeks. Her friends said she had moved to a different city and didn't want to be contacted, so left no forwarding information. Her work place knew nothing other than she had left without giving them a two-week notice. Next, he went to the nearest ATM to get some cash, but all he got was an insufficient funds notice. He had the ATM check his bank balance. It showed that he had one dollar in his account. After that, he went to his bank to see what was going on. They informed him that about two weeks ago, the joint account holder had taken all the money out of both their checking and savings account, leaving only one dollar in the checking and thirty dollars in the savings just to keep the accounts open. He was also told that he couldn't take the thirty dollars from the savings account unless he wanted to close the account down. He did not want to do that. He went back to his parent's house.

His parents let him stay in his old room. They also had an old car he could use until he found his truck, or whatever worked out. He called the police to report his truck stolen. A few days later, he got a call from the police saying that his truck had been left at a Budget Rental parking lot for several days. The Budget Rental manager thought it had been abandoned, so had it towed. His truck was in a holding yard. He contacted the tow company. They confirmed that they had his truck, and he could have it after paying the towing and storage fees that came to two-hundred-twenty dollars. Fan-fucking-tastic. His parents loaned him the money and he retrieved his truck.

Well, at least he had his truck back. And he had his dive gear and tools, so he could still work. That is just what he did. He went back overseas for several hitches. When he was at home, between overseas hitches, he took whatever work he could get through the Vancouver office. I kept in loose touch with him over the next few years. To my knowledge, he never found out where his girlfriend had run off to, nor had he recovered any of his money or belongings. He lost over one-hundred-fifty thousand dollars all said and done. After hearing his story, I had decided to not have joint accounts with girlfriends.

I know girlfriends weren't the only ones capable of doing that to divers. Most divers I knew had been married and divorced at least once. It was very rare to find someone who had been in the dive industry for more than ten years and still be married to their one and only spouse. Usually, the divorces were much harder on the diver than the spouse too. It is easy for the spouse to show evidence that the diver is away from home and the kids, if they have any, more often than being present. Lots of times the spouse doesn't work outside the home, so the diver usually has to pay child support and alimony. I know the diving industry isn't the only work environment like that. Any job that requires the employee to be away from home a lot has the same issues. We are all in the same sinking boat. There are people out there who can make it work, but it is a rare and beautiful thing. It takes a special kind of strength and trust to survive that lifestyle.

*　　*　　*

In July I married the woman from Brasil. When we met, I didn't speak any Portuguese and she didn't speak much English. We joked that the only things she knew how to say in English were "Oh, my

God," and "I love you." Well, what else do you need to know how to say? Right. To say the least, we had many misunderstandings. I had told her I was a diver, a commercial diver, translated more like "professional diver" which she understood as "Lifeguard." Kind of funny if you think about it, but very far from the reality. She didn't know that I would be working away from home for days or weeks at a time. She soon realized the actual situation though, and I'm not sure she ever liked it much. That marriage only lasted nine years.

I met my third and current wife in two-thousand-two, while I was working on a dam in Montana. I moved in to her house that same year. Two years later we got married. We had some growing pains due to my dive career. She wasn't a fan of me working away from home for weeks at a time, but we worked it out and are still together. Like I said, it takes a special person to be able to handle a spouse who makes a career out of commercial diving.

I would always tell the tenders working under me, that they would need to think seriously about what they wanted out of life. Do you really want to be a diver at the expense of relationships with your spouse, children, and everybody else important in your life? Many people start a career in commercial diving, but few actually make it their life long endeavor.

*   *   *

A BRIDGE TOO FAR
Chapter Six

In August nineteen-ninety-two, I went on a job at the Champion lumber yard in Bonner, Montana, just east of Missoula. I had worked at the dam just down-stream from there several times. I was familiar with the hotels and restaurants there. On the job with me was a young kid from the Hope, Idaho area that I had worked with on several jobs, and a guy I had never worked with before who was originally from Boston. The guy from Boston had more dive experience than I did, so he was the designated supervisor.

The lumber yard was on the bank of the Blackfoot river just upstream from where it joined the Clark Fork River. Their fire control system used water from the river. They had two large water pumps that each had a thirty-six-inch suction pipe in a pond just off the river. So much silt had settled in the pond that the water flow to the fire protection system was restricted to the point where the system couldn't be effective. Our job was to clear the sediment from the pond and make sure the intakes were clear. It didn't sound like a huge job, but it ended up taking us a full week to complete.

Our plan was to use an airlift to suck the sediment out of the pond and blow it towards the middle of the river, where it would flow downstream. We had a hand jetting package with us also, which ended up being a good thing. The sediment was really fine mud that had packed into the pond like clay. The airlift would suck it out, but very slowly. It was like sticking a vacuum hose into soft clay. It would suck perfectly round holes, making the bottom look like Swiss cheese. It was very labor intensive and slow work. Boston came up with the idea to let the airlift run on its own, unattended more or less, and the diver would use the hand jet to break up the mud and wash it towards the mouth of the airlift. That process actually worked very well, but it caused an issue that neither I, nor the kid from Hope had encountered before.

The water in the pond was shallow, about ten feet, but should have been closer to twenty feet deep. So, we had five to ten feet of mud to remove. Even though it was sunny and warm while we were there, the water was cold enough that we needed to wear wetsuits to keep warm. When wearing a wetsuit, you need to wear a weight belt to counteract the buoyancy of the neoprene. The funny thing about buoyancy is that it changes when the density of the water solution you are in changes. You know, you are more buoyant in salt water than you are in fresh water. You are **really** buoyant in the Great Salt Lake and the Dead Sea because the salt content in the water is very high. The water in the pond we were working in is fresh water, relatively low buoyancy. My weight belt and ankle weights supplied plenty of weight to keep me on the bottom. That is, until I started hand jetting. The hand jet supplies a powerful stream of water, like that coming out of your garden hose at full blast, that easily cut through the mud. The hand jetting broke the mud up into teeny weeny particles that became suspended in the water. This increased turbidity. Turbid water causes super buoyancy. The result was, that even though I had plenty of weight for normal work, I was now rising towards the surface. I couldn't stay on bottom, which meant I couldn't stay on task. I had to put more weight on.

I informed topside of the issue and got out of the water. I didn't have enough weight with me, so I borrowed Hope's weight belt. Boston wouldn't let us use his weight belt. He had a Miller weight belt and plenty of additional weight to add to it that he was heavy enough when he dove. Both Hope and I were using SCUBA type weight belts. Boston gave us a hard time for not being real divers. I guess he didn't consider me a "real diver" because I hadn't broken out as a diver in the Gulf of Mexico.

Anyway, after putting on the second weight belt, I didn't have any problem staying on the bottom and getting the work done. That was the first time I, or Hope, had done any hand jetting in that kind of mud. Boston had obviously worked in those conditions before. We got the job done to the client's satisfaction and they talked to us about making this an annual commitment. Sadly, Champion shut down their yard a couple years later, so I never went back there.

*   *   *

I worked a few more small jobs in Montana for the Montana Power Company and Washington Water Power. Our office guy in Spokane had secured the service contract for WDOT (Washington state Department of Transportation) which meant that our company, United Marine Services, would be doing all the Washington State Ferry inspections as well as the inspections required on all the bridges on roads owned by Washington state. Yeah, our company had changed its name from United Marine Divers to United Marine Services last year.

I didn't know why, and didn't really care, the work was the same. At the same time, Can-Dive had changed its name to Can-Dive Ninety-One. So what?

The federal government had a requirement where every bridge had to be inspected once every five years. That meant that all the bridge footings in water needed to be inspected by divers. The service contract was for two years. Each year there would be four to six months of bridge footing inspections. This year we would inspect bridges during September, October, November, and December. The job required a three-man crew and a way to get to all the bridge footings. UMS had the use of a jetboat that we could fit a shallow water dive package in which was perfect for that kind of work.

Towards the end of September, I had just finished up a small job in Montana and went home for the weekend. The following Tuesday, I got a call from the office guy asking me if I got along with the guy from Boston and could I work with him. I told him, sure, no problem. Then he asked if I would like to go on a bridge inspection job on Wednesday, tomorrow. I said I would. He told me to meet the dive crew, headed by Boston, at a hotel in a small town on the west side of the Cascade mountains, that night if possible. He also told me I didn't need to bring any dive gear. Okay. The weather was warm and sunny, so I decided to ride my scooter to the motel. I could be there in time for dinner. I had dinner with Boston. I always took my dive gear with me when I went on a job no matter what the office said. You never know what might happen. I could carry it all on my motorcycle. It had to be packed just right though.

We caught up a little over dinner. He explained to me how the job worked. We would be working strict eight-hour days. That included drive time, set up time, break down time and time spent preparing for the next day's work. There would be zero overtime. The nice thing was that drive time included driving to the job from home Monday morning and driving back home Friday afternoon. Also, every Monday morning we would get five days per diem for the week's motel and food, paid in cash. That sounded pretty good to me. I asked him why I was coming in during the middle of the week. This was the second week they had been doing these bridge inspections. The three-man crew had been picked a week-and-a-half ago. I had already been slated for work in Montana. Boston told me that one of the guys just didn't work out. I guess he was a new guy and ended up not liking the work or something.

The next morning, I got up and grabbed breakfast at McDonald's and met the other two guys at the truck. The WDOT representative, who was present at all of the inspections, met us at the truck a few minutes later. We caravanned to the bridge and surveyed the area to see how to set up for the inspection. A boat launch just downstream from the bridge was where we put the jet boat in the water. We got everything set up and ready to go. The client rep observed us from the beach. We motored up to the bridge and tied off to one of the piers. There were only two piers to inspect and the deepest depth was just under fifteen feet. Boston dove and I logged his description of the footings. We were looking for cracks, spalling, scouring and any other damage that might be present. The two footings were close enough together that the diver could just swim over to the next pier and inspect it without us having to move the boat. Same deal there, he inspected and I recorded his descriptions. There was no damage, so we got the diver back in the boat.

We went back to the boat launch and put the boat back on the trailer. While I and the other new guy secured the boat and dive gear, Boston gave his report to the client. The client was satisfied and gave us the location of the next bridge. It wasn't too far. We drove to the next site and looked over the situation. This bridge crossed a small irrigation ditch. There was only one pier in the water and the depth was about five feet. I would be doing the diving here. We would not be launching the boat for this one.

In fact, I didn't really see the need for a dive helmet. Couldn't I just put on a SCUBA mask and do this one breath-holding? After discussing it for a few minutes, we decided that a dive helmet would be best, so I would not have to keep popping up for air. We parked the truck with the boat on its trailer off to the side of the road at one end of the little bridge. The dive package was set up in the boat so that we could use the boat as the dive command whether it was in the water or not. Boston ran the radio, dive rack, and kept the log. The other guy tended me from the river bank off the boat. This inspection took less than an hour. There was no damage to report, so it was another fairly quick inspection. If there was damage, we had an underwater video camera and gear to record and make a visual record of it for our client. We didn't need that here. The client had a still camera and always took photos of the bridge being inspected so he had proof that the inspections were actually completed. After securing everything, we drove to a nearby motel to spend the night.

We arrived at the hotel with about an hour left in our eight-hour day. We were using a bank of K-bottles for our air supply. We had a small hp air compressor in the back of the truck that we used to refill the K-bottles. It took about forty-five minutes to fill an empty K-bottle with that compressor, so we had just enough time to fill out the rest of our day doing that. When the only bottle we had used was filled, we went to dinner at a local restaurant. The next day was Friday and we would be driving home in the afternoon. That meant we could do one more bridge inspection in the morning.

It took us about an hour to drive to the bridge the next morning. Boston did the diving and I ran the rack, radio, and kept the log. The new guy just tended. This inspection went about the same as the others. We launched the boat at a nearby boat launch, motored to the bridge, tied off to one of the piers, and did the inspection. There were two piers on this bridge to inspect, so it took us a couple hours to complete. The depth was less than twenty-five feet. I could see that this was not going to be a very exciting job, but it would be very steady; almost like a regular forty-hour-per-week job except that we wouldn't be home on the weeknights.

After we completed the inspection to the client's satisfaction, we secured the dive gear and boat. The client gave us the location of the bridge that we would be inspecting on Monday. It was a four-hour drive from Seattle, where the client travelled from, so we would meet at the bridge around noon. Boston was living near Issaquah, Washington, so his drive time would be close to the client's. Both the other guy and I were from the Spokane area, so we would drive together. Boston had his own truck, I was on my motorcycle, leaving the other guy to drive the company truck and boat back to the yard in Spokane.

Monday morning, I went to the yard in Spokane to get the truck and boat. I double-checked all the equipment and restocked the consumables. I was told the new guy wouldn't be joining me. A different third guy, from western Washington would be coming over with the guy from Boston. I didn't think much of it, dive crews changed all the time. Sometimes it could be a pain to change personnel when the crew was cohesive and got along real well with each other, but there didn't seem to be much cohesion in our crew from the previous week. Besides, I would just as soon travel by myself. It was no fun being stuck in a vehicle with someone who's company one didn't enjoy. That afternoon I met Boston, our new guy, and the WDOT client at a bridge in central Washington somewhere.

*   *   *

Boston and I finished out the year working on that bridge

inspection contract. The third crew member changed every two to three weeks. One or two lasted less than a week. One might wonder why it was hard to keep a guy on this job. I mean, it was steady, it was easy, there was diving every day, and we got to be home every weekend. We also didn't work any national holidays. So, we got Veteran's Day off, Thanksgiving too. And it was a set schedule, so we could plan around the work. That was a rare thing for the dive industry. Boston was in charge, following the client's lead. I suppose he could be a little hard to get along with. I didn't have any issues with him. He knew what he was doing. He always took the first dive of the day, which often would be the only dive of the day. I didn't care, I didn't feel the need to dive every day. I suppose that bothered some of the guys.

He also always wanted everything done his way, whether it was the best way or not. In his mind, his way was the best way. I also didn't mind that. His way, his responsibility. If something went wrong it was on him. We didn't have any problems though, so his way always worked fine. Divers tend to have strong personalities, so there is a fair amount of head-butting and chest pounding in our industry. The only problem with that is when it comes from a guy who doesn't know what he is doing or just can't get the work done. At least Boston got stuff done and done well.

Remember the guy from Poulsbo, Washington who said he knew everything there was to know about ROVs? Well, he ended up working with us for a little while on the bridge inspections. The office guy had access to a side scan sonar and had suggested to the WDOT representative that we could do scans of the bridge piers. He also said we could print out those scans so they would have an actual picture of the bridge footings and surrounding channel bottom. Guess who got sent out to operate the side scan. Yeah, the know-it-all ROV guy. Wonderful. Oh well, he wasn't really interested in the diving, so Boston and I would do all that.

The know-it-all didn't like riding in the truck with me, pulling the trailer with the boat because it wasn't a very comfortable ride. He preferred riding in Boston's truck. Fine with me. He also wasn't as familiar with the side scan sonar as Boston was. He often couldn't get it to print the scans and would have to ask for help. The scans weren't all that great either. After a few failed attempts to get good scans, the WDOT rep decided it wasn't worth the time, so we quit using it for the rest of the year.

A couple weeks later, we were driving between bridge inspection sites in eastern Washington. I was driving the work truck and trailer combo, following Boston in his truck with Poulsbo riding shotgun. The sky was blue and the air was hot. We were driving through an area of rolling hills covered in dried grass. Small rock formations dotted the countryside and sagebrush popped up here and there. I was listening to a rock-n-roll station on the radio. I was drinking Mountain Dew, eating Twinkies, and enjoying the drive.

All of a sudden, Boston pulled over to the side of the road, jumped out of his truck and ran into the field. He had a pistol in his hands and fired off several shots. I pulled over behind him, shut off my truck, and got out to see what was going on. Poulsbo jumped out of the passenger side of Boston's truck and came running back to me. His eyes were wide and he looked very stressed. He tried to open the passenger door on the truck that I was driving, but it was locked. He started yelling, begging to ride with me. I said sure, whatever you want and unlocked the passenger door for him..

Boston was far off the road in the grass field, looking around. Poulsbo was sitting in the passenger seat of the company truck. I walked to the back of the company truck to a cooler I had there and got out a Mountain Dew. I asked Poulsbo if he wanted one, but he declined my offer. I gulped my Mountain Dew down and grabbed another. I asked Poulsbo what was going on. He was still shaking as he responded that he was afraid for his life. He tells me Boston has threatened to shoot him. Yeah, sure.

I was about half done with my second Mountain Dew when Boston came back to his truck. He asked me if I had seen them. Seen what? I enquired. He said there were some pheasants out in the field and he had tried to shoot one. He missed, he said. Well, he **was** using a pistol. I didn't see any pheasant, but it was the perfect environment for them. I was sure there would be pheasant in the area. Is that really why he had his gun out and was firing shots? Did he really threaten to shoot Poulsbo? Did he just need to vent? I don't know. I asked him if he wanted a Mountain Dew. He said no thanks, he had stuff to drink in his truck.

I asked if he was ready to get going and he replied that he was. He asked where Poulsbo was and I responded that he was sitting shotgun in my truck. Okay, let's go. We got back on the road and headed to the next inspection site. By the time we got there, everybody was calmed down and behaving like nothing had happened. We finished the inspection and moved on to the next site. We finished out the week, but the following Monday, we had a new tender with us. I never heard anything more about the incident and I didn't tell anyone about it. Nobody got hurt, and what was going on between the other two guys wasn't really any of my business. I got along with Boston just fine. No issues between he and I.

*   *   *

We had to inspect all the bridges that the WDOT was responsible for. That includes the little teeny ones that crossed a muddy ditch to the very large bridges crossing the Snake and Columbia rivers. On one warm and sunny day, the bridge to be inspected was across the Snake River by Lyon's Ferry state park. The river was deep here and there were four piers and footings to inspect. It would take us a couple days to get this inspection done. Boston took the first dive on the first pier as normal. His deepest depth was just under sixty feet and he finished the inspection of that pier in one dive.

On these deeper dives, we would start at the bottom and work our way up. We used Oceaneering's "re-pet up" dive tables. The premise on those tables was that you could dive deep, say ninety feet for example. At ninety feet, a diver can stay on the bottom for thirty minutes. The diver can then do a re-pet dive to say fifty feet, where he would have a bottom time of one hundred minutes minus the re-pet time from the ninety-foot dive. Thirty-four minutes allowed at fifty feet if the diver had spent a full thirty minutes at ninety feet. This way a single diver would have more dive time to complete the task at hand. For you technical divers out there, you have to come up at least a whole atmosphere, that is ten meters or thirty-three feet, between depths used in your calculations. That means you can't re-pet up from ninety feet to eighty feet, or seventy feet, not even sixty feet really. From ninety feet, you could re-pet up to fifty feet or shallower. And basically, by the time you got up to thirty feet, you could spend all day, no matter what depth you started at, as long as you kept the times with-in the no-deco limits. Whew! Too much technical stuff, sorry. I get carried away sometimes.

Back to the job at hand. Boston completed the inspection on the first pier. I was up to dive on the second pier. It was at least a hundred feet from the first pier. We would have to move the boat. We motored to the second pier and looked for a place to tie off the boat. Sometimes there would be an eyebolt poking out of the pier, or maybe a piece of exposed rebar or something like that. The second pier had no such feature for us to use. We would have to float a line around the pier, sort of lasso the pier and tie off that way.

We put the line in the water on the upstream end on one side of the pier. We let the line float downstream while at the same time we motored around the other side of the pier, trying to let enough slack in the water that we could grab the bitter end from the water on the down-stream end of the pier. I was on the port bow leaning way out over the water trying to pick up the end of the rope floating in the water. More than half my body was hanging out over the water and I was keeping myself in the boat with my feet. Suddenly Boston gunned the motor and the boat rammed the pier. I went flying into the water.

I grabbed the side of the boat and pulled myself back in so quickly I don't even think my underwear got wet. Boston said I looked like a cat jumping back in the boat. He said he had never seen me move that quick. It was just a reflex action from me. I asked Boston why he would do that. I was going to get wet anyway. I didn't need my clothes all wet. He swore up and down it was an accident. Sure, whatever you say. Tradition required me to buy a bottle of booze for the crew for falling in the water by accident. Even though I didn't technically fall in, I was knocked in, I still bought a bottle of Rum for us to share that evening. Even if Boston did it on purpose, it was done in fun and I didn't get hurt. As I have said before, we liked to give each other a hard time when we could. We all had a good laugh about it.

Anyway, we got the boat tied off and I made my dive. I started the inspection at a depth of ninety-five feet. It was dark down there, but with my dive light I could see about ten feet. The only fish I saw was a little catfish about twelve inches in length. It didn't move when I came upon it, but its eyes followed my every move. The bottom was rocky and the pier footing was in good condition. I re-petted up the pier, doing my inspection on the way up. All said and done it took me about an hour-and-forty-five minutes to inspect the whole pier and footing. After I got out of the water and back into the boat, we had just enough time left in the day to get back to the beach, load the boat, secure the dive gear, and get back to the motel. Our day ended at four-thirty and we had a couple hours of a warm sunny day left. We went to a restaurant that had a nice outdoor patio for dinner. Over dinner we shared the bottle of Rum, but we didn't finish it off, it would last us a few days. The next day we would finish the inspections of the last two pier footings and that would complete the week for us.

*　　　*　　　*

Another bridge we had to inspect crossed the Touchet River in Dayton, Washington. One of the fun things about this bridge inspection contract was that we got to go to places one would rarely go. Boston liked to look for top-rated restaurants where-ever we were working. I suppose good food and a good dining experience was something to be enjoyed. It was better than eating at McDonald's or Booger King all the time. I liked looking for the best breakfast places around. I also searched out the best ice cream parlors, or at least the best milkshakes where-ever we went. My favorite milkshakes are Huckleberry or Chocolate Malts with extra chocolate and extra malt. A Chuckleberry shake could be good too, if it was made with real huckleberries. Needless to say, we ate pretty well when we were on this job.

Anyway, Boston had read about some five-star restaurant on the north side of Dayton. It had been written up in some travel magazine and was touted as a "not to be missed" dining experience. So, of course, when the bridge in Dayton was to be inspected, we knew where we would be dining.

I don't remember the name of the restaurant, and I don't know if it is even open anymore. But at the time, reservations were required to enjoy their dining experience. Boston made the reservations. After we finished our diving for the day and had secured all our equipment, we went to our motel and got cleaned up. We got to the restaurant about ten minutes before our reservation time. We were clean, wearing button-up shirts, but still in jeans. I was wearing my purple high-top tennies like I always did. When we entered the restaurant, we were immediately told, by the hostess, that we had to have reservations in order to dine there. Boston assured her that we did and gave her his name. She found it on the roster and gave him a little frown. Good, she said, it will be just a few minutes. After about forty minutes, we were finally led to our table which was in the back corner, out of view from the entrance. Hmpf. Whatever, I didn't really care where we were seated. We got our menus, water and a basket of breadsticks right away. Actually, that stuff was already on the table as we were seated.

It was Italian. That's good, I hadn't had Italian food in a while. I decided on chicken parmesan. I don't remember what the other guys ordered, but I do remember it took close to half-an-hour before the waiter came and took our order. Then it took almost an hour for our food to arrive. First was a tiny little salad accompanied by a small cup of soup with some stringy garnish. My main dish was a very small portion on a large plate. The other dishes had small portions that were drizzled with differently colored sauces looking more like some French artistic dish then a meal that would leave you satisfied. We had dessert, also. I ordered strawberry cheesecake. When it came, it was half the size of a normal piece, like they cut the cheesecake into twenty-four slices rather than the normal twelve or so. Then the bill came. Are you *kidding* me?! It was priced higher than the meals in the Space Needle in Seattle. Ach du Lieber Gott! Whatever. Let's pay the bill and go get a cheeseburger to fill us up. I think Boston actually liked it, but I sure didn't. I didn't care for the way we were treated either, but maybe that's just me. Oh well, like I said before, one of the perks of this job was to try different restaurants around the state. That didn't mean that all our dining experiences would be good ones.

*   *   *

The following week we did inspect mostly small bridges with only one or two pier footings in the water. The majority of the bridges crossed little muddy ditches that were less than three feet deep. There really was no need to wear a dive helmet for these. We did wear our dive suits though, because we would be splashing around in the watery muck on our hands and knees. We still had to get our eyes on the whole footing, so we would be putting our head in the water. A SCUBA mask would be utilized. It seemed funny to me that we would inspect those footings rather than the WDOT representative, as diving wasn't necessary to do the actual inspections.

Yes, we wore dive suits, yes, we splashed around in muddy water, stinking of dead fish and rotten seaweed afterwards, but really, it didn't take any type of special training or equipment to do that. We still charged dive time and got our wet pay for the time we spent splashing around in the mud, even though we weren't diving. That couldn't have been cost-effective for the state. I mean, the WDOT guy did the inspections of the bridge piers and footings that were out of the water on his own. Even if a bridge we inspected had some piers in the water and others on land, we only did the ones in the water. If it was raining, he probably got just as wet as we did when we inspected these super shallow footings. Oh well, work is work, and money is money. In the long run we didn't mind.

That is until we received our paychecks and there was no wet pay on them. What the Hell?! It seems that the WDOT guy had made some complaint to our office about being charged for diving when we didn't do any actual diving. That kind of made sense from the client's point of view, but it made no real sense from our point of view. We still donned our dive suits and got wet to do the inspections. We argued with our office guy about it and he agreed to talk to the WDOT about it. In the mean time we would be paid the wet pay that we figured we were owed, at least the state agreed to that. The following week we were informed by our office guy that we would only be paid wet pay if we were actually wearing our dive hat. It no longer mattered whether or not our head went under the water. The state's argument was that if we didn't have our helmet on, how could we be diving. They didn't pay dive pay for just getting wet and sticking your head under the water. Okay, your game, your rules. We decided we would put our dive helmets on for any and all footings we were asked to inspect.

The next super shallow footings we did with our helmets on and the WDOT guy asked why we were doing that. He could see that it really made no sense and was much more strenuous for us to do the inspections that way. He also thought the inspections might have been completed faster if we weren't in our dive gear. Why the heck were we wearing our dive gear to do those footings, he enquired. We explained to him about how our pay worked. He seemed to understand but after that, we didn't do any more inspections on those footings in very shallow waterways. We found out later that the WDOT guy was supposed to have done those shallow ones on his own. It seems he just didn't want to splash around in the smelly, muddy, muck and figured we were being paid to do just that.

*　　　*　　　*

Another group of bridges we had to inspect crossed some stagnant canals located on the peninsula of Washington state.

There were several bridges to inspect so we were in this area for several days. The weather was fairly warm even though it was late fall. I don't think it ever gets really cold there, but I suppose "really cold" is a subjective feeling. Regardless, the water was a little warmer than a lot of the water we dove in. The canals weren't very deep, ten to fifteen feet is all, but there were quite a few pier footings to inspect.

The canals were covered in green, fuzzy algae. They didn't smell very good either. The water under the algae was really murky, visibility was less than three feet. It wasn't silt in the water reducing the visibility, it was algae. All different kinds of algae. There were long floating hairs of algae, little green balls, bigger green balls, along with little blobs of bluish-green fluff floating around. Yuck, yuck, YUCK!

I was glad I had decided to wear my dry suit for this dive. This was probably the grossest water I had ever done any diving in up to this point. That made me think of those poor divers who dove in poop. Yes, divers dive in poop. Somebody has to do the work in the city sewers when they have issues. Not me though, no way, no how. This was bad enough for me. Little did I know. More on that later though. At this point, this was the grossest water I had ever been in, and it was the grossest water I hoped I ever would be in. When I got out of the water, Boston told me I needed to rinse off before I got out of my suit. We didn't have any way of doing that though. I removed my dive hat and looked at myself. Oh, Gross! There were all kinds of worms and water bugs slithering all over my suit.

We took great care getting me out of my gear and wrapped it in plastic so we could keep the muck and worms contained until we got back to the motel where we could wash the muck and smell off my gear. We tried to keep all our contaminated gear contained until we could give it a good cleaning. That took a little time out of our day, but we didn't care. I was glad to finish up that group of bridges. Gross, at least it would be another five years before we might have to inspect those bridges again.

I think I would let someone else inspect those bridges when it came time to do them again.

We finished up the inspections for the year in mid-December, just before Christmas. It was a nice way to fill out the year, and also the first time I'd had steady work into the winter. It seems dive work was becoming less seasonal in the Northwest. Boston and I also did the bridge inspections the following fall. He and I did most of the inspections, while several other divers rotated through as our third crew member.

*   *   *

In late December, I got called into our Spokane office for a meeting with several of the other guys, our core group of divers, the Secret Squirrel Club you might say. I thought this was kind of weird, because we had never had a group meeting like this before. We had Christmas parties every year, where everyone would get together and have a good meal, with drinks afterward. But never a serious meeting with the core group. All of us wondered what was up.

After all of us arrived and sat down at a conference table, the office guy came in and said he had some things to talk about. He wanted to know where we all stood on what he was about to say. It seems Can-Dive was having trouble paying its bills, that was the reason for the name change the previous year. Now the banks in Canada had frozen all of Can-Dive's accounts and was in the process of seizing all their assets, meaning all our assets also. Oh, Great! What does that mean for us? We were still owed pay from the previous two weeks. What about the jobs that some of us were working on? What about the jobs we had scheduled to start after Christmas? What about the service contracts we had with Montana Power Company,

Washington Water Power, and WDOT? We anticipated lots of work from those contracts in the coming year.

We were worried about our monthly bills. I had just purchased a new car for my new wife. One of the guys had just bought a house for his young family. All of us had all the monthly expenses that all working Americans had. Work in the dive industry isn't as regular and predictable as most other work, but at least we normally knew when work was about to end. This felt like the rug was being pulled out from under us.

Not to worry, said the office guy. He had talked to the banks and organizations who were in charge of freezing the accounts and seizing assets. He had been reassured that all paychecks would be honored and that we could continue using the equipment that we had on working jobs. It seems that our office was the only part of Can-Dive that was actually turning a profit. We only had a couple jobs worth of equipment out in the field, but we figured we could hide whatever equipment we might need for our upcoming work in our personal garages. I hid a dive package in my dad's garage since my own garage was full.

The office guy also told us that, starting in January, we would no longer be United Marine Services. We would be Norwesco Marine instead, and we wouldn't be owned by Can-Dive. It seems our office guy had started an equipment supply company a couple years ago and was now in a position to buy the needed assets from Can-Dive to continue our work. He said the work would continue on just like nothing had happened. Pay would still be the same, work would still be the same, and we would keep all our upcoming work and service contracts. If nothing else, it seems our office guy was a good businessman, and now he would be the owner of the company and our boss. That was fine with me. All it really meant for me was that I would be wearing a different t-shirt at work. It was a relief to learn that we still had work. In fact, I think we started getting more work. I know we started working in the winters more.

The only slow times for us from here on out were during the fish closures on the rivers in the Northwest. "Fish closures" were when all work was stopped on the rivers where the salmon and steelhead ran. The EPA passed some laws that no construction work could be done on the rivers that might interfere with the spawning fish. What that meant for us was that there would be a two to three week shut-down of work in the spring when the fish swam upstream to spawn, and then close again in the fall for a couple weeks when the baby fish headed down river and out to sea. The EPA also restricted how low the water levels in the reservoirs behind the dams could go. It used to be that when work was required on dam units, head gates, trash racks, or whatever, the company would just lower the water level to a point where the work could be done in the dry. Well, that destroys lots of fish habitat and breeding areas. So now when the work needed to be done, it was to be done by divers rather than lowering the pond level.

*   *   *

The third Friday in January, nineteen-ninety-three, I got called to go on a wheel inspection job for a Washington State ferry. It was in Seattle at the ferry dock there. Nobody else was available to go on that job for some reason. It was an "emergency" job and according to our contract with WDOT, we had to be able to answer a call to work within twenty-four hours. It was also in our contract that all work on weekends or holidays would be paid at the union overtime rate. Also, divers required on the job would get paid for drive time if they came from outside a sixty-mile radius from the union hall. For me, on this job, it meant that I would get paid eight hours drive time to the Seattle ferry docks, eight hours dive pay for the dive, and eight hours drive time back home to Spokane. I could hardly say no to that. The boss said I would meet one other diver at the ferry dock and one of the ferry workers would fill in as our third guy. Okay, sounds good to me.

I made the drive that Friday evening and spent the night at my sister's house in Seattle. I met the other diver at the ferry dock Saturday morning. He was a friendly well-fed guy from Texas. He was about my same age and had about the same amount of time in the dive industry as I did. This was his first job in the Northwest. He said he would gladly let me have the dive since I had driven all the way over from Spokane. That was nice of him. We finished the job in a couple hours. I gave the report to the WDOT representative and got the necessary signatures on our paperwork. The Texan and I went out to lunch to give us a chance to get to know each other better. He ended up becoming a very good friend of mine, whom I worked with quite a bit over the next six or seven years. After lunch, I drove back home. I earned almost as much for that one job as I did in a normal week of work. Gotta love that.

*   *   *

About half-way through the second year of the bridge inspections, our third guy came from eastern Canada. He had worked for the Can-Dive office in Toronto, or Montreal, or where-ever it was, but they didn't have enough work for him. Our boss, the owner of Norwesco, still used Can-Dive to supply personnel when needed, he was half French-Canadian himself, so no real surprise there. Anyway, this guy from back east came to work for us in Spokane. He, supposedly, was some great engineer and computer expert type guy. He had come up with some plan using side scan sonar to make super detailed scans of the channel bottoms and bridge footings. He assured everyone that the printed scans would be so detailed that there wouldn't be a need for divers anymore. Okay, sure, I've heard that before.

Boston and I had been working together for a while now. We had our routine down and worked well together regardless of how the third guy turned out. Except for this engineer guy. He came on board and decided he was going to run everything his way. He told us he was a diver and he did help move gear and equipment around. But it was blatantly obvious that he thought he was smarter than the rest of us. Sure, whatever you say. He did know his way around the computers. Boston was pretty good with computers too. I definitely was not. Boston still took the first dive every day, and I still did the other diving.

The engineer from Montreal wasn't real hip on diving, but he did put himself in charge of the computer. Since we were now going to be doing more with the sonar, we were taking more direction from him. We spent a lot of time positioning the sonar head in specific spots to take scans. The engineer, Montreal, would put all the scans on the computer to try and come up with three-dimensional renditions of the bridge piers, footings, and surrounding channel. Sometimes it worked and sometimes it didn't. It was taking more time to set up and do the scans than it used to take just doing the actual dive. In order to render the three-D drawing, the computer needed at least six scans. The more scans the better. Sometimes we would set up to eight, ten, or even twelve scans depending on the size of the channel. The WDOT representative decided he wanted us to dive on the piers as well as have the sonar scans. Now we were spending quite a bit more time on each bridge than we had in the past. I was thinking to myself, "Why take a good thing and mess with it?" The service contract was coming up for renewal the following year, and if we ended up being too expensive, we wouldn't get it. That would be sad because it was such a nice gig.

I was involved in the bridge inspections until mid-summer of the second year that we had the WDOT service contract.

Montreal didn't stay with us on the bridge inspections the whole time. I think his sonar project ended up being more costly than what the WDOT wanted to endure. Sadly, we didn't get the service contract the following year, some other dive company got it. I missed that work a little. There was enough other work for me, keeping me busy enough that I didn't think about it too much.

*   *   *

WHAT WE HAVE HERE IS A
FAILURE TO COMMUNICATE
Chapter Seven

In the early March of nineteen-ninety-three, Montana Power Company called us back to Madison dam, near Ennis, for the annual cleaning of the trash racks. They informed us that the automated system needed a little more work than usual so we would need to plan two to three days for the work to be completed. Our three-man crew consisted of me, Blanchard and Boston. We all got along well and enjoyed each other's company for the most part. We did still give each other a hard time all the time though.

Montana Power Company owned and operated thirteen dams

across Montana. I had worked on most of them. The MPC employees were great to work with, they bent over backwards to help us out anyway they could. Madison dam had an automated system of pins on chains that was designed to self-clean the trash rack. The chains had a gear driven drum at the top of the rack and a roller at the bottom. The pins would collect debris, as the chains travelled around the rack, and raise it to the top, effectively cleaning the rack.

The issue was that, in the spring, huge mats of algae would flow down the Madison River from the lake by Ennis and overwhelm the cleaning system. Our job was to remove the mats of algae, inspect the pin and chain system, then re-align or replace the chains as necessary. Usually, the chains only needed to be untwisted, and the few broken pins replaced with new ones. Normally we could take care of this in one day, with two dives. The bottom of the trash racks was at twenty-eight feet and the river bottom under the racks was thirty-one feet. That meant a diver could spend all day down there. We dove in four-hour blocks, so it was a two-diver project.

This year though, several of the chains had broken, most of the others had twisted, and the MPC employees thought that a couple of the rollers on the bottom of the rack probably needed to be replaced. We designated three days to do the job. We would rotate the diving, so every three days, each of us would get two dives. We stayed in a motel just south of Ennis, which consisted of log cabins. They looked pretty rustic on the outside, but were very nice on the inside. We each got our own room, paid for by MPC. We also got twenty-six dollars a day for food. Our days started at eight in the morning and we finished by four-thirty in the afternoon. This left lots of sunny time for us in the evening.

After work we would go back to the Motel and clean up. Then we would do something fun for a couple hours, and after that go to Ennis for dinner and maybe a beer or five. This part of Montana has lots of history and outdoor recreation. It is well-known world-wide for fishing. There is excellent hiking in the area, it is only a couple hours northwest of Yellowstone National Park. It's also only about a half-hour drive to the living ghost town and past capitol of Montana; Virginia City. Also, quite a bit of gold mining by use of river dredges had been done in the area back in the late eighteen-hundreds and into the nineteen-twenties. There were huge mounds of dirt, gravel, and rock lining the smaller creeks and rivers in the area. It just so happened that Blanchard had an interest in panning for gold. He said that the best place to find placer gold is where it had been found before. He researched the area and had discovered a couple spots that he felt might have some gold.

He wanted to spend a couple hours at the end of our work day panning for gold. We only had one truck between the three of us, so our choice was to go with him or stay at the motel. I suppose we could walk somewhere from the motel, but Ennis was about three miles north. Both Boston and I decided to go along with him. We figured we could hike around the area a little, there were trees and hills all around the creeks. Lots of dredging equipment had been left along the river banks, and was rusting away. Or maybe we could play at panning for gold too (but we didn't). After the first day of watching Blanchard panning for gold, Boston and I were a little bored with it. Blanchard wanted to go panning again the second day. Oh joy. I thought it would be more fun to visit Virginia City, so did Boston, but Blanchard really wanted to go gold panning. Okay, one more day of it.

The next day, Blanchard took the first dive. While he was in the water, the other two of us got to talking. We had a couple damaged brass fittings in our tool box. Boston took one of those damaged fittings and started smashing it with one of our little four-pound sledge hammers. He pounded it into a small pile of flakes and bits. He showed the little pile to me and asked if I thought it looked like gold dust. I looked at it and told him not really, but if it was mixed in a pan with other dirt and pebbles, it might shine enough to fool someone. We both smiled. Boston wrapped the small pile in a little cloth and put it in his pocket, saving it for later.

We finished the day's work and headed back to the motel. On the way there, Blanchard confirmed with us that we would do the gold panning thing again. We reassured him that we were okay with it. After cleaning up, we went out to the same area we had been in the previous day. We all got out of the truck and started looking around. Boston headed down to the creek while Blanchard gathered his gold panning stuff. I slowed him down a bit with idle talk and questions, giving Boston time to sprinkle the crushed brass in a part of the creek that looked good for panning. When he was done, I left Blanchard and walked to another part of the creek. Boston and I both watched Blanchard head right for the spot where the brass had been left.

We tried not to watch Blanchard too much. We didn't want him to become suspicious of anything. We both walked around bending down here and there as if we were searching for gold, or garnets. There actually did happen to be small bits of garnet mixed in the dirt. I think Boston actually found a couple little garnets as we were messing around. All of a sudden, we heard a whoop and a yell.

We both looked up and saw that Blanchard had a huge smile on his face. He was saying he found some gold flakes and it looked like it might amount to close to an ounce of gold. Of course, we both walked over to where he was. He was looking at the stuff in his pan and flicking it around with one of his fingers. By the time we got there, he wasn't smiling quite so big. Then he asked us to look at what was in his pan and tell him what we thought. I told him I wasn't familiar enough with gold dust to know what it really looked like. Boston said he didn't know either, but it sure shined like yellow gold.

Blanchard shook his head and said it looks quite a bit like gold, but didn't really act like it. He said it didn't go to the bottom of the sand in his pan like it should. I couldn't keep a straight face anymore, and just as soon as I let out a little laugh, Boston laughed. Then Blanchard knew we had been up to something. We fessed up and we all got a good laugh about it. We went back to the truck and drove into Ennis where we had dinner at the Longbranch Saloon. They had excellent food and a great bar. We had another good laugh about the brass and decided that the following day we would go visit Virginia City.

*　　*　　*

In May the same crew, Blanchard, Boston, and I went to Lake Washington in Seattle to work on a job for the WDOT. The state was putting in a new floating bridge from Mercer Island to Bellevue. The project would add three lanes of traffic, thereby doubling the size of Interstate-Ninety across the lake. Our job was to inspect the bottoms of the concrete pontoons making up the bridge and also inspect the anchor cables that went from the pontoons to the bottom of the lake. We would be on this job for over a month.

This was also a job where there would be no overtime paid. The union in Seattle had a deal where wet pay was paid in a four-six-eight-hour schedule daily. That means that if you dove less than four hours, you would get paid four hours wet pay. If you dove four-and-a-half hours to six hours, you would get paid for six hours. In order to get eight hours of wet pay, you would have to dive over six hours. On the east side of the state, we got paid four and four. That may not seem like a big deal, but it turned into a big deal for us.

Since we were working straight eight-hour days, there was only about six hours of dive time per day. It took us almost an hour to get in position and set-up ready to dive and then another hour to break down and get back to the beach. Normally we would dive one guy in the morning and another guy in the afternoon, after lunch. That would be two four-hour divers. But our boss decided he would only pay for six hours of dive time per day whether we dove one guy or two, because that is what the union would allow him to do. It probably saved him somewhere around two hundred dollars a day.

At that time, the IRS allowance for per diem in Seattle was right at one hundred and twenty dollars per day. But the union-required per diem was only twenty-eight dollars per day, and that was payable only if the work was more than sixty miles from our union hall. That meant that Blanchard and I should have received the per diem, but since there was a diver's union in Seattle, our boss wouldn't pay it. Again, he said if we didn't like it, we didn't have to go on the job. When we expressed our dissatisfaction, our boss would just say that we should thank him for the work because it was he who kept us working and we should be happy that we were working at all. I don't think he appreciated the fact that he only got the work because his company had a good reputation of getting work done well and on time, and that was because of us, the guys working for him. If we all refused to work for him, he would have to get guys with less experience to do the work and his reputation would go down the drain.

The inspections we were doing involved a lot of swimming. We had to inspect the whole bottom surface of the concrete pontoons. To do this we ran a rope under the pontoon and up each side. A guy on top of the pontoon would move the line along six feet at a time, while the diver would swim along the line under the pontoon inspecting as he went. The water was pretty cold too. Even though we were wearing dry suits, we would get chilled after three hours in the water. The boss wouldn't pay for us to use hot water either. In those conditions, the diver's effectiveness really went down after three-and-a-half hours.

Our boss wouldn't listen to anything we said about the conditions. He would only pay six hours wet pay per day, if we didn't like it, he would find other divers who would do it. All three of us stayed on the job. We dove two guys every day anyway. We logged the dives for the office in a way where we all got paid evenly even though on paper it looked like only one guy was diving each day. The only time we could get paid for two four-hour divers was when we were inspecting the anchor cables. They were deep enough that the diver's actual dive time would be limited by the depth and re-pet tables.

The anchor cables went down to very large concrete block anchors on the bottom of the lake. The deepest anchors were in one-hundred-forty feet to one-hundred-twenty feet. We used the No-Decompression tables when diving on the cables. We were diving out of the company jetboat which didn't have room for a Decompression Chamber on board so we couldn't use the Sur-D-O2 (surface decompression using oxygen) tables. That limited our bottom time to ten minutes.

The diver would grab on to the cable and follow it down to the bottom as fast as possible. Once the diver reached the bottom, he would inspect the cable connection to the anchor. Then the diver would inspect the cable on the way back to the surface, taking the time to do a good inspection. The diver would stop at ten feet of depth and do a five minute "safety stop" to help keep from getting the bends. Those dives were great, because they were easy, short, and paid well. Along with the four-hours of dive pay, we would get depth pay which was a dollar a foot from fifty to a hundred feet and a dollar-fifty a foot from a hundred to a hundred-and-fifty feet. All three of us would dive on those days.

We worked on the floating bridge about six weeks. When we finished, the WDOT asked us to inspect the piers and footings of the bridge on the west side of the lake where the bridge transitioned from the pontoons to a traditional bridge. The access to the water wasn't very good on the west side of the lake. The bank was pretty steep and the parking lot we were allowed to use was a short hike up the bank from the water. The trail up the bank was mostly paved and there were so many trees around it that you couldn't see the cars in the parking lot until you actually got into the parking lot. Blanchard and Boston were sharing our company van, so all their gear and most of the company gear went in the van. I had my white nineteen-sixty-four Chevy pick-up on the job. We had to make quite a few trips up and down the trail to get all our gear loaded in our rigs. The last Friday of the job we were loading all the gear into our respective rigs.

The other two guys had discovered paintball guns and decided they would have a little fun with them. Blanchard was loaded with pink paintballs and Boston was loaded with green ones. I wasn't into paintballing. Anyway, on my second trip to my truck, I noticed a few pink spots on my truck. I didn't say anything and went down for my next load. When I returned to the parking lot, I saw a few green spots added to the pink spots. I still didn't say anything. I had to make about four more trips up and down the bank.

Each time I returned to my truck there were more paint blotches on my truck. I acted like nothing was going on, like I hadn't noticed the paint marks. By the time we had all the equipment loaded, my truck was so covered in pink and green spots you couldn't tell the truck was white. I kept smiling like nothing was going on. We said our good-byes and that we looked forward to the next job. Those two guys were giving me the weirdest looks. As I turned back to my truck, they asked if I noticed anything strange. I turned back to them and answered no, nothing strange. They looked flabbergasted. They asked if

I had noticed the change in color of my truck. I looked at my truck and then looked back at them and said "Yeah, I see the pink and green. I know it is just water-based paintball marks and will wash right off, no worries." They just shook their heads and laughed. I laughed too. They were hoping for some huge reaction, but I didn't give them the satisfaction. Who got who on that one?!

*   *   *

I spent the next couple months working in Montana. Montana Rail Link had some bridges that needed footings inspected, so I did some of those. I worked for Montana Power Company quite a bit. In late July, we got called to do a job in Trout Creek, Montana. A train had derailed and one of its cars carrying crude oil had rolled into the Clark Fork river and ruptured, spilling almost ten-thousand gallons of crude into the river.

Crude oil sinks in water, especially when it gets cold. It turns into a very sticky black goo that sinks and even works its way under any loose sand. The EPA required Montana Rail Link to remove all the oil spilled in the river and along the river bank. Montana Rail Link had removed the damaged rail car from the river. They hired a crane to scoop the blobs of spilled crude off the river bank and out of the water. Their problem was that they couldn't see where the oil blobs were on the river bottom. We got called in to help the crane operator locate the crude oil that was in the river. Joining me on the job was the young kid from Hope and a new guy that was living in the Kalispel area.

We were using our normal, for us, shallow water dive package that consisted of a Quincy Three-twenty-five compressor, volume tank, rack box, radio, two dive hoses and a K-bottle filled with air for our back up air supply. I don't know what other dive companies Kalispell had worked with before, but he did not like our dive set up. He told me he had gone to dive school in Houston, Texas. I had heard of that school and thought they did a better, more honest job of getting their graduates ready for the dive industry than DIT in Seattle did. They trained their students for work in the Gulf of Mexico, though, which was quite a bit different from how we did things in the inland northwest.

Anyway, our set up made this new guy nervous. It didn't help that Hope had started our air compressor without checking the fuel. It died within minutes of starting and wouldn't restart. I asked if he had checked the fuel. Sheepishly, he said no. We filled the fuel tank and the compressor fired right up. It had a Honda motor powering it, so was very dependable. I usually like to dive my new guys right off the bat so I can get a feeling for how they perform and how they listen to direction, but since Kalispel was a little shook, I had Hope go first.

We spent a whole week working at that site retrieving blobs of crude oil. The majority of the spill had been cleaned up with the crane and our help in the first two days. There were still a lot of small blobs of crude spread all over about a hundred feet of river bottom. The crane wasn't useful with the small stuff. We used six-mil plastic bags to collect the smaller stuff. We had to pick up the small blobs and stuff them into the bags until the bags were about seventy percent full. Then we would drag the bag back to the river bank squeeze out most of the water and seal the bag. This was a slow and tedious process.

After a few days, the oil had started to sink below the sand. This forced us to sift through the sand searching for the hidden oil. A representative from the EPA was on site and was recording how much of the spilled oil had been collected. We couldn't consider the job finished until he signed off on the collection. He had been measuring how much crude was being collected and said he wouldn't sign off until we had recovered at least ninety-five percent of what had been spilled.

To retrieve that much oil, we had to crawl around the river bottom on our hands and knees, sifting through the sand with hand trowels. This caused little drops of crude to float around in the water and get all over our suits. The droplets of crude also covered all areas of exposed skin. It was a real pain to clean ourselves at the end of the day, especially around our necks. The oil would stick to the hairs on our arms and necks and not really come off in the shower. This caused me to think about how much crude oil was transported by rail and by truck and how hazardous that method of transport is. The spills from pipelines are considerably smaller and less frequent than spills from trains, trucks, and boats.

*   *   *

In mid-August I had just finished a job in Montana. I was asked to replace a guy on a job that had been going on for a couple weeks on Lake Pend Oreille in north Idaho. A job had been secured by a non-union dive company from California. They had been hired by the U.S. Navy's Acoustic Research Detachment in Bayview, Idaho. The Californian company was required by the union to hire a certain percentage of workers from the union. They also needed to rent a couple boats to transport their personnel from the beach to the work site at the deepest part of the lake. Our boss could supply both the boat and the union personnel required, so his company was hired by the company from California.

I think four divers were hired along with the jetboat. The contract said that the Californian company would pay for all the fuel, servicing, and upkeep of the jetboat. The divers hired were responsible for operating the jet boat and helping out with the diving as required. It turned out that the divers from California were using SCUBA. A fair amount of the diving to be done was at depths of forty to seventy feet. One of our shallow water dive packages was also hired by the Californian company. We did all the diving deeper than fifty feet as well as any of the diving that would take more than an hour to do. That diving didn't start until later on in the job though. The first four to six weeks didn't include much diving for our guys.

Two of the guys that started that work were Boston and the Rancher guy from central Washington. Both of them wanted to dive and didn't like working on jobs that didn't have much diving. They both wanted off this job as soon as they found out how little diving was going to happen. Neither of those guys really like working in Montana either, that was one of the reasons I worked in Montana so much.

Anyway, as soon as I finished my work in Montana, the Rancher left the Pend Oreille job and I took his place. Within a few days, Boston was replaced by the guy from Texas that I had worked with in Seattle. We worked a minimum of twelve hours a day, seven days a week. Many of the days went fourteen hours and a few lasted sixteen hours. Mostly driving the jetboat around. The jetboat operator had a radio and would be called whenever needed to move personnel, supplies, and small equipment back and forth from the beach to the work site. We were, basically, a water taxi service. It was an easy job that paid well. I didn't really understand why the other guys didn't like it.

Since this job was out of town, we were paid per diem. The IRS rate for the area was eighty-four dollars per day, but our union per diem rate was still only twenty-eight dollars. We had finally got our boss to pay fifty dollars per day for lodging and food when we worked out of town, but for some reason, he only wanted to pay the twenty-eight dollars as mandated by the union on this job. The California company had rented a Boy Scout lodge on the lake and let their guys sleep there. I suppose that is why our boss thought we didn't need to pay for hotel. I decided it was better to stay in Spokane and drive back and forth every day. My wife was eight and a half months pregnant with the baby due August twenty-eighth. I wanted to be home as much as possible just in case. Everybody on the job knew that I wouldn't be working when my wife went into labor. That didn't happen until the second week of September, my daughter was born two weeks late, after a long, hard labor.

Working on this job, I became well acquainted with most of the California guys, as you do on any out-of-town job. Several of the guys had worked for Oceaneering in the late seventies and early eighties and had been part of the team that developed the Rat Hat. We had a lot to talk about. When my daughter was born, they made it very easy for me to have the time off to be present at the birth. Being born late had caused some issues with my daughter, so she had to spend ten days in the infant ICU. My wife stayed with her during the day, and I stayed with her every night. After she was released from the hospital, I wanted to be as near as possible, but I still needed to work. My dad had a camper on the back of a pickup and let me borrow it. For the next two months, we lived at a campsite on the lake close to Bayview. The California crew let me check on my little family every couple of hours.

It also came out in a conversation with the California office guys that we were being paid eighty-four dollars per diem. I told them I was only getting twenty-eight. They got really upset and contacted my boss. He fought it a little, but then had to give in, because legally per diem wasn't pay and if it was being paid to the company for the employees, the boss was legally required to pay it to his employees. That would be us. He was required by law to pay us for all the back per diem that he hadn't been paying. That ended up being an almost three-thousand-dollar check for me. Nice. Of course, that really pissed off my boss and he accused me of conspiring with the Californian company.

I didn't understand how he thought what he was doing was okay. From my point of view, he was stealing money from me in order to make a bigger profit. He told me again, that I should be thankful he was giving me any work at all and it was in my best interest to help him make as much money as possible. I agreed that I should help him be successful, but not if it cost me money, and especially not if it meant he was stealing money from me. Needless to say, this caused a rift between the two of us. He ended up kicking me off the job a week before it ended. At that point, I didn't care. I made plans to visit Brasil for Christmas and introduce my daughter to her Brasilian family. I also got a pair of Kissy-Lips tattooed on my butt so I could moon my boss when he called me back into his office.

I took my little family to Brasil in early December. I stayed there until May of the following year. The owner of Norwesco had been calling my dad since late March, trying to find out where I was, when I would be back, and when I would be ready to go back to work. In late May I called him from Brasil and he told me he had lots of work and could really use me. The sooner I got back, the better for him. Okay. I guess we weren't at odds anymore. I returned to the states, but had to leave my wife in Brasil because of paperwork issues. We decided it was better to leave my daughter with her mom. It would take almost a year to get them back home.

*   *   *

One of my first jobs when I got back was at Madison dam. Joining me this time were Kalispel and a guy whom I can't remember really. I usually stayed at the Rainbow Valley Lodge south of Ennis. They had enough rooms for our crew usually and they were recommended by Montana Power Company. This is where we all usually stayed. There was quite a bit of repair to do on the trash rack cleaning system, we were told, so it looked like we would be here about a week.

This was both Kalispel's and the other guy's first time working at Madison Dam. Also, this was my first job of the year, so I hadn't seen these guys in a little while. Those two didn't want to stay at the Rainbow. They had found a cheaper place to stay. Somebody in Ennis had a single wide mobile home that they rented out to fishermen and tourists. It had two bedrooms and I guess it was enough cheaper that both guys felt it would be worth it to stay there. Okay, we don't all have to stay at the same place, it's just easier if we do. I thought that was a little weird, but whatever, these guys were still kind of new to the dive industry and our way of doing things.

The job started out like it always did. We set up our dive station on the dam inside the Gate Operator's shack. It was heated, so it was a nice dry place to change in and out of our dive gear. I went over the trash rack cleaning system with both guys. I showed them how everything was supposed to work and what it was supposed to look like when it was in perfect shape. I explained what we would be doing to repair the broken chains and replace the broken pins. I also talked about re-aligning the chains in the pulleys at the bottom of the trash racks. Kalispel was a little nervous about diving inside the trash racks because there would be nothing to keep the diver from going down the Penstock Pipe if the Head Gate was open. I assured him that the Head Gate was closed, the power was shut off and the machinery tagged out so there was no way the Head Gate could open up until after we were done and gave the keys to the

Lockout back to the dam crew. He was satisfied with that.

I dove Kalispel first. I already knew he could dive well and was pretty comfortable in the water. He was a good worker and a good welder, both topside and under water. I liked having him on my crew. The work went well for the day. The other guy was only tending, so I dove in the afternoon while Kalispel ran the radio. Our work station here was so small it was easy for the radio operator to help with topside work and still be able to hear the diver on the radio and see the depth and breathing air pressure gages. We got quite a bit done the first day.

When we were done, we headed back to our lodgings. I asked them if they wanted to get together for dinner and both of them said no. Really? Yeah, they said, they both had decided to eat in their rental, it had a full kitchen. Okay. I then asked if they wanted to get together later for a beer. The Rainbow was south of Ennis and I had to drive there, but I was doing that for dinner anyway. They both declined. Okay. That was really weird, because it was the norm for me and the crew to eat together and share a drink or two. I guess I hadn't worked with Kalispel enough yet to know whether or not he drank. For all I knew, he was a teetotaler. Whatever. I would enjoy dinner by myself and have a few beers anyway. I came to Ennis often enough that I knew the owners of the restaurant and also several of the bar tenders and servers at all three bars in town.

The next day at the dam, everything was the same. Kalispel dove first. I asked the other guy if they did anything the previous night. He replied that they just made dinner in the trailer. He also said it had satellite television, so they just watched that for a while. That's a good thing, I guess. I dove in the afternoon. It was pretty much the same as the day before. We were making good progress though. We would probably be done the next day, Wednesday. At the end of the work day, we headed back to our lodgings. I asked if they wanted to get together for dinner and maybe have a beer afterward. They both declined again. Fine. I'll eat by myself again then.

In the morning, I packed up everything in my hotel room and checked out. I knew we would be finishing up here today. We were heading to Hebgen Dam to work the next day. Hebgen Dam was not quite an hour south of Ennis, if you drove the speed limit. Montana Power Company had a house right across the highway from the dam where they let us stay when we worked there. That was great because it was a three-bedroom house and kept up very nicely, and they didn't charge us anything to stay there. I loved it.

I had informed the other two that we would be leaving for Hebgen after we were done with the work at Madison. They needed to be packed up and ready to go. They weren't real happy, because they had rented the trailer for five nights. I told them that they shouldn't have committed to a whole week when we didn't know for sure how long the job would last. Just because Montana Power Company had hired us for the week didn't mean we would be at the same dam all week. It all depended on how the work went. The trailer rental ended up breaking even in cost as my three nights in the Rainbow lodge, so they weren't really out any more money than they would have been if they had stayed at the Rainbow Valley Lodge with me.

That day we finished up at Madison. Everything was in good shape and MPC was happy with us, as always. We drove down to Hebgen Dam that evening. There was nothing really close to Hebgen Dam for dinner. There was the Blue Moon Saloon about half-way between Ennis and Hebgen Dam where we could stop and have dinner. Or we could get settled into the house MPC was letting us use and then go into West Yellowstone for dinner; but that was twenty-two miles away from Hebgen. We opted for the Blue Moon. They had good food and cheap beer. We only had one or two beers though, because we still had to drive after dinner. The guys seemed a little anxious at dinner. I asked if they were doing okay or if something was wrong. They looked at each other, then Kalispel piped up with "The Boss told us to make sure and not fraternize with you. He said the crew wasn't supposed to eat with or drink with the supervisor after hours. He said it was company policy."

"What are you talking about?!" I asked, "We have no such policy here."

"yeah, that's what he said" the other guy agreed with Kalispel.

"Well, that is a bunch of Bull," I replied. "In Montana, and on *All* my jobs, we work together, we eat together, we drink together, we keep each other alive. The boss is not here and he doesn't tell us what to do or how to do it. All that matters is that we get the job done to the customer's satisfaction and we keep each other alive and well. We don't want any accidents or people getting hurt. We do the job in a way that we can make that happen. No matter what. Other than that, we do what we want." Everybody relaxed and we had an enjoyable dinner. When we were done there, we drove the rest of the way to the house by Hebgen. The caretaker of the house was there to let us in and show us around. He recognized me from the last time I had worked there.

In the morning we went over to Hebgen Dam. We met with an engineer from MPC. He had a couple guys from the Rainbow Dam shop with him to assist us. Lots of water was leaking through the Stop Logs in position on the two gates. They wanted us to plug the leaks. This dam is not a hydroelectric dam. It is just for flood control on the Madison River. We could walk into the dam from the downstream side and actually look at the stop logs from the backside. That way we could see how bad the leakage was and where the leaks actually were. That would give the diver a good idea of what to watch out for. This would actually make the diving a little safer for us. All three of us walked in to look at the leakage, even though Kalispel and I would be the only divers. The other guy wanted to see it and how often do you get a chance to see the inside of a dam behind the head gates? I thought it was great that he wanted to check it out.

The leaks were so bad that it could easily take us two days to plug them all up. The engineer said we didn't have to stop the leaks one hundred percent, but hoped we would be able to stop about ninety to ninety-five percent in the two days we had to do the job. I told him we would give it our best shot. I knew that we could easily stop ninety-five percent of the leaks in two days. I let Kalispel dive first, that is what he preferred and I didn't have a preference one way or the other. The diving was shallow, because we didn't have to go to the bottom of the dam. The bottom of the stop logs was at twenty-two feet, so the diver could stay down all day. We would make two three-and-a-half hour dives per day. I was sure that would be plenty. There were two gates about twelve feet wide by ten feet tall. Kalispel did a good job plugging the leaks. We just used rags, knotted and unknotted, stuffed in the cracks. We would sprinkle slag from Colstrip on top of the rags. The reddish ash would get sucked up by the water leaking through the rags and stop the leaks. Realistically we could get about ninety-seven percent of the leaks stopped using this method. When we didn't have slag to use, MPC would supply us with bags of compressed wood pellets, for pellet stoves. Those worked great, because they were slightly heavier than water and would sink. Shortly after getting wet, they would start to expand and come apart turning into soggy sawdust that did a great job of sealing leaks too. The wood pellets were actually better because they would swell with time. If we got the leaks stopped to about ninety-five percent or more, it wouldn't be strange for the leaks to stop one hundred percent within a couple days. We kind of spoiled the MPC guys that way.

The weather was good for us. We didn't have any issues with the diving. We finished up early Friday afternoon. When we had finished plugging the leaks, we looked over the downstream side of the dam. There was still quite a bit of water flowing. It was down about seventy-five percent from where it was before we started, but there was still a bit of flow. We walked back inside the dam and could see that hardly any water was leaking by the stop logs. We did discover all kinds of water coming through cracks in the concrete and also coming up from the bottom of the water chamber though.

The engineer said he was very happy with what we had accomplished, but would want us to come back at a later date to do an in-depth inspection of the outside of the dam. I told him we would be happy to do that for him. We had left most of the dive station in the back of the truck because we could drive on the dam and park very close to where we actually went in the water. This made for a very quick load up of our gear when we were done. We made it back to Spokane in decent time. Not in time for a normal dinner, but well before midnight.

*   *   *

I worked all over the Northwest the summer of nineteen-ninety-four. One of the jobs I worked on was on Hungry Horse Dam just on the west side of Glacier National Park. Kalispell went on that job with me as well as a few of our other regular guys; Blanchard, the Greek, the Texan and Boston along with a couple other semi-regulars. We were hired to do the wet work of a large construction job.

The job was to remove the old head gate system and install a new system that would allow the dam to draw water through the intakes from different levels of the water. I think it was called a Slide Gate System. The idea was that they would be able to regulate the down river water temperature by choosing water from different levels in the reservoir. I worked on that job for about a month. While there, Kalispell and I camped at a campground on the downstream side of the dam. There was a good little restaurant in Hungry Horse that I frequented often for dinner. They had fantastic Huckleberry shakes and good Huckleberry pie. They also had Huckleberry ice cream, a nice treat on hot, sunny evenings.

The job was lots of fun because we did a lot of different types of work. We did some concrete cutting, core drilling, and steel installation. Some of the work was fairly deep for surface supply work. We tried to keep within the No-Deco limits, but had to get a decompression chamber on site so we could do a few surface-decompression using oxygen (Sur-D-O2) dives. I had operated the chamber on quite a few of those type of dives when I had worked in the Gulf of Mexico. Also, Blanchard, the Greek, Boston, and the Texan had a lot of experience in the Gulf with Sur-D-O2. There was a lot of work to do so we ran two shifts. Our boss also brought in a Canadian, who worked for Can-Dive, to run one of the shifts. He thought he knew what he was doing, but he really didn't. I don't think he had a good understanding of how the decompression tables worked; either that or he just didn't care. Lots of divers got bent diving for him. He was also quite full of himself, so I was glad I wasn't on his crew. He had a nickname for himself, but I'll just refer to him as "Big Load" because that's about what I thought of him.

Before the job was completed, I was sent on another set of small jobs for the Montana Power Company. I worked at the Thompson Falls dam, Hauser dam, and a couple of the dams near Great Falls. I enjoyed working on the little jobs. I thought it was fun to spend a couple days at one location then move on to another project. Most of the divers I knew preferred to get on one long project rather than a bunch of little ones. They were always hoping for work with deeper dives too. It wasn't only the wet pay they liked; it was the depth pay as well.

*　　*　　*

In late August, the office secured a substantial contract for work on Libby Dam just outside of Libby, Montana. The job was to replace ten-thousand bolts that secured the head gate guides to the sides of the head gate slots. The placement of the bolts went from the surface to a depth of two-hundred-twenty feet. The actual work on the dam wouldn't start until November, but there was plenty of set-up and prep-work to do in getting ready for the job. The dam was owned and operated by the Army Corps of Engineers; Seattle office. I had worked plenty of jobs for the ACoE and knew their protocol well. That didn't get me on the job though.

The replacement of the bolts required a four-step process. First, a hole had to be drilled through the steel of the gate guide. Next, a sixteen-inch-deep hole would have to be core-drilled into the concrete behind the gate guide. Then the replacement bolt would have to be positioned and secured in the hole. Lastly, nuts and washers would be threaded onto the bolts and torqued. It was going to be a time and labor-intensive job. It appeared there was going to be a large number of deep dives required for its completion. Not only would divers make a lot of money on this job, but it was going to cost the company a lot to get the work done. Our boss was looking for ways to keep his costs to a minimum.

With this in mind, the boss consulted with the engineer from eastern Canada. Remember him? The guy from Montreal who wasn't as good an engineer as he thought he was? Anyway, they came up with an idea for a robotic machine, operated by pneumatics and hydraulics, that would position itself, drill the holes in the steel, drill the holes in the concrete, then move to the next position and repeat the process.

They called it the "Drill Frame." We called it "Frankenstein." It would require the use of a crane to lower it into position and lower it all the way down the slot. The crane would also be needed to bring it back to the surface when it was finished with the slot. It required a tool-air compressor to operate the positioning and securing mechanisms. It also required a hydraulic unit to power the steel drills and core drills. In theory it was a wonderful thing. I don't know how much the boss spent on materials for the "Drill Frame" but it was probably somewhere around ten-thousand dollars. If it worked, though, it would save him a couple hundred thousand dollars in dive pay. Of course, the divers weren't happy about that.

At the end of August, Montreal required a dive to be made on Libby dam for some needed measurements. I went to Libby dam with Kalispell and the Rancher from central Washington. The Rancher was very excited about the dives he thought he would be making to two-hundred-twenty-five feet. The deepest dive we made to take measurements ended up only being to sixty feet though. The reservoir level was low at this time of year. We lowered an aluminum skiff, loaded with dive gear and two divers, down from the top of the dam; a one-hundred-sixty-foot crane ride. The Rancher wasn't too upset, he was still looking forward to all the dives in the future of that job, and he figured if he were here in the beginning, he would be here to do the work throughout the job. We got the needed measurements and information and delivered it to Montreal the Engineer. I went back to the smaller jobs for the Montana Power Company.

At the beginning of November, Kalispell and the Rancher went back to Libby dam to start setting up the job. The main contractor was from Missoula and would supply extra tenders when they were needed. By the third week of November, there was more work to handle than could be done by just those two guys. I had finished up the small jobs I had been on, so the boss asked if I would help with the set-up in Libby. I told him that I would. He wanted me to meet at the office Friday to gather some gear and fill out some paperwork for me to work on that particular job. I was to be on site the following Monday morning at eight.

I thought it was weird to have to fill out special paperwork for a job like this, but maybe it had something to do with working on an ACoE job. I had to get special clearances to work on the Pend Oreille job, so maybe this dam required something like that. I met with the boss and he said that the union pay rate for this job in Montana would be eighty percent of our union rate in eastern Washington. He wanted me to sign a document agreeing to the reduced rate of pay. I told him that I wanted to talk to our union representative before I agreed to that. He said that was fine.

I called Kalispell to see if he had signed such a document and he told me that he had; everybody who wanted to work on that job had signed such a document. Then I called our union rep to see if it really was okay with the union or if our boss was trying to pull a fast one. All my other work in Montana paid our eastern Washington rate. The union rep confirmed the boss's statement. He told me that because this job was being crewed up from the Missoula union, it would be paid at Missoula rates which were eighty-percent of our eastern Washington rates. Okay. I went back to the boss and told him I would sign the document for that job, but not for any other work. He was satisfied and gave me the document to sign. I signed it. At the time, our tender pay was twenty-two dollars per hour, meaning we should be making seventeen-sixty per hour. I started working that job the following Monday.

When I got there the set-up was pretty much complete. The guys were ready to start using the "Drill Frame." Our crew consisted of Kalispell, the Rancher, a professional tender from Alaska, and me. There was a crane with a designated operator from Montana at our disposal. If we needed any other hands to help tend lines, we could request them from the crew working for the prime contractor. Every day at the end of the shift, we had to give the foreman of the construction company a report on our progress and the hours each of us had worked that day. We were working ten-hour days at that time.

Wednesday, some guy I had never seen before drove up to the dam in one of our company trucks pulling a flatbed trailer. He jumped out of the truck and sauntered down the dam to where we were working. In a loud, almost threatening voice he announced he was so-and-so and he worked for our boss at Norwesco Marine. He was there to deliver some equipment and supplies and wanted to know where he could unload it. Kalispell and I looked at each other and busted out laughing at his intensely animated determination. We showed him where he could back the trailer to and start unloading the supplies. He backed the truck and trailer combo to the unloading point, jumped out of the truck and started throwing stuff off the trailer like a madman. Whoa, whoa, whoa we both said. Slow down and let us unload this stuff in an organized manner. He said he was in a hurry because he needed to get back to the office before the end of the day. We helped him unload everything quickly, but carefully. That was my introduction to a young kid from Coeur D'Alene, Idaho, who had just started working with us, and would continue to work with us for the next six years. Oh boy.

The Drill Frame was very awkward to work with. It was eight feet tall and eighteen feet wide, and about a foot-and-a-half thick. It weighed several hundred pounds, being a steel frame with two positioning pins, four hydraulic drills, six pneumatic pistons, and all the required fittings and hoses attached. Now you know why we called it "Frankenstein." A bundle of four hydraulic hoses and two pneumatic hoses made up the umbilical that we had to feed into the slot as "Frankenstein" was lowered down.

The machine worked fine on the holes out of the water. At this point, Montreal had decided that his machine was working, and would continue to work, as he had designed it. The drill frame even did okay with the holes down to about twenty feet, although the positioning wasn't as easy when we couldn't see the positioning pins. Montreal's solution to this issue was to install a couple underwater cameras; one showing each positioning pin. Wonderful, that's all we needed, more cables to raise and lower, as well as all the equipment required to operate the cameras. No thanks. Kalispell, the Rancher, and I assured Montreal that we could do it by feel just as well. Montreal agreed to that.

We discovered that the hydraulic unit wouldn't operate all four drills at the same time. It wouldn't even operate two of the drills at the same time. There was enough line loss that we could only operate one drill at a time. This put uneven stress on the frame causing it to tilt just enough to misalign the holes so only one hole would be properly aligned for the second drilling operation; the core drilling. Montreal had left us to our own devices and went on to bigger and better things. He told the boss that his machine was working fine when he left it and that it was up to the crew at the dam to keep it working properly.

I talked with the other two divers and told them that, obviously, Montreal hadn't taken into account the line loss due to friction of the hydraulics. I did the calculations for the hydraulic output that was required for each drill and determined that, not only did the engineer not take into account the line loss, he hadn't taken into account the actual output of the power unit. If the theoretical output numbers were used, and you didn't take into account the friction coefficient, then Frankenstein would work as designed. The problem was we were working in the real world, not a theoretical world.

I also told the guys that the air compressor wouldn't supply enough pressure to work the pistons below ninety feet. We needed them to work down to two-hundred-twenty-five feet, a depth requiring a minimum of one-hundred-ten pounds per square inch just to overcome bottom pressure. Tool air compressors put out about two-hundred psi at the source, so with the line loss at depth, there wouldn't be enough pressure to operate the piston cylinders. At this point, the Rancher was not liking the job at all. If Frankenstein worked, there would be no deep dives, if any dives at all. Frankenstein wasn't any fun to work with. We had been attempting to drill for two weeks by now and were woefully behind schedule. The boss was giving us all grief for being so far behind schedule. He gave us permission to alter the drill frame as needed to get it to work.

The Rancher quit the job in a huff the Wednesday before Thanksgiving. We didn't need a diver to fill his spot, so the boss asked if I or Kalispell knew anyone that could take the Rancher's place. I had a friend in Spokane, who worked as a commercial fisherman in Alaska, that would be happy to fill the position. Kalispell was a good welder, so we cut up the drill frame a little and re-welded it, modifying it to make it work better. That helped a little, but not much. We modified it a little almost every other day. We were getting further and further behind schedule. The foreman of the construction company was not happy and our boss was even less so. About this time, I looked at my paychecks. I was only getting paid fourteen dollars and ten cents per hour. That did not seem right to me.

I thought I was supposed to be making eighteen dollars an

hour. I asked Kalispell what he was making. He showed me that we were earning the same pay, and that is how much he had been earning since the start of the job. Since I had been filing the paperwork with the foreman every day, I had to go into his job shack. I looked at the bulletin board where all the safety and other announcements were posted. A pay schedule was posted in the upper right-hand corner of the board. It had to be since this was a union job.

The lowest rate on the schedule was sixteen-seventy an hour for the laborers. We, as diver tenders, were only getting fourteen-ten per hour. How could that be? I asked the job foreman about it and he showed me his pay schedule. He said that at a minimum we should be getting sixteen-seventy, but he had thought we were getting seventeen-sixty per hour. I showed him my pay stub and he just smiled and shook his head. Something wasn't right. He let me make a copy of the job pay schedule. I highlighted the laborer's rate and the tender rate. I included that in a letter to my boss, saying that I thought there was an issue with our pay.

The boss called me into his office. I skipped a day of work to meet with him in his office. He showed me the paper I had signed stating that I would work for eighty percent of the regular pay. I told him that was eighty percent of eastern Washington pay, not eighty percent of Missoula pay. He said I had signed the document and he was going to hold me to it. I told him, that what he was paying us was less than what the laborers were getting paid and that was not right. We were skilled workers and worth more than that. Again, he told me that I had agreed to the lower pay. I shook my head and told him I wasn't going back on that job.

He told me I had to go back since I had agreed to that pay. I laughed. I told him I didn't **have** to do anything he told me to do and I hadn't agreed to fourteen dollars an hour. He said he didn't have anyone to take my place. I informed him that wasn't my problem. He told me again that it was in my best interest to keep his jobs profitable and I should be thankful for the work. I laughed again, I was almost at the point of bending over, pulling my pants down and showing him my new tattoo. But I didn't do that. Instead, I walked out the door and told him not to call me anymore.

He called after me and said fine, he would pay the seventeen dollars per hour if I would go back to the job the next day. I told him, no, I wasn't interested. I was angry that he had been shorting my pay for the past month. He asked why not, and I told him that he owed me all that back pay. I said that if he wanted me to go back to that job, he would have to pay me the seventeen-sixty per hour that I had agreed to plus all the back pay he owed. On top of that, he would have to pay Kalispell and the new tender the same thing. He said fine, but he wouldn't pay any per diem. That irked me even more because I knew that, since this was an ACoE contract, he was getting reimbursed for the per diem according to the IRS schedule. The IRS had designated eighty-four dollars per day for that area at that time. He was only paying us forty dollars per day as per the union schedule.

I just shook my head, said no thanks and turned to walk out the door. Okay, fine, he said. He would pay the seventeen-sixty per hour, he would keep paying the per diem, but the new tender, my friend, would only get paid the laborer rate of sixteen-seventy. That was okay with me, my friend wasn't a diver and was only doing laborer type work anyway.

I went back to the job and worked up until the Friday before Christmas. We were supposed to go back to work on December twenty-seventh, the Wednesday after Christmas. Tuesday, I got a call from our office saying that I wasn't on the job anymore, the Rancher had come back to take my place. Fine with me, it was a shitty job anyway.

The following Saturday, I got a call from the boss asking if I was available to go back to Libby dam the following Monday. I told him not really. He asked why not. He wanted to know if I had something else going on. I told him no, I didn't, but I didn't want to deal with the crap on that job anymore. He told me he would pay the eastern Washington rate if I would go back. I asked him why, had somebody left? He told me the Rancher didn't want to work there anymore. I thought about it a minute or so, then told him I would be there Monday morning at eight.

Monday morning when I showed up, Kalispell was all smiles. Just before Christmas he had received a check for all his missing back pay since he had started the job, plus he was getting the eastern Washington pay rate. Good deal. We were still way, way behind schedule on the number of holes we had drilled. Something needed to be done. I was looking down stream over the edge of the dam when I saw the boneyard.

That is where the ACoE kept equipment and large spare parts. I also saw a pile of concrete stop logs. I went into the job shack and had a talk with the foreman. I asked him why he hadn't had the ACoE install the stop logs in front of the head gates we were working on. I mean, that would hold all the water back from the head gate slot and the work could be done in the dry. Was there a reason that wasn't being done, I asked. He looked at me with the deer in the headlights eyes. Nobody had mentioned that possibility to him. I asked him if we could ask the ACoE guys in charge if that might be a possibility. He said he would look into it.

The next day, the foreman told me that the ACoE told him it would be no problem at all to install the stop logs and dry out the head gate slots. They spent the day doing just that. I told Kalispell what was going on and that we would no longer be using "Frankenstein." He asked me what the plan going forward was then. I told him we would get some spider scaffolding like the construction crew was using on another part of the dam.

We would put two guys in it, one at each end, and they would do the drilling and bolt installing all in one go. That should save us plenty of time, allowing us to make up for being so far behind. At the current rate of production, we had figured the job wouldn't be completed until the following August or September, barely meeting the deadline of the job. I figured if all went well, we should be able to finish in May or June, July at the worst. Kalispell laughed and replied that anything would be better than continued work with the Drill Frame.

That week Montreal came back out to the job site to see the progress. I guess the boss had told him that things weren't going according to plan and maybe he should make an appearance to see what was going on. When he saw what we had done to his beloved Drill Frame, his face turned white and it looked like he was going to cry. When he heard us refer to it as "Frankenstein" he turned around and walked off the dam. I didn't see him on the dam for the rest of the job.

We got the spider scaffolding and set it up. We had a meeting with our crew, which now consisted of Kalispell, my friend from Spokane, one other laborer from Libby, and me. We went over what needed to be done and how we saw it working. The two laborers got into the spider stage and started work. The plan worked well, exceptionally well in fact. We started installing bolts at an incredible rate compared to what we had been doing. At the end of that day, I figured we should easily be able to complete the job by the end of May, or early June.

We were using an annular cutter bit to drill the holes through the steel. They were expensive and would become dull enough not to work well after about twenty holes. This was going to be a very expensive project if we couldn't come up with a way to get more life out of the bits. The boss was already complaining about how many bits we were going through. The laborer from Libby said he knew a machinist in Libby who might be able to help us out. Kalispell took a couple of the specialty bits in to Libby and talked to the machinist. The machinist said he could sharpen the bits for us for a minimal fee. That worked for us. He ended up being able to sharpen the bits four or five times before they were useless. That ended up saving us a bunch of money, not to mention the time wasted waiting for new bits to show up.

The divers that were hoping to get on this job weren't very happy with me. There were now less than two hundred bolts to replace at the bottom of the head gate slots. Those bolts didn't secure the head gate guides, rather they secured steel plates at the bottoms of the penstock intakes and couldn't be accessed in the dry without lowering the level of the reservoir two hundred and thirty feet. The boss talked to Can-Dive and made some deal to utilize their Newt Suit to do the work. None of the divers that worked for us were trained and certified to use the Newt Suit. It would be a fully Canadian team that would come in and do the deepest bolts. Even though I had plenty of experience being part of the support crew for the Newt Suit, I didn't get on that part of the job. I didn't actually want to, because the Newt Suit work would be overseen by the Canadian that had led one of the crews at Hungry Horse dam – Big Load. I didn't like working around him at all.

Anyway, that meant that there wasn't going to be any diving for us on this project at all. I was okay with that, because my philosophy on diving is that you only put a diver in the water when there is no other way to do the work. I caught a fair amount of grief from the divers for taking away the diving on this job. I thought it was strange that they were upset with me, when the boss and the engineer had designed a Drill Frame that, if it had worked, would have left no need for any diving on this job anyway. Well, I suppose you can't win for losing.

The first week of February nineteen-ninety-five we had got ourselves back on schedule. The use of the spider staging was working better than we had hoped. I got all the equipment we had needed for the Drill Frame, as well as any equipment needed for diving loaded up and sent back to the yard in

Spokane. It was obvious by then that no wet work was going to be done by us. The Rancher had left in a huff before Christmas because of the lack of diving and now Kalispell was ready to leave. We were utilizing a four-man crew, one of which needed to be the supervisor type and the other three didn't need any special training. That meant that the boss didn't need two diver/tenders on the job. He could save money by replacing either me or Kalispell with another laborer from Libby. I didn't care either way, we had some other little dive work coming up soon anyway. Kalispell was anxious to get off the job though. He'd had enough of the non-diving work. He left, I stayed. He and I worked well together so it was a little sad to see him go.

Another laborer came in to fill his spot and we carried on. We were making great progress. I pushed the guys hard to get us on schedule and then to try and get ahead. I kept their morale up by setting goals and buying them dinner and drinks at the end of the day every time we met those goals. By the end of February, we were way ahead of schedule. It looked like we would complete the work in May, possibly April. I kept pushing the guys and they kept performing very well. We actually replaced the last bolt at the end of March. It took us the first week of April to get all the equipment cleared out and our part of the job site cleaned up.

It was a Friday morning when the job was all said and done. The boss had come to Libby that Thursday so he could have a meeting with the construction foreman Friday morning. Everybody seemed happy with the work and completion time. I know the construction foreman was ecstatic, because we had finished our part four months ahead of schedule. My boss didn't say much to me. He didn't even say "job well done" or even "thank you" for getting the work done in time. I thought that was a little odd, because just in January we were three months behind schedule and it was looking like we were going to be on the job all spring and summer. I also knew I had saved him a ton of money. Some companies gave their employees bonuses for that kind of performance.

That Friday afternoon, my friend from Spokane and I, went back to the motel and collected all our gear. We had checked out that morning, but they let us store our luggage in their office while we finished up our last day at the dam. We stopped by a little restaurant on the west side of Libby for dinner. We had been doing this for the past couple months on our way home for the weekends. This would be our last time we had dinner there. When we entered the restaurant, we spotted the boss sitting at a corner table by himself. I waved to him. He waved back but didn't say anything. We sat at our own table and had dinner. Before we had ordered, the boss left the restaurant. He didn't even say good-bye on his way out. Weird, I thought. We had our meal, a hamburger and a bowl of soup. After we finished, we went to pay the cashier and were told that our meal had been paid for by the gentleman that was seated by himself in the corner. I guess that was his way of thanking us for the completion of the job. Thanks, boss man. I did thank him for the meal in person the next time I saw him, which was the following week.

*   *   *

Later on, I got sent to Seattle for a job in Puget Sound. I didn't work in Seattle a whole lot because my boss, the owner of Norwesco, didn't like paying per diem for employees from out of the area to work in Seattle. He didn't have to pay per diem for divers working out of the Seattle union to work on jobs in and around Seattle. In the past, I could stay at my sister's house when I worked in Seattle, so per diem there wasn't a huge deal for me. She had gotten married a couple years earlier and had a new baby. It was no longer comfortable for her and her family to have me stay there. Now, when I worked in the Seattle area, I required per diem just like all the other out of area workers.

There was a lot of dive work going on at this time. All the dive companies were pretty busy, so the pool of available divers in western Washington was small. We had dive crews all over the place and our regular guys that lived in Seattle were unavailable for this job. The boss even had to call a couple guys down from Canada to fill the crew requirements. The union per diem was up to forty dollars by now, while the IRS scheduled per diem for King County was one-hundred-seventy dollars. I was in the union, so couldn't really expect more than what the union rate was, but the Canadians weren't in the local union. There were three of them needed, but they made it clear that they would not come down unless they got the IRS rate for per diem. They also wanted our union rate of pay because they would be working in Seattle; *and* it was higher than what their Canadian rate of pay was. Not fair to me, or any of the other American guys hired for that work.

The cheapest motel I could find in the area was thirty-eight dollars per night. That left me two dollars a day for food. McDonald's anyone? No matter how much I talked to the boss about it, he wouldn't give in. I told him it didn't make any sense for me to work for him if it cost me money to do so. He told me, *again*, that it was in my best interest to keep his jobs profitable. If he was awarded contracts and got work, then I would keep working. All I could do was shake my head. I reiterated that if it cost me money to work, there was no reason for me to do so. My problem was that I enjoyed the diving industry and loved working under water. Don't tell anybody, but I would have done it for minimum wage! Not really, I have always been aware that our work is worth a lot more because of the knowledge and the skill set that is required to do what we do.

We were working at Shilshole Marina near Ballard. The Canadians were all staying at a motel up the hill and off highway ninety-nine a couple blocks. Their motel had a large parking area that we were allowed to use as a staging area. I didn't want to stay there because it cost eighty-seven dollars a night, no breakfast included. My motel was a few blocks away. I would meet them at their motel every morning, after getting a breakfast burrito from McDonald's, to prep for the day's work. The Canadians were kind of a pain to work with, because we were only getting paid for eight-hour days. The prime contractor at Shilshole wanted us on site at eight in the morning and expected us to stay until four-thirty in the afternoon. We got half an hour for lunch. The Canadians wanted us to start our day when we met in the parking lot of their motel. It would take fifteen to twenty minutes to meet and load the needed equipment for the day's work. That meant we wouldn't get to the actual worksite until after eight-thirty. That upset the prime contractor. I tried to get the Canadians to meet at seven-thirty in the morning, but they wouldn't agree to that. They would agree to staying later at the marina as long as they got paid for the extra time. I wasn't running the job, so it wasn't my problem.

My problem was being at the job site on time. I told the Canadians that I would be at the marina, ready to go, at oh-eight-hundred. Whatever time they arrived at the marina was none of my concern. They were fine with that, since one of them was doing the supervising. I was just trying to keep the peace with the prime contractor. There was about half-an-hour's-worth of set up every morning at the marina to get going anyway. I took it upon myself to have everything ready to go by the time the Canadians arrived. That worked for everyone concerned.

The marina work lasted about three weeks. It was pretty

shallow, so even though we were diving every day, each diver didn't do that much diving. The Canadians took as much of the diving as possible, so I ended up only diving once or twice a week. Happily for me, the job only lasted three weeks.

*   *   *

I'M A DAM DIVER DOING A DAM JOB IN A DAM TOWN

Drinking in a Dam Bar!

Chapter Eight

At the end of March nineteen-ninety-five, I went back to Madison dam for our annual spring cleaning. I was accompanied by Blanchard and the Coeur D'Alene Kid. The Kid had just got out of dive school the previous year. He was the excited guy who had brought the equipment to me and Kalispell working on Libby Dam. He had gone to DIT in Seattle. His parents bought him brand new dive gear for graduating dive school. We gave him a hard time about how shiny his dive helmet was, not a scratch on it and never been in the water. We told him it was so shiny we had to wear sunglasses to look at it. He didn't appreciate the joking.

There was enough work to be done on the trash rack system for two days. We would be spending the night in Ennis. The boss didn't want the Kid to do any diving yet, because he was fresh out of school. I thought that was kind of silly. In the northwest we didn't really have designated tenders and there wasn't any type of traditional apprenticeship or breakout like there was in the Gulf of Mexico. Here we all did everything for the most part. There were a few guys that had a stick up their butt about it and didn't like to put newer guys in the water.

We usually only had three-man crews, so if there was a lot of diving to be done, everyone on the crew might be expected to dive. I preferred to dive my new guys on easy stuff so I could get a feel for how they performed in the water. I mean, if I was doing the diving, ran into trouble, and ended up needing a standby diver to jump in and help me, I would be depending on them to save me. I preferred to know that they were comfortable enough in the water that they would actually be a help rather than a hinderance.

Some guys didn't see it that way though, or maybe they just didn't think about it. Or, maybe they, like many divers, thought they were invincible and could not die. There did tend to be two kinds of divers; those who thought they were bullet-proof and nothing could hurt them, and the others who had some sort of death wish and were hoping, maybe subconsciously, that they would die under the water. Anyway, I liked to know how a guy worked in the water for my own peace of mind.

Regardless, all the diving at Madison dam this time was done by me and Blanchard. At the end of the first day, we went to the Longbranch Saloon for dinner. They had excellent food and service and we knew the owners, a husband-and-wife team who did all the cooking. Dining there had become a regular thing since we had been working in Ennis at least a couple times a year for the past several years. There weren't a lot of options for food in Ennis then. We usually had breakfast at the

Ennis Café and dinner at the Longbranch. Our favorite place for drinks at the end of the day was the Silver Dollar.

At dinner we found out how spoiled and rude the new kid was. The restaurant offered Montana raised beef, fresh trout from the Madison river and a few other specialties. I'm not much of a fish eater, so I ordered steak. Blanchard tried different dishes all the time and the Kid ordered the trout. The meal came with soup and salad and a couple sides. It was always very good. The Kid ate the salad, grimacing as he did so. After one sip of the soup, he pushed the bowl aside and stated loudly enough for the entire restaurant to hear that it wasn't very good. Then he started in on his meal. After two bites, he threw his silverware on the plate with a loud clanging. Everybody in the restaurant looked over to see what was going on. Next, he announced to the whole place, kitchen and all, that the fish dish was the worst he had ever had.

He rudely pushed his plate away and stated that he hoped he wasn't expected to pay for such garbage. I hoped no one could see me. Blanchard turned red. What the heck, dude?! These are our friends and the food is good. What is your problem?! He just got up and walked out of the restaurant. Whatever. We let him go. We apologized for his behavior and finished our meals. Then we had dessert. When the bill came, we paid for his meal and left a large tip for the waitress and the chef. We apologized again and promised never to bring that guy back into their place. I still don't understand how some people can be so rude.

That wasn't the only time the Kid made a scene in a restaurant. Almost every time we had a sit-down meal at any restaurant when we worked out of town, he acted more or less the same. I guess the only person who cooked food good enough for that kid was his mom. After a few times like that, I refused to eat with him. The Kid was a good worker though, and he had a desire to learn. He did seem to want to be a good diver. He did what he was asked to do and busted his butt, so I didn't mind having him on my jobs, even if I didn't want to share a meal with him.

*   *   *

About this time, I was getting shit from a few other divers for not having my own dive helmet. I was still diving one of the Rat Hats that we had on loan from Can-Dive. Also, the Canadians were always trying to use my Rat Hat whenever I worked with them because I kept it in very good working condition. I figured the Canadians could use one of the other Rat Hats. Supposedly they knew how to service and maintain them so why should I let them use the one I kept in good shape for me. I think we had six or seven other Rat Hats, that I kept maintained, but not regularly used. My boss was more on the Canadians' side than mine. I decided to start looking for my own hat.

I liked the Miller the best, but it didn't fit my head very well. I liked the Savoie also, but it was hard to find and hard to get parts for. The most common dive helmet in use was the Kirby-Morgan Superlite Seventeen, either A or B. I could buy a new one, but they cost around four-thousand dollars. I was in the market for a used one. Used Seventeens in good shape went for fifteen hundred to twenty-five hundred, much more in my price range. My friend from Texas had one that he had used for the past couple years. Before that he was diving a Savoie.

Anyway, he had found an almost new Superlite Seventeen for around twenty-five hundred dollars. It had only six dives on it. He wanted to buy it, but couldn't justify having two of the same dive hats. He talked to me about buying his Superlite, but they are not my favorite hat. I have a slightly fat head so the Seventeen fits fairly tightly on me. The Texan said he would let me use it on the next job we went on and I could decide whether or not I wanted to buy it. That sounded good to me. We just so happened to be going on a job together on Ross dam on the Skagit river in the north Cascades. The diving was to be done on the trash racks, the bottom of which were at one-hundred-eighty feet or so. That would be an excellent place to test the hat.

The job started on a Monday. I met the crew at the dam around seven-thirty in the morning. It was a nice summer day. We had a fairly large crew because the diving was so deep. Boston was there, Blanchard was there, as was the Coeur D'Alene Kid. There were a couple other guys too. We had a chamber on site so we could utilize surface decompression using oxygen if required. There was a crane with a man basket for us to get the diver in and out of the water. The water surface was around thirty feet below the top of the dam where we got the dive station set up. I had my Rat Hat with me, but planned on diving my friend's Superlite as much as possible since he had brought both of his.

We got everything set up and ready to dive. Boston made the first dive and established our down line. Blanchard was supervising and set up the dive schedule. We went to work. I made sure all my bailout bottle fittings and dry suit whips matched up to the Superlite. I was ready to go when my dive came up. Mine would be a quick dive to the bottom of the trash rack to take a couple measurements. We would try to do it with minimal in-water decompression. In-water decompression would be easy to control with the use of the man basket at the end of the crane wire so I wasn't worried.

I got dressed in. The padding inside the helmet was squishing my face. I figured if I bought the hat, I would thin the foam padding in the liner and make it fit better. The hat breathed well. I got to the bottom of the trash racks and topside checked my depth: one-hundred-seventy-six feet. Using the altitude adjustment and adding the two-foot safety margin put me on the one-hundred-ninety-foot table. I was at depth for twelve minutes. That gave me a four-minute deco stop at twenty feet and a seven-minute stop at ten feet. It was my practice to extend the decompression times a little just to reduce the risk of getting bent. I asked for a ten-minute stop at twenty feet and a fifteen-minute stop at ten feet.

One of the things about making these quick pops to deeper depths is that your sinuses don't get much time to equalize with the pressure changes; especially if you are a little stuffed up. I was a little stuffed up when I made this dive. More than I realized. My nose was a little runny at the start of the day, but it didn't feel plugged up. I didn't have any issues clearing on the way down, so I didn't think I would have any issues during decompression. Ha!

I didn't really have any issues coming up. I mean my ears popped like they normally do. I did feel a little pressure in my sinuses at about forty feet, but not painful or anything. By the time I got to my twenty-foot stop, the pressure was more intense, but still not painful. My sinuses weren't clearing like they usually did. At the marked time, I moved up to my ten-foot stop. Still no pain, but definitely more pressure. Then all of a sudden, I felt a huge blob of snot flow out my nose. It was warm and runny. Boy did that feel good. I couldn't see the goo and that was probably a very good thing.

When I reached the surface and stepped out of the man basket, the Texan was there to help me get out of my gear. I unlatched the hat and removed it from my head. I felt more slimy boogers slide out of my nose and into the oral-nasal mask. Oh yeah! That feels *sooo* good. Oh, Gross! It does not look so good though. There was a very large slimy blob of yellow and green snot mixed with bright red blood. My friend from Texas saw it and turned to the edge of the dam to puke. He didn't actually puke, but he said he hoped I wanted to buy the hat because he didn't want to put that hat on his head ever again.

I laughed and told him it would clean up. He shook his head saying it didn't matter and if I wanted it, he would sell it to me for nineteen-hundred dollars right then and there. He would even throw in the helmet bag. I shook my head no and told him I wasn't sure I wanted to buy it after all since it was bright yellow. I preferred a different color. He just looked at me like I was insane. After a bit, he told me that I could paint it whatever color I wanted. I laughed some more and told him I would happily take the hat off his hands for the nineteen-hundred.

I got out of my dive gear, dressed into my topside work clothes and rinsed out the dive hat. At the end of the work day, we went back to the motel we were staying at and cleaned up. We met for dinner and I paid my friend the nineteen-hundred dollars for the Superlite. I told him he could keep the hat bag because I didn't need it. I preferred a hard case and had a couple of them at home. Later, at the bar, we had a few beers and laughed about the booger bomb. And that, my friends, is how I came into possession of my Superlite Seventeen B.

*   *   *

I finished out the week at Ross dam. There were some shorter jobs to do over the next few weeks on several dams. Since I didn't mind moving around a lot, I was taken off the Ross dam project to run the little jobs. That weekend I returned to the yard in Spokane and loaded a shallow water package into our dive van. There were quite a few jobs to do scheduled over the next three weeks. My team and I cleaned some trash racks, unclogged some irrigation intakes, and sealed leaks in some spill gates. I also returned to Wanapum dam and helped them install stop logs so they could do their required maintenance.

After finishing that little tour of work, I had a couple weeks off. I decided to use this time off to go through my new hat. I wanted to replace all the O-rings, the diaphragm, and valve seats. I completely disassembled the helmet to do this. I looked at it and decided this would be a perfect time to change its color. What color would that be? Well, my favorite color is purple, electric violet actually, but purple none the less. I wanted a tough coat of paint on it since it was a working hat. Napa would put any car color in spray cans. Automobile paint should be tough enough to do the trick. My favorite car color? Plum Crazy from the Dodge Roadrunner. I went down to the local Napa and had them make up three cans. That should be enough to do my hat and bailout bottle.

I sanded down the shell of my helmet and the bailout bottle. Then I sprayed both with four coats of grey primer. After drying and sanding, I applied the Plum Crazy. I gave them three coats with light sanding in between. I let the paint dry for a couple days then reassembled my hat. It was a thing of beauty, at least to me. When my friends saw it, some laughed, some shook their heads, and a couple just said I was crazy. I didn't care, I liked it. I wasn't the only diver who had personalized his hat by a long shot anyway. At the time, you could buy them new in Yellow, Red, Green, and Blue. Purple wasn't that big a deal to me. Some guys even put pinstriping on their dive hats. Others painted little pictures like mermaids, fish, or other stuff. I liked purple and everybody would know whose hat it was. Shortly after I got my hat back together, I got called out to do another job. I would be going to Montana for the week.

Friday morning, I went into the shop to load the truck for the jobs I was going on. I unloaded my personal gear from my truck and set it at the edge of the parking lot by the office door. Then I went into the garage and started gathering the equipment that I would need for the upcoming work. Blanchard was out in the parking lot loading up his own job. He had seen my new paint job already, but our boss had not.

I opened the garage door so I could back the truck I would be using up to the garage, getting ready to load it.

The boss was standing outside talking to Blanchard. I heard the boss ask if I really had painted my dive hat purple. Blanchard nodded his head and flipped open my hat box. There it was, all bright and shiny brand new, never been dived purple. The boss looked at it for about one second then started swearing and jumping up and down. He got real red in the face and looked at me. "How unprofessional can you be?!" he screamed. I just looked at him and replied that I didn't see the big deal. Lots of people had personalized dive hats. He answered "Yes, but not Purple!"

I looked at Blanchard, who was wearing a black t-shirt emblazoned with United Marine Divers in Hot Pink and Chartreuse Green. I really didn't see how my purple hat was any less professional than a t-shirt in those colors that the boss was okay with. To me, Hot Pink was much less professional than purple. Maybe they were about the same, though. I think the boss ranted and raved for about forty-five minutes before shaking his head and walking back into his office. After he was gone, Blanchard laughed. I just shrugged my shoulders and went back to work. The boss didn't pay for my hat, so he had no right to tell me what color it could or could not be.

*   *   *

The following Sunday I headed to Montana. Montana Power Company had scheduled work at three of the dams along the Missouri river just east of Great Falls. I checked into the O'Haire Motel after arriving in Great Falls. MPC had a deal with that motel for special low rates for their sub-contractors. The motel bar, the Sip 'N Dip Lounge, was a Tiki bar with a swimming pool window behind the bar. When you walked into the bar, it was like stepping back into the late fifties or early sixties.

I don't think the decorations had been changed since the place was built. They even had a piano in the middle of the bar and a lady piano player who had been playing there since nineteen-sixty-three. On Friday and Saturday nights there was a mermaid swimming in the pool. The place was clean, the bar was fun, the piano player was great, and the drinks were cheap. It was our favorite place to stay when we worked in Great Falls. There are five dams right there, so we had a fair amount of work in that town.

Monday morning, my crew of two and I met at the Rainbow dam maintenance shop. That is where the offices for all of MPC's dam maintenance and repair are. All work, above and beyond normal maintenance, was dispatched from this shop. If we were working on any one of the five dams in Great Falls, we would meet at that shop every morning at eight. The foreman would go over the work to be done that day and designate the crews to work on each project. The crew assigned to the work we were to be doing would join us in the work shop to gather the tools, equipment, and any parts we might need to complete the task.

One of the coolest pieces of equipment that they had for us to use was a World War II Duck. For those of you who don't know, a Duck is an amphibious vehicle designed to transport soldiers and equipment across areas of land with small bodies of water that need to be crossed. It has six-wheel drive and floats. The two-man cab could be sealed up to make a water tight compartment. The back of this particular Duck was an empty truck bed with sides that were about three feet high. There was plenty of room to load a complete shallow water dive package, air compressor, two dive hoses, and all.

This was an invaluable piece of equipment for us because it

allowed us access to the dams we wouldn't otherwise have. We would load the Duck with all our equipment and ride to the dam to be worked on. When we arrived at the dam, the Duck driver would drive down the river bank and into the reservoir behind the dam. Once in the water we would motor over to the dam and tie up to where we would be working. Most of the work we did out of the Duck was spill gate sealing, but we would use it to do work anywhere we needed that we couldn't drive to.

After the melting of the snowpack in the spring, the dam operators would want to conserve as much water as possible. Lots of water leaked by the spill gates after they were shut and we would be hired to seal the leaks. The Duck could motor right up to the spill gate slot putting us as close to the work site as possible. The MPC guys had custom built a ladder for us to climb in and out of the Duck.

The deepest depth at the bottom of most of the spill gates was thirty or forty feet. We had to use altitude adjustment tables for decompression which added ten feet on to our bottom depth. This put our deepest diving on the spill gates on a fifty-foot table. With a three-man dive team, we had plenty of dive time to work a complete eight-hour day. The MPC management didn't like to pay overtime, but they had no problem keeping us working all week long. It might take us two or three weeks to seal all the spill gates on the dams in the Great Falls area. We would go home on the weekends, so the dam guys would usually want to finish up around noon on Friday. If the roads were clear, we would be home in time for a late dinner.

This particular week, two guys from Seattle whom I had never worked with before met me at the hotel late Sunday evening. I explained to them what the work would entail and what we were expected to do. Early Monday morning we grabbed breakfast and lunch on the way to the maintenance shop. They were pretty impressed with the Duck. We got all our equipment loaded, including all their personal dive gear. One of them had a Superlite Seventeen and the other had a Miller dive helmet. The diver with the Seventeen obviously had much more experience than the guy with the Miller. They both said they had plenty of dive experience and would have no issues.

I didn't like having two guys I had never worked with on a three-man crew. I had no idea what kind of divers they would turn out to be. I didn't know if I could depend on them to run the dive when I was in the water. I had no idea if they knew their way around a dam. Did they know to keep their fingers and toes away from the leaks in the gates? Did they know how to tend the dive hose when working around leaky dams? Would they pay attention to what the diver was saying over the radio? It made me nervous, but I didn't let them know that. I planned to make both of them dive before I would dive so I could get a feel for how they worked and dove. That was my normal mode of operation.

The first dam we went to was Morony dam. It was the furthest east of the five Great Falls dams. We rode in the back of the Duck on the way to the dam. When we got there, I had a little meeting with the dam operator to go over my work plan for the day. It looked like we would be working at that dam for two days, unless we ran into some issues. I had done this same work at this dam the previous three years without any issues and didn't expect any issues this year. After signing the required documents for the operator, I went back to the Duck. My crew and I got into the back of the Duck while the Duck driver and one other MPC employee climbed into the cab and drove us down the river bank and into the forebay. We motored over to the far right side of the reservoir where we would start the work. We got the hats online, putting mine on the standby hose so I could dive the other two guys first and minimize how many times we would connect and disconnect the dive helmets.

We decided the guy with the Superlite would dive first. We went over all the predive checks and everything checked out fine. The diver splashed and followed the right side of the gate down to the bottom which was twenty-six feet below the surface. I added my three-foot safety margin and the extra ten-foot altitude adjustment which gave me a calculated depth of thirty-nine feet. This put the diver on a forty-foot table for decompression. I explained my process to the guy with the Miller hat, so he would know how to plan the dive and follow the paperwork. He didn't get the three-foot safety margin. I explained that the norm for the U.S. Navy decompression tables was to add a two-foot safety margin to the depth indicated on the pneumo gauge in case the gauge wasn't right on.

I told him I always added an extra foot to that because I wanted to reduce the risk of the bends as much as possible. I told him that I also shortened the bottom time shown on the No-D tables by having the diver leave bottom three to five minutes before the end of the table. Since we were using a forty-foot table on this dive, the table allowed us two-hundred minutes at that depth, but I would have the diver leave at one-hundred-ninety-five minutes. He shook his head, not getting it. He said everywhere else he worked they pushed the tables right up to the end. I told him that was fine, but on my jobs, I expected him to run the tables the way I wanted. I wanted to reduce the risk of the bends and this was my way of doing that out here. If we had to treat for bends, we would require a Hyperbaric chamber. There was one at the Air Force base in Great Falls, but that was at least a half-hour drive from these dams. The next closest chamber was at Virginia Mason hospital in Seattle and that would require a helicopter flight of several hours. Neither of those were good options, so it was up to me to reduce the risk as much as possible.

The guy in the water was doing well. He had obviously worked around sucking water before and knew to keep his umbilical away from the suction. He was doing well plugging the leaks. Here the leaks were small enough that we started with knotted rags for the bigger gaps and unknotted rags for the smaller ones. After we stuffed rags in all the leaks, we would add a layer of cinders behind the rags. MPC got the cinders from the coal-fired electric plants they owned and operated in eastern Montana. The cinders would stop ninety-five percent of the leaking.

There are nine spill gates on Morony dam for us to seal. The guy with the Seventeen got three of the gates sealed up in his dive time. I was happy with his performance. He communicated well when he was in the water and took direction well. I could work with this guy again. We didn't need to take breaks for this kind of dive work. The topside guys could get a drink, or eat a snack, even eat lunch while a guy was in the water without slowing the progress. The only time we had an actual break in work was when we swapped divers. When the Superlite guy got back on board the Duck, we swapped his hat for the Miller. We started going through the pre-dive checks and found that the comms didn't seem to be working on the Miller.

The "comms" is the two-wire communications system consisting of a microphone and two speakers wired to a junction block in the dive hat with two external posts. A comm cable is attached to the external posts and runs up the umbilical to the dive radio at the dive control station. It is a pretty simple set-up and easy to keep in working order. I always have a spare radio and spare batteries for the radio on each job. Both radios were working. The comm cable in the umbilical can fail, but it usually has four wires and the only places that commonly fail are at the ends which can easily be checked and redone if needed. The comm cable was working fine. The mic and speakers in the hat go out on a fairly regular basis. Most divers carried spares just in case this happened.

A well-maintained hat rarely has issues. This guy's Miller

looked good and well-maintained, but that was because he had just rebuilt it. The wiring was all messed up and he admitted that he didn't know what he was doing when he rebuilt his hat. Why, why, why would you rebuild your own hat if you didn't know what you were doing. I mean, it's not like your life depends on that particular piece of equipment working, does it?!

We spent a little while trying to get it working, but I wasn't comfortable having this guy dive with an untested hat, especially if he didn't know what he was doing. We wasted about half-an-hour with the Miller and that didn't really make us look good in front of the customer. I was not happy, but said I would do the next dive. The guy with the Superlite said he would loan his hat to the Miller guy for his dive. I was okay with that. Of course, now I didn't have much of an expectation for the quality of the Miller guy's work. He lived up to, or down to as the case may be, my expectations. He spent his whole dive, and the rest of our work day, on one spill gate and didn't even get it sealed up well enough to move on to the next gate the next morning.

We went back to the hotel after work that day. The two guys from Seattle spent all evening trying to get the communications in the Miller working. They were not successful. The next morning, we met at the Rainbow shop and went directly to the Duck. We didn't have to go to the meeting because our task and MPC crew had been designated for the week. We met the Duck driver and the other guy at the Duck. Our gear was already loaded, so we just climbed aboard and headed to the dam. About an hour later we were moored in the fourth spill gate slot. I jumped in the water and finished sealing that spill gate. I did two more before I finished my dive time and got back in the Duck. The Superlite guy ran the radio and filled out the dive log. He did just fine and I was happy with his work. I had him dive next. He got the last three spill gates sealed up on his dive. We had completed the scheduled work on Morony dam. We would find out what our next project was tomorrow morning.

Wednesday morning, we went into the Rainbow shop for the morning meeting. We were to seal the spill gates on Ryan dam. It was predicted that we would spend the rest of the week there and hopefully get all the gates sealed by the end of the day Friday. Again, we rode to the dam in the back of the Duck. When we got to the dam, I had my little meeting with the operator and got the necessary paperwork signed. Back in the Duck, and into the reservoir we went. I let the guy with the Superlite dive the first dive, I took the second dive. I decided not to let the guy with the Miller dive for the rest of the week. I had demoted him to full-time tender. He wasn't happy, but he didn't say anything to me about it. He just cried to the guy with the Superlite, who asked me to reconsider my decision. I didn't reconsider. The guy couldn't get his hat working and he didn't perform well in the water. I needed to get the work done and my best chance of that was to split the dives between the Superlite guy and myself. We did finish up the work at Ryan dam that Friday. We were asked to return the following Monday to continue work on the Great Falls dams. I told my boss that I didn't want the Miller guy back, he said he'd see what he could do. I always gave my boss a list of guys that I wanted on my crew, sometimes I got them, sometimes I didn't. I did get my boss to give me his word that I would only get one new guy at a time from here on out.

*　　*　　*

The following Sunday, nobody met me at the motel. Monday Kalispell and the Coeur D' Alene Kid met me at the Rainbow shop. This was a crew that I liked to work with. We were designated to work at Cochrane dam this week. We went down to the Duck with the same two MPC guys that we had worked with the previous week. I knew this would be a productive week.

Cochrane dam has seven spill gates. The deepest depth here was twenty-eight feet. With the altitude adjustment and my safety margin, we would be decompressing on a fifty-foot table. All three of us dove each day. It only took us two days to get the spill gates sealed. Wednesday we were asked to dive on one of the head gates on Cochrane dam. The MPC crew needed to do some maintenance in the turbine chamber of one of the units. We needed to seal the gate well enough that they could drain the chamber and keep it dry enough for them to work inside it.

The head gate sealed up very well along the sides. The issue was that the gate didn't always set flat on the concrete pad at the bottom. Sometimes it sat a little cattywampus with the right side set tight on the bottom, but the left side stopped about one inch off the concrete pad. I had sealed this leak for them several times in the past years. It only took about fifteen minutes to seal it up. The way we did it was to take a twelve-foot section of CP hose (you remember, the red rubber hose used for pneumatic tools) to the bottom, stuff one end into the bottom left corner and let the water flow grab the hose and suck it into the leak.

The big issue here is that the bottom of the gate is at seventy feet below the surface. That calculates to over thirty pounds per square inch of pressure. A gap at least ten feet long with an average width of half-an-inch gives a differential of something like one-hundred-eighty pounds. If your umbilical, foot, or hand gets stuck in there, you are not getting it out. Needless to say, the diver only had one chance to set the hose and seal the gate and he better make sure everything is out of the way of the hose. So much water flowed through that gap that at about thirty feet you could hear it roaring. The closer you got to the gap, the louder the roar. Oh, did I forget to tell you that visibility in this forebay was zilch? Well, it is pitch black in there. Below five feet, you can't see anything and the water is so silty that even with a light you only see a brownish-yellow glow in your faceplate.

For this dive, we set up the dive station on the top of the trash racks. There was a trapdoor at the top of the racks that we could use to get inside the head gate slot. The diver would climb down the trash rack frame, so as not to be free-falling to the bottom. It normally took three or four minutes to climb down because you had to thread yourself through the framework while holding onto the CP hose with one hand. The bottom of the trash racks was about six feet below the bottom of the head gate, so it was easy to sneak up on the sucking gap.

The topside crew would keep a little tension on the diver's umbilical to ensure it wouldn't get sucked through the gap. I was prepared to make the dive, but offered it to the other guys on my crew. The Coeur D' Alene Kid had no interest in making that dive. Kalispell wanted to do it. Okay. I explained to him exactly what to do. There was no need to panic or freak-out to complete this task. All the diver needed to do was keep calm and be aware of where his umbilical and the CP hose were. Also make sure he kept his fingers and toes away from the monster sucker.

A depth of seventy feet here meant that we would be using a ninety-foot schedule for diver's decompression. That gave us a bottom time of thirty minutes, or twenty-five minutes with my safety factor. We got the dive station set-up and dressed in Kalispell. He entered the water and we handed him the long section of CP hose. He left the surface. He got down to thirty feet just fine. I could hear the roaring of the monster sucker through the radio. I asked him how he was doing. He said he was fine, but his descent had slowed considerably. He asked me what his depth was, I told him he was at thirty feet, not quite half way. He continued on down.

When he reached fifty feet he stopped again. I asked if everything was okay and he responded that he was fine, but thought he had passed the leak. I told him he was only at fifty feet and had another twenty to go. I heard him inhale and exhale loudly. The roar of the water flow was getting fairly loud. He asked if I was sure the gap was only an inch. Maybe the head gate wasn't set all the way down. The dam has a marker on the head gate shaft, so the topside crew could tell exactly how far down the gate was. I assured him that the gate was set on the bottom. I also reminded him that we had a limited bottom time and no chamber, so any decompression stops would be made in water.

He continued on down. The roar was quite loud. When he reached sixty-five feet, I told him he was close. It had only taken him twelve minutes to get there. His dive time was half over. I said nothing about that. I asked if he was okay and if he had located the left-side of the head gate. He said he had and that the gap was so big he could see white water flowing through it. I reminded him to watch his fingers and toes. He laughed, "No Shit!" He poked an end of the CP hose into the left corner and gave a short yell. I asked if everything was okay. The roaring had stopped. He responded that he was fine, he just didn't expect the sucker to grab the hose out of his hands with such force. It gave him a start. I told him he had completed the task and could return to the surface. He left bottom with a time of nineteen minutes. Good job. He was out of the water about three minutes later. The next part of this job was to check the seal on the tail race gates on the downstream side of the dam. We loaded all our dive gear back into our truck and headed down to the base of the dam.

We set up our dive gear on the deck next to the tail race. There are two tail races on this dam. They are concrete tunnels, square tubes that were fourteen feet high by twenty feet wide, extending down-stream about fifty feet. The tail race gates are at the beginning of the tunnels. The river level is about fifteen feet above the top of the tail race tunnels, so you can't see the tunnels or the gate slots from the surface. The dam crew had a carry deck (small mobile crane) and a man basket to lower us into the water which was about twenty feet below the deck of the dam. The Coeur D'Alene Kid would make this dive.

The first time I dove on the tail race to check the seals on the gate was several years previous. It was the first time our dive company had made this dive for MPC. We had just started working for MPC, before that they had used another small company from Spokane that had been around since the seventies. I tried to get a job with that little company when I first graduated dive school, but the owner just looked at me and laughed. He said he only used older experienced divers. I later found out that the divers he used were just SCUBA diving buddies of his. Anyway, he had done the diving for MPC in the past, but MPC was having issues with him. That is why we were working for MPC now.

Back to my first-time diving on the tail race gate at Cochrane dam. I was lowered to the water in the man basket at the end of the wire of the carry deck. I got in the water and followed the crane wire, from the gantry crane used to raise and lower the tail race gate, down to the top of the gate. The Gate slid through a slot in the top of the concrete tunnel. The slot was about two feet wide and ran the width of the tunnel, roughly twenty feet. The gate fit down inside the tunnel. There was a gap on the down-stream side of the slot between the top of the gate and the bottom of the tunnel top. The top of the tunnel was eighteen inches thick. The gap between the top of the gate and the tunnel top was about fourteen inches; just big enough for me to get my legs through. I sat on the top of the gate with my legs through the gap, hanging over the down-stream side of the gate. I had been told by the MPC crew that I could just squeeze through that gap and inspect the sides and bottom of the gate to make sure it was sealed. Ha! There was no way I could fit through that gap.

I told topside that there was no way I could get through the gap with all my dive gear on. I didn't even think my helmet would fit through that gap. If I took all my dive gear off, I might be able to squeeze through, but not with my helmet on. They said the diver from the other company had done it many times. I laughed at that. I told them that there was no way that other diver fit through that gap because I knew him and he was fatter than I was. I told them that the only way I could get in to check the gate was to enter the tunnel from the downstream side and crawl up the tunnel to the gate. The problem here was that there was a lot of turbulence around the end of the tail race. I told them I would try it and see what I could do. I crawled down-stream along the edge of the tail race tube. When I reached the opening, I tried to climb down the side but the turbulence was too much. I got washed off the tube and swirled around in the turbulence. My topside crew pulled on my umbilical and got me to the edge of the dam deck. The MPC crew moved the carry deck as far down stream on the dam as they could and lowered the man basket into the water. I got in and was brought back on deck. I told the guys I could do it I just needed more weight. That was no problem, I just borrowed a weight belt from another diver on my crew. I donned the second weight belt and got back into the water.

I made it down to the bottom of the tail race and was able to crawl upstream to the gate. It was quite easy to go upstream because the turbulence actually pushed me that way on one side of the tunnel. It flowed the opposite way on the other side of the tunnel. The problem the MPC crew had with this gate sealing was that stones from the river bottom would get washed up the tail race and settle along the bottom sealing surface of the gate. Upon inspection of the gate, I found several stones stuck between the bottom of the gate and the tail race bottom. I had the gantry crane operator come up on the gate a foot or so, enabling me to remove the stones. That was all it took to get the gate to seal properly. We didn't even need to use rags or anything to make it seal better. From then on, we jumped in and inspected the sealing areas before they set the gate. This could be done by going through the slot because without the gate there, a diver could fit through and inspect all the sealing surfaces. After the gate was set, we would crawl in from the down-stream opening and double check that the gate was on bottom and sealing like it should.

Another time I had to seal the leaks on this unit at Cochrane dam, nobody wanted to make the dive on the head gate, so I did it. That was fine, but it meant that one of the other divers would have to do the dive on the tail race. I explained to the diver going in what the process was. He did fine inspecting the gate slot before the gate was set. When it came time for him to crawl up the tail race though, he got a little nervous. He wasn't comfortable diving in all the turbulence. He said he would do it though. He made it to the top of the tail race and inside the tunnel. Then he really started freaking out and screaming that he was being "Sucked into the dam!" I told him there was no way he could get sucked into the dam from the down-stream side. I mean, think about it man.

Water flows from the up-stream side of the dam down-stream. The amount of water on the upstream side made it physically impossible to get "sucked into the dam." I told him it was just turbulence and there were no worries. But he was too freaked out. His screaming stopped making sense, so I had to pull him out of the water. I had the other guy on my crew finish the dive. The guy that freaked out never really got over that experience. I don't really know what made the experience so traumatic for him, but something did. Anyway, he told our boss that he never wanted to dive on the dams in Montana again; and he never did.

Back to this day with Kalispell and the Coeur D'Alene Kid. We got our dive station set up and the MPC crew got their equipment ready. They had the tail race gate hanging off the gantry crane over the slot as usual. That made it easy for us to locate the slot. If we didn't have the gate hanging above the slot, the turbulence and lack of visibility made it difficult to get to the slot. A diver could easily get disoriented or lost in those conditions. It had happened before. I explained all this to the kid so he would have a good idea of what was expected of him.

He just looked at the hanging gate, then back at me. Then he asked what would happen if the crane cables snapped. I told him the gate would fall, of course. He stared at me. So, if the crane wire parted while the diver was in the slot or anywhere under the gate, the diver would get squished. I responded in the affirmative. "Yes, I suppose the diver would get squished like a grape." He didn't think that was funny. I reassured him that MPC did a very good job with their maintenance and regularly inspected all the crane wires for damage. We have never had any issues with any of their equipment.

That did not reassure him. He said he wanted the gate chained off with safety chains before he dove. I told him I would see what we could do. I went to the foreman of the MPC crew and told him of my diver's concerns. He said okay, he would have his crew take care of that. They did and the kid made his dive. He was very nervous the whole dive. He was concerned with the turbulence and it bothered him that the visibility was so bad. He ended up completing both tasks to everyone's satisfaction, so I was happy for that. With all that messing around, that was the longest day I ever had sealing those two gates.

Wednesday morning, the head manager of the Rainbow shop asked me if we could clear some debris that was keeping one of the spill gates on Rainbow dam from closing all the way. I told him we could take a look at it and see. We were to spend the rest of the week sealing the spill gates on Rainbow dam, so his question fit right into the work schedule. He took me out to the spill gates for a look. It wasn't "debris" that was keeping the gate from going all the way down, it was a LOG! A big log, about sixteen feet long and two feet in diameter. The amount of water that was flowing under the bottom of the gate was incredible.

He wanted us to dive in front of **that** and try to free the log?! Was he crazy?! He had been working on dams for close to thirty years, so he had to know about pressure differential and how much force flowing water had. There was no way we could dive on that. I asked him why he didn't just raise the gate a little and let the water flow flush the log through. He said they had tried, but he figured that when his crew had closed the gate on the log, they had jammed it into the bottom corner. The water flow wouldn't budge the log. I told him again there was no way we could dive on that gate.

He was not happy. We returned to the shop and I started getting our gear set up in the back of our truck so it could be used as a mobile dive station. The spill gates on Rainbow dam were easier accessed from the top of the dam. The MPC crew would use the carry deck with the man basket to get the diver in and out of the water. While I was doing that, the shop manager took Kalispell out to look at the log stuck in the gate. He tried to convince Kalispell that it should be safe enough for us to dive on it. Thankfully, Kalispell told him the same thing I did. I am sure that his dive on the head gate at Cochrane dam was still fresh in his mind. He was well aware of what problems such a leak could present a diver. We finally convinced the manager to get his crew to figure out how to do it without us.

We got set up on the left side of Rainbow's spill gates and started our work. We rotated the diving between the three of us. The depth here was less than twenty-five feet, so we were decompressing on a forty-foot table. That gave the diver plenty of bottom time. We dove two divers a day. The MPC crew had successfully dislodged the log by the end of the day Thursday. By noon on Friday, we had finished our task of sealing all the spill gates on Rainbow dam. The MPC crew was happy. It was a nice day, so they decided to have a Bar-

B-Que for lunch and asked us to join them. We did and it was excellent. They supplied everything; burgers with all the trimmings, chips, and pop. That was a great way to end the week and kick off the weekend.

*   *   *

The following June, after I finished the annual spring work in Montana, I returned to the yard and unloaded my gear. That same day, a Friday, the boss came out and asked me to start loading up my gear for a job on Lower Granite Dam. It was going to be quite a big job. There would be a night shift and a day shift. There might be two crews on the day shift. Blanchard had been working on the mobilization of this job all week.

We were going to install a test fish collection system on the upstream side of the dam. That would involve core drilling utilizing a core drilling machine used in mining. We would also use pneumatic hammer drills, and a host of other pneumatic and hand tools. We would be doing some underwater welding and burning. We were going to be there awhile. The job was scheduled to be done in steps. Plus, this was just a test system. Depending on how it worked out, the unit might be expanded, or even removed and replaced. Little did we know, but we would be working on most of the dams on the Columbia and Snake rivers installing fish protection and collection systems for the next five years. It was good work to get involved in.

This job required a lot of set up before we could do any diving. We put work barges together made up of Flexi-Floats. Flexi-Floats are sectional metal floats that are eight-and-a-half feet wide by thirty feet long (or ten by forty). They can pin together on all sides so you can make any size barge in just about any configuration you can imagine. We put together a couple barges that were twenty-four feet by thirty feet. We put a boom truck on one. We set up the dive station in a Conex. We had another Conex where we stored our dive gear and used it as a dressing room to change in and out of our gear when we were diving. We also had a Deck Decompression Chamber (DDC) on the top of the dam, in case anybody got bent, or had any other hyperbaric injury. It was mostly set up when I got there the following Monday. To start, there would only be a day shift. After a few weeks and getting all the kinks worked out, we added a night shift.

I would be working on the night shift as night co-supervisor with the Rancher from central Washington as the other co-supervisor. I met the crew at the dam around four p.m. Several new guys had been hired to fill out the crews on both shifts. The new guys weren't "new" as in fresh out of dive school, they were just new to working with us. Night shift consisted of myself, the Rancher, the Coeur D'Alene Kid, a guy from Santa Barbara, California (who was the son of the head dive supervisor on the job at Lake Pend Oreille three years earlier), and another guy from western Washington who was a navy-trained Seabee diver. I later learned that the guy from SoCal was also a navy-trained salvage diver, but had gone to a commercial dive school after being released from the U.S. Navy. It is difficult for navy-trained divers to break into the commercial field. The navy has a different way of doing things and it can be hard for the navy guys to accept the way things are done on the commercial side of underwater work. I had spent four years in the U.S. Navy, and we had always joked that, when doing things, there was the right way, the wrong way, and the Navy way! Ha ha.

The Coeur D'Alene Kid and I had shown up on sight before the day shift had ended. I met with Blanchard, who was running the day shift, and we went over what the plan was for the night shift. We kept an eye out for the new guys coming on board. We liked to watch them unload their gear to try to get a feel for how they might be on the crew. The first new guy to show up was driving a minivan with a personalized license plate; DVR4HIRE. Blanchard and I just looked at each other and laughed. What kind of clown was this? Back then, personalized license plates were called "Vanity Plates" and not a lot of people had them. We wondered how full of himself this new guy must be to have a plate like that.

I went up to the top of the dam to meet him and help him get his gear onto the barge. He was tall, skinny, kind of goofy looking. and seemed really young, but must have been in his mid-twenties. He carried more gear in his van than most other divers on the project. He said he had brought everything with him because he was hoping to move to the northwest if he could find enough dive work to keep him going. He wasn't planning on putting all his gear on the dive barge. That was good because we had limited storage space in the Conex boxes. Each diver had space on a shelf just big enough for his hat, dive underwear, and personal stuff. We hung our dive suits in another Conex that had a heater in it to help them dry after the dive. Our bailout bottles and weight belts were kept outside. This guy with the vanity plate was the guy from SoCal and he turned out to be a good worker and good diver. Getting to know him reminded me not to judge a book by its cover.

The next guy to show up was the ex-Seabee. He was small, stocky and quiet. He hadn't worked with any of us before and kept to himself. He had minimal dive gear, but accepted help in getting it loaded onto the barge. He turned out to be a pretty good worker. He knew how to tie more knots than most of the other divers combined. Of course, we only used a few knots on a regular basis; the Bowline, the Clove Hitch, the Square Knot, and the Trucker's Hitch. There wasn't any need for the other fancier knots, but this guy could tie them all. He had Monkey Fists on his zipper pulls and lanyards for all his tools done with eye-splices or square knot chains. He could also tell you the load ratings of all the different ropes and chains we used.

The last guy to show up was the Rancher. He arrived at our normal start time of four p.m. Day shift ran from eight in the morning until four p.m. and night shift would run from four p.m. to midnight. If nightshift finished the assigned tasks before midnight, we could leave early. We weren't allowed to start any tasks that we couldn't finish before the end of our shift. The plan for the night crew tonight was to move a drill template to a new location.

The drill template was a four-foot by six-foot sheet of quarter-inch steel. It had four holes across the top, four holes along the bottom, and three more holes evenly spaced down each side that were used to mount the plate to the dam with rock bolts. The plate had mounting bolts on it that we used to secure the core drill to the plate. This way we could drill the holes into the dam exactly as the engineers of the project required. The holes we were drilling were three-and-a-half inches in diameter and fourteen feet deep. William's bolts would be inserted into the holes and used to mount the fish collection system to the dam.

We were all staying at a Hotel in Pullman, Washington. It took us between twenty and thirty minutes to get from the Hotel to the dam, or vice versa, depending on weather and traffic. Traffic was mostly farm equipment or cattle on the road. The job spanned a couple years, so weather could be rainy, sunny, or snowy. Sometimes nightshift would run out of projects well before our scheduled knock off time. On those occasions we were allowed to go back to the hotel early. When this happened, we ended up with more free time. Different people like to do different things to occupy themselves during their free time.

Some people like to sleep, some like to read, others like to see movies, some even like to work out. Being divers, most of us at that time in the mid-nineties, liked to drink. Some of us liked to drink in our rooms, others liked to drink in bars. Once in a while we would all go out as a group – the whole crew. Five divers getting drunk and blowing off steam. Not necessarily the best or safest of circumstances. Divers are a fairly tight-knit group of individuals. We tend to take care of each other both on and off the job, even if we don't really like each other. We never leave a guy behind if we can help it. We tend to have a "one for all, and all for one" mentality.

Pullman is a college town, home of Washington State University, the Cougars. Being a college town, there are a lot of bars and these bars are frequented by college students. As a whole, college students are not good drinkers. They haven't had years of experience, they don't know when to stop, and they don't always behave well. They are usually far away from home and parents, so feel they can sow their wild oats. Many of the young men are trying to impress the young girls and show them how manly they are, especially if slightly older guys are around that the young girls find attractive. This can lead to confrontations, sometimes violent ones and sometimes the police get involved.

One Thursday night we finished up early. It was mid-October, but the weather was mild. The roads were good and there was no traffic between the dam and the hotel. We got back to the hotel around nine p.m. We had time to get cleaned up and make it to a restaurant for dinner before closing time. This was a somewhat rare occurrence so we decided to go out as a group to this Mexican restaurant that we all liked. The food was excellent and the drinks were cheap. We had dinner and several beers.

The restaurant closed at ten, but they didn't kick good, paying customers out until ten-thirty or so. By this time, we were feeling no pain and none of us wanted to quit drinking. The bars were open until two a.m., so we had plenty of time to continue making merry. The youngest in our group was the Coeur D' Alene Kid, he was about the same age as the average college student. The two ex-navy guys were in their late twenties and the Rancher and I were in our early thirties. We were a fairly responsible crew even if we did drink fairly heavily. The Coeur D' Alene Kid didn't drink anywhere near as much as the rest of us, not that that has any bearing on anything or adds to nor diminishes the events of the evening.

The restaurant closed and we went outside. We were trying to decide where to go. Pullman is a small town, so we could walk everywhere we wanted to go, which was good, because that meant we wouldn't have to worry about driving drunk. Or maybe that was bad, because it meant we didn't need a designated driver with a level head who could keep us out of trouble. We weren't out "cruising chicks," we just wanted to drink, get to know each other better, do a little people watching, maybe play some pool or something. I had heard of a bar called "the Cave." It was in the basement of some building and supposed to be a pretty fun place to go. So off we headed up the hill to the Cave. We found it after about a twenty-minute walk. Needless to say, we were ready for a drink, and not just one.

We went through a door and down some stairs where a guy sitting on a stool stopped us. He was checking IDs. All of us were legal to drink, so he opened another door and let us in. Thursday was Ladies Night. It was packed, and it was noisy. I squeezed my way to the bar, bought a round of beer for us all and made my way back to the group. The tables and places at the bar were all taken up, it was standing room only and elbow to elbow at that. There were a couple dart boards on the walls and a couple pool tables, but there were so many people in the place that there was no room for players. It didn't look like anyone wanted to play those games anyway. The girls were all trying to look pretty and the boys were doing all they could to look suave and manly. We just wanted to relax and have a drink or five. I told the guys we should try another place less crowded after we finished our drinks. One of our group had just bought another round for us though. Well, we had to finish that drink before leaving.

We were standing in a very tight circle, trying not to get bumped into or bumping into any other patrons. The tall guy from SoCal was drinking a mixed drink out of a tumbler. A short girl behind him stumbled backwards and fell into him, causing him to spill his drink all over the front of his shirt. He spun around quickly, his elbow inadvertently smacking the girl on her cheek. She was on her way to falling on the floor, when the guy next to her caught her and kept her on her feet. He yelled at SoCal demanding he apologize for smacking this girl.

SoCal looked aghast and said "Look what she did! She spilled my drink all over my shirt! I think she owes me a drink."

"You had better apologize to her, or you will be sorry!" yelled the college guy.

"No, she should apologize and buy me another drink" my friend stated.

By now a crowd of college boys was closing in and I suggested we leave the bar before things got out of hand. The college boy pushed SoCal and SoCal pushed back. I stepped in between the two and guided my SoCal friend out of the bar. We were closely followed by the rest of our little crew. The doorman asked if everything was alright as we left and I told him everything was fine, we just wanted to leave before anybody started fighting. He thought that was a good idea, and kept the loud-mouthed college boy from following us.

We walked up the stairs and out of the building. At the street level, we looked around and saw another bar just to the right of us across the street. That is where we headed. This bar wasn't nearly as crowded. We sat at the bar, ordered a round of beer and looked around the bar. It was pretty dead and there was no pool table. After we finished our beer, but before we ordered another round, a couple guys in our crew wanted to try a

213

different place. This place was actually a tavern and served only beer and wine. A couple of us liked hard liquor better. We headed out to look for a bar better suited to what we were after. We headed to a place that was on the other side of the Cave - the place where we had the little issue.

As we were crossing the street, who do we see on the corner but the loud-mouthed guy who wanted to defend the drunk girl's honor and he had about five friends with him. They had left the Cave looking for us. They wanted to teach us a lesson. They started yelling at us and making derogatory comments. I told our crew we should just ignore them and keep on heading to the next bar. The college boys had a different idea. They blocked our way and started calling us dumb hicks and old men who couldn't perform.

The Coeur D' Alene Kid just wanted to go back to the hotel. SoCal and the Seabee were taunting the college boys. I was trying to keep everybody calm and the Rancher told the college boys they better shut their mouths and leave us alone or he would pull out his Smith and Wesson and settle everything once and for all. I didn't know why he said that and gave him a funny look. Less than a minute after that, five cops showed up with their hands on their pistols. They asked what was going on and who had the gun. The college boys and a couple of our guys were still yelling at each other.

I went up to the officer who seemed to be in charge and explained what was going on and that we didn't want any trouble. He said that was good, but wanted to know who had the gun. Nobody has a gun I told him. Nobody was waving a gun around and people were just hyped up. I told him things were being said that nobody really meant because they were all drunk. The officer told me that was good and since he didn't see any gun and nobody had hit anybody yet, he would let us all go as long as we left the bars close to the campus and headed back towards our hotel, while the college boys were told to go back to their dorm rooms.

The cops threatened the college boys with a night in the drunk tank if they didn't comply. We were allowed to go on our way. We walked to a bar close to our hotel. On the walk back the Rancher and SoCal said they didn't know I was such a good negotiator with the cops. I told them I really wasn't, I was just telling the truth. The Rancher said no I wasn't as he pulled his Smith and Wesson out of his back pocket. I about fell over. I had no idea he was packing. I asked him why he was carrying a pistol and he told me you never know when you might need it. My idea on that is if you're not carrying it, you won't need it – when you're going drinking anyway. Guns and Alcohol do Not mix. I like guns and strongly support the Second Amendment of the U.S. Constitution. People need to be responsible about it though.

*   *   *

Another thing we did on dams in the nineties was set and install Fish Sensors. These were radio transmitter/receivers that picked up signals from radio-tagged Salmon. NOAA (National Oceanic and Atmospheric Administration) required that all the dams on the Columbia and Snake Rivers installed them for both the Spring and Fall Salmon runs. It was a job where you would only spend a day, maybe two, at each dam site.

Some sensors were mounted right on the upstream side of the dam by the spill gates, others were set up in the forebay (the pond upstream of the dam) and could be as much as a quarter mile from the dam itself. This meant that they were fairly deep – over one-hundred feet. Which isn't really deep for a commercial diver, but in order to keep costs down we tried to do that work using the No-D (U.S. Navy No Decompression) tables. Otherwise, if decompression was planned, we were required to have a Deck Decompression Chamber on site.

The rules and laws have changed a lot since I started diving. Look at how the USN decompression tables have changed. When I started diving, the tables we were using were based on data gathered during World War II and shortly thereafter. When I went to commercial dive school in the mid-eighties, the Navy just published Revision One, but I don't know of any divers who even paid attention to the changes. In twenty-eighteen, the navy released Revision Seven, Change A. Science. Also, I think now if you work on government projects, you are required to have a DDC on all jobs done in over fifty feet of water.

It didn't used to be that way. Hell, when I first started, government jobs could be done on SCUBA with a two-man team. Stupid. I usually spoke up about mitigating risk, but got shut down a lot. Surface supplied diving doesn't really take that much more than SCUBA and it is a thousand times safer. I mean look, you've got an unlimited supply of air, you've got hard-wire communications to the surface, you have a life-line built right into the umbilical which also serves as a focal point when you are on bottom, making it extremely hard to get lost, unless you are an Idiot. I've worked with my fair share of those through the years. They usually don't last long though – unless they are really good at kissing the boss's ass or good at blaming other people for their mistakes. I always owned up to my errors and mistakes. That got me kicked off more than one job. At least I could sleep at night.

Anyway, back to No-D tables and installing fish counters in forebays at depths over one hundred feet (thirty-three meters). If you look at the USN No-D tables we were using in ninety-five (Revision Two) you would see that the diver only had twenty-five minutes to complete the dive. That means from the moment you leave the surface, you have Twenty-Five Minutes to get to the bottom, find the location to set up the sensor, get the sensor set up and leave bottom without getting tangled in anything. Remember we are working in a river. Granted it is in the forebay of a dam, so there isn't much current, but there is still some. There is all kinds of debris on the bottom; trees, rocks, trash (like boat hulls, motors, cars, etc.). And it's DARK. The rivers in the Pacific Northwest were more polluted back then and that meant that light didn't penetrate as far as it does in clean water. Ninety percent of the work I did in fresh water was done in the Black. Sometimes it was so murky that even if you had a light, you could only see a few inches if you were lucky.

This particular job I was working on was at Wanapum Dam on the Columbia River by Vantage, Washington. The water wasn't too murky. It was black by the time you hit twenty feet, but with a light you could see over five feet. The current was minimal. The depth at the base of the dam was just at one hundred feet, maybe one hundred and one, maybe ninety-nine. It was our common practice to add a table, meaning go up one table. I usually added a three-foot safety factor to the pneumo reading. If my depth gage showed ninety-nine feet, I'd add three feet to make it one hundred-two feet. That meant I would be using a one-hundred-ten-foot decompression table. Now we're down to a bottom time of twenty minutes.

The sensors further upstream were in about one-hundred-fifteen feet, add three feet making it one hundred-eighteen feet. I would be using a one-hundred-twenty-foot table. That meant the diver only had fifteen minutes to get everything done. On this particular dam there were fourteen sensors to be set up. Typically, a diver would make one dive and then he was done diving for the day, mostly because of how the re-pet tables worked (repetitive dive tables). That meant I needed fourteen divers to complete this job in a day. Wow. Try to find fourteen divers who are willing to go out for a one-day job several hours from home. The company that owned the dam had told me that I had a twelve-hour window to get the job done. I might be able to re-pet a couple, maybe three divers if I planned the dives well. I still needed eleven divers minimum.

To do this job, I would have to work with a bunch of guys I hadn't worked with before. Wonderful. I needed divers who were competent, compatible, and not afraid of the dark or giant catfish. There weren't giant catfish in these rivers, but there were Sturgeon. Some divers were afraid of them (for no good reason) and that inhibited their ability to get the job done. If all that wasn't bad enough, the dive company I worked for at the time, Norwesco, didn't want to pay per diem or overtime.

Divers don't like driving hours for free, especially for a one-day job. We also wouldn't pay for a hotel room out of our pockets. Overtime pay, especially overtime wet pay, made it easier to find divers for a job like this. But, remember, the dive company didn't want to pay overtime. In fact, for this job, I had been informed that my divers would be working a split shift. That is, half of them would work from six a.m. until two p.m. and the other half would work from ten a.m. until six p.m. I would be the only one getting overtime as I would be working from six a.m. through to six p.m., my reward for running the job. Thank you *so* much. Grimace. We didn't get any more pay for running the jobs than the guys working with us got paid. We did get to do **ALL** the paperwork **and** take responsibility for the whole job though. Our incentive was that we could dive as we wanted. Which many times pissed off the other divers, because the "supervisor" might take the easiest, shortest, highest paying dive no matter where it fell in the dive rotation. I didn't do that. I didn't like causing grief and anger amongst my dive crew for the sake of a few bucks. Instead, I tried to get the dive company to pony up for a little extra pay, or maybe a per diem thrown in so I could spend the night on one end of the job and not have to kill myself driving all night.

Sometimes it worked, other times it didn't. The owners of the dive companies really had no idea how lucky they were that I, and others like me, loved our jobs so much. Or maybe they did and just took advantage of us anyway.

So, I have fourteen sensors to install and set up. I get an eleven-man crew (I would say eleven-person crew, but at this time, only guys were diving in the northwest), five showing up at six in the morning, leaving at two in the afternoon, another five showing up at ten in the morning, working until six at night. And me. I only recognized a few of the names on the crew list. Most of the guys I liked working with were on other jobs. I had been taken off a longer job to run this one. Lots of new names, meant lots of guys I hadn't worked with before. Not my favorite way to work a job. Oh well. I would do what I could and hopefully I would meet some good guys.

The Seabee was due to show up at six. That would be good, he was a good worker. A couple other guys I knew, who were okay, another who was a PIA, but I could deal with him. At least there was nobody I knew of who I wouldn't work with. At least my boss respected my wishes when I gave him the name of someone I would not work with. The resumé of one of the new guys stated that he spoke Portuguese. Hmm. I had a hard time judging a person by their resumé alone, because half the time it was a load of B.S. I had worked with guys who had really good-looking resumés stating all kinds of experience, but when they got on the job, they didn't know their ass from a hole in the ground. By the same token some resumés were super simple but the worker was top-notch.

So, this guy shows up, tells me his name and I respond in Portuguese. My Portuguese isn't perfect, but I am fluent. This guy is taken aback at first, but answers my questions in Portuguese. We have a little conversation and the rest of the crew is just looking at us dumbstruck. Okay, I think to myself, at least this guy can speak Portuguese like his resumé says. It turns out he was half-Brasilian. We ended up getting along really well and working together quite a bit over the next several years.

All the morning guys showed up by a quarter to six or so except for the Seabee. We got the boat loaded and ready to go. We were working out of a twenty-four-foot jet boat. It was crowded, but it worked. I wanted to set the deep sensors out in the forebay first. We were all loaded up and ready to launch the boat by six-thirty; still no Seabee. I couldn't wait around, besides, in the dive industry at this time, if you were late and missed the boat, you missed the job. Too bad, so sad Seabee.

We boated out to the first location and Brazil wanted to dive first, so I let him. He did a good job, found the sensor at a hundred-fourteen feet and got it taken care of. Job well done. Next was a guy who had been in Desert Storm. He spent more time talking about that than anything else. He jumped in, but couldn't find anything. He spent fifteen minutes flailing around in the dark before I pulled him up. That sucks. I think he may have had PTSD, even though nobody was talking about that back then. I wasn't too hard on him. I figured I'd just re-pet him later in the day on one of the dam-mounted sensors where I knew he wouldn't get lost. Because I was down a man, I had to dive in the morning. I didn't like doing my dive early on when I had a bunch of divers I didn't know, because I liked to keep myself as sort of an Ace in the Hole to make sure I could get the job done as required. I trusted Brazil to run my dive.

By nine-thirty we had all the sensors in the forebay located and set up. We headed back to the beach to meet with the rest of the crew and move to the top of the dam where we would work from to place the rest of the sensors. Some would be at the bottom of the dam; others would be at progressively shallower depths. The Seabee was with the ten-a.m. crew. He said he was told to show up at ten. Fair enough, it just meant that I had been working a man short the whole morning. Everything was going well, so far though, so that was good.

We had to use a hydraulic drill to put some holes in the pier faces so we could set some rock bolts to attach the clips to that held the sensors and the cables going to them. Some divers were really good at drilling those holes and some not so much. I got extended bottom times with the good divers by re-petting them up. That means sending them to the bottom to work and when they finished, if they had any time left, they would head to the next work level. If it was at least an atmosphere (thirty-three feet) shallower, I could recalculate their bottom time on the re-pet table. If we were lucky, they would have time to get more work done. A couple of the divers were good enough that they could finish a whole column in one dive. That saved me from having to re-pet many divers. In fact, I only had to re-pet one diver from the morning. We ended up getting the whole job done before five p.m. That was great for me. Some of the guys who started at ten were worried that they wouldn't be getting a whole day's pay, eight hours, but I assured them everybody would be getting a full eight hours; four hours wet pay and four hours tender pay. Everybody went home happy. I even got back to my home in Spokane before midnight after dropping all the dive equipment back at the shop.

*   *   *

OIL SPILLS – TRAINS, TRUCKS AND BOATS
Chapter Nine

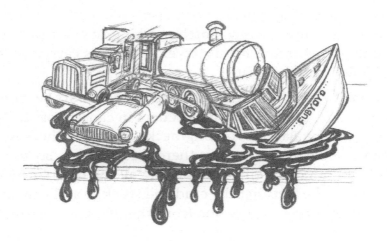

There are all sorts of Oil Spills; both natural and manmade or a combination of both. The first time an oil spill affected my dive career was in nineteen-eighty-nine. It was the Exxon Valdez that wrecked in Prince William Sound, Alaska. I wanted to go up there and work as did every other diver in the United States! I never got up there to work on that though. As I look back on my career it was probably a good thing. So many people went up there that not enough people were left in the continental U.S. to do all the work. What that meant for me was that I had more work than I knew what to do with. It really helped boost my dive career.

The second time an oil spill affected my career was in Montana. Trout Creek, Montana to be exact. I already told you about that job; with Kalispel and Hope.

The third time I had to deal with an oil spill was also in Montana. This time it was just outside of Plains, Montana. It was an "emergency job" because, like in Trout Creek, a train derailed and cars carrying crude oil ruptured spilling their contents into the Clark Fork River. Not this again! This time Boston would be running the job. There was a *lot* of oil spilled, so we had a double sized dive crew. Plus, we would be using boats because the oil spread further into the middle of the river. Some carloads of Corn also spilled all over making a very large bright yellow blotch marking the location of the derailment. Also, fun for us, several box cars carrying Coors Beer spilled into the river.

There were a *lot*, and I mean a **LOT** of cases of Coors Beer on the river bottom. There was regular Coors in cans, Coors Light in cans, and Coors Banquet in long-necked bottles. There was so much oil spilled that we were there three weeks. Boston had talked Montana Rail Link into buying all the divers new dry-suits due to the fact that the crude oil stuck to and ruined our suits. That was a nice bonus from the job, but not the best bonus.

Like most of our jobs out of town, we stayed in a local motel fairly close to the job. We ate at the restaurants and we drank at the bars after work. That's how this job started out, but as soon as we discovered the motherlode of Coors on the river bed our pattern changed. We still got up early in the morning and went somewhere for breakfast and bought something for lunch. We still showed up at the job site and did our job. We spent a good solid eight hours scooping up crude oil and putting it in the waste containers. We did this more or less the same way we had done at Trout Creek. We would guide a crane in to scoop up the large blobs of crude. The smaller patches of crude we scooped into heavy-duty plastic bags. This is where the crude got all over our suits, hats and any exposed skin. What was different was that after our eight hours of work for the day was completed, we spent a couple hours retrieving cases of Coors from the river bottom and loading them into our trucks.

We didn't start retrieving the beer until the fourth day. Boston had looked into it and discovered that Coors didn't want the beer and so whatever we salvaged was ours. Yeehaw! Several Boxcars of Coors beer on the river bottom split between six divers. Wow. You don't realize how much beer can fit in a Boxcar until you start taking cases out of the river and loading them into pickups. Every day we filled two pickup beds with cases of beer. I never counted how many fit in a pickup bed, but it was a lot. Way more than we could drink. So, what did we do with it? Well, it was summer.

That's actually why the train derailed. The rails warped in the heat of the Montana summer sun causing the train to derail. The summer days were long, sunny and warm. Perfect for having a beer or twenty in the city park. All the townspeople knew about the derailment, the cleanup and the boxcars of beer. When the train first derailed, some of the cases of beer had floated down the river and ended up along the banks leading into town. The local fisherman and kids had, of course, found the beer. So, when we went to the park with two pickups full of beer, everybody knew. That's why we went to the park in the first place. We figured we would share the beer with the town. Needless to say, we were the most popular people in town for a couple weeks. It was a lot of fun and we made quite a few friends.

*   *   *

I never spent any time cleaning up oil spills after that last job in Plains. I did work in the oilfields though, after promising myself that I never would again. The next time that an oil spill affected my work wasn't until twenty-ten. That was the Deepwater Horizon rig explosion and fire followed by the subsequent oil spill. In the mid-two-thousands up until twenty-ten I had been working in the Gulf of Mexico on the Boa Deep C and other vessels. There are stories there for later.

The Deepwater Horizon incident put a stop to a lot of work in the gulf for me. It didn't bother me too much though. A friend of mine and I had planned a Motorcycle trip through Europe for the spring of twenty-ten and the Deepwater Horizon incident took place in April. We left for Europe in May, so weren't planning on working for a while anyway. The volcanic explosion in Iceland that spring actually had a bigger impact on me that year, but that is a story for another time and a different book.

*   *   *

The last time that my work was directly affected by an oil spill was in the fall of twenty-eleven. Flooding on the Yellowstone River had caused debris to float down and take out some bridges and a couple oil pipelines by Laurel, Montana near Billings. We were hired by Exxon to help repair the pipeline crossing the river there. We also had a second crew working on a BP pipeline just upstream of the Exxon pipeline. The flooding had occurred in the early summer. The pipeline was broken in early July. Exxon shut the flow of oil down, but not before a significant amount of oil had flowed into the Yellowstone.

I had nothing to do with the clean-up. But I was involved in the repair of the pipe crossing the river. Originally Exxon had told Global that the repair would commence in August. I was working for Global Diving & Salvage at this time with a bunch of guys that I used to work with at Norwesco Marine.

Norwesco had some major issues in nineteen-ninety-nine and ended up changing their name to preserve their safety record. Most of the good divers left that company after that, but the company still held on and kept working in the northwest. More on that later. This story is out of sequence, but it fits in this chapter better than any other, so, here it is.

I was working with the Coeur D' Alene Kid and three other guys I met later on. One was a good friend from Illinois who had moved to Idaho in two-thousand. Another was a guy who was from Spokane and had worked in the Gulf of Mexico as a tender before moving back to the northwest in the hopes of becoming a diver. He started out weak, but turned into a pretty good diver. The trick was to keep him off the booze. I'll refer to him as "Duck Fart." You'll find out later in the book when I formally introduce him why he is Duck Fart. The final guy on the crew was from Temecula, Californy and started working with Global after Ivan hit the Gulf of Mexico, damaging a lot of older oil rigs – also stories for later.

Okay, the work is supposed to start in August. The crew has been chosen. Illinois is going to be the supervisor and the Coeur D' Alene Kid is the superintendent of the job. There is a lesson here about the dive industry and probably all construction jobs. There is no set path from tender to supervisor, superintendent, and beyond. There are a lot of factors involved. Skill and job performance are not the deciding factors and seniority has very little to do with promotion. I was the supervisor when the Coeur D' Alene Kid made his first paid dive and moved up to diver from tender. Now here, fifteen years later or so, he was the superintendent and I was just a tender slash standby diver. Duck Fart and Temecula would be the divers. I ended up running the dives and the radio because the guy from Illinois couldn't stand running the dive when Temecula was in the water. Plus, he would rather be more involved with the actual workings of the job than sitting on the radio babysitting the divers.

September rolled around and still the job hadn't started. Don't the guys from Exxon know that it gets cold in Montana? It snows. The ground freezes. The rivers freeze over. Equipment gets cold and doesn't always start. It gets very cold. Our first snow usually falls in the middle of September. The Exxon guys were from Louisiana. I guess they didn't have any idea about working in winter conditions. They were about to learn though. I was doing other jobs while waiting for this one to start.

October came and still the job hadn't started. I asked if the job was going to be pushed back to the following summer. No, I was told, it was going to happen this year. I just shook my head. Okay, whatever you say. Finally. I got notice the job was about to start in late October. A little late I thought. We would be dealing with snow, ice, and frozen Everything. It would slow the progress of the job, but that's okay I suppose. I would make more money and it would be a better Christmas.

It was cold when we set up the dive area. The river water temperature was thirty-four degrees Fahrenheit; just above freezing. At least we had hot water for the divers. The dive station was inside a Conex and we had a couple good heaters in there, so at least Dive Control was comfortable. The dive hoses and standby gear were set up outside. The river wasn't frozen solid where we were working, but it had already frozen upstream and there was new and thicker ice every morning along the banks. Because it would warm up during the day, huge chunks of snowy ice would float down the river. They were usually balls of frozen slush about six feet in diameter. The divers had to dodge them as they floated by, because they were big enough and heavy enough to knock the diver around.

It wasn't bad for the divers while they were working close to the river banks, not much water flowed there. Out in the middle of the river though, the current was stronger, about a knot-and-a-half I figured, and that is where the Giant Slush Balls traveled. It was really bad for the divers because they were usually facing downstream as they worked. They couldn't see the slush balls coming at them. There was a berm between the edge of the river and the dive control station, so I couldn't see the divers in the river. We had cameras and lights mounted to the dive helmets, letting me see what the diver was seeing. The water was very clean and very clear. The deepest depth we were working in was twenty-four feet. If the diver lay on the bottom and looked up, I could see blue sky through his camera. That didn't help with the slush balls. Other workers on the jobsite tried to let me know if they saw slush balls coming down the river. Sometimes there were just too many though, and many times nobody was watching for them. Sorry divers, you need to be aware of your surroundings!

In this part of the river, the bottom was bedrock so the pipeline just lay across on top of the bed rock. Usually there was no issue, but when huge trees and sections of bridges and pieces of buildings were washed downriver during the flooding, that was what took out the pipelines. The new pipe would be laid in the same position on top of the bedrock. That could be done without divers. What we were hired to do was place huge bags of gravel along the sides and on top of the pipeline, basically burying it, in order to protect it from debris flowing down. The bags Exxon had us use were white woven polypropylene bags that could hold thirty cubic feet of gravel and sand. A full bag weighed about three thousand pounds. You don't want a bag like that hanging over your head from the crane especially as a diver.

A crane was used to lift the bags of gravel out over the river and down to the diver. The clear water made this extremely easy for the diver because he wouldn't have to surface to locate the bag, or search around in the dark for a bag already on the bottom. The crane operator would hang the bag over the diver and the diver could guide the crane from the bottom. It worked great. Except for the diver from Temecula. I don't know if he was afraid to look up, or couldn't bend back far enough to see the bag, or what his deal was. The crane operator would start lowering the bag and I would tell Temecula that it was coming down and he would start yelling "I can't see it! I can't see it! Stop! Stop!" He did this every time. This is what drove Illinois crazy and why he couldn't run the radio when Temecula was in the water. Illinois told me that running Temecula's dive made him want to jab pencils into his eyes. Ha ha. You just need a little patience to deal with a guy like Temecula.

Exxon hired a Crane Company from Billings to supply the cranes we needed. That was good for us, because they were used to the winters in Montana and the Billings area. Winters in Billings were not as cold as other parts of Montana, but it still snowed and everything still froze. The cranes, and all the equipment rented from Montana companies had heaters, block heaters and whatever else they required to start and run, in winter conditions. The equipment that Exxon had brought up from down south, and there was a lot of it, was not prepped for winter conditions. To get the job done, Exxon needed boats in the river. They didn't want to use prop boats, which made sense for several reasons; divers in the water, debris in the water, shallow conditions, boulders hiding below the water surface to name a few.

They didn't want to use jet boats. They had been told that the jets would freeze up in the cold water. That was true. The jet drive could freeze if water was left in it and it got cold enough. Also, slush could clog the jet drive if the water was cold enough; which it would be in the Yellowstone River in winter. Instead, they brought up Fan Boats from Louisiana. Okay, those are cool, lots of fun to ride in and they could travel in very shallow water. The Exxon guys in charge even figured they would be able to skim right over the snow and ice. Yeah, not so much.

Part of the problem there was the boats did fine until the water on the hull froze to the snow or ice they were trying to traverse. That slowed those boats right down. Another issue with those boats was they had no heaters. They didn't start in the mornings until Exxon bought and installed block heaters for them all. Also. it was very cold for the people in the boat. Another problem was that, if the boats were left in the water overnight, which they were, the river water would freeze around them effectively anchoring the boats to the river bank. It took hours to free them on the cold mornings.

This Exxon pipeline ran under Riverside Park just south of Laurel and crossed the Yellowstone River just east of the Highway Two-Twelve bridge. The city of Laurel let us set up all of our work sites in the park. It was temporarily closed to the public. It made for very nice scenery. This park was pretty much closed in the winter months anyway. It did have a couple toilets, but the city shut them down through the winter months so they didn't have to worry about frozen pipes. That meant Exxon needed to rent a bunch of Honey Buckets. You know, those blue plastic Port-a-John things. We, the guys from the inland northwest, tried to tell them to make sure they got heated Honey Buckets. They laughed at us. Asked us if we were weenies who couldn't sit on a cold toilet seat. I told them they didn't know what a cold toilet seat was.

Exxon brought in about twenty Honey Buckets, more than enough for the number of people working on the job. About three weeks into the job, Exxon discovered why we suggested they get heated port-a-potties because they all froze. They froze Solid. Yeah, a big block of Blue Ice wrapped in a brittle grey plastic box. When you pooped or peed on the block of blue ice, your excreta (poop and piss) would freeze before melting any of the blue ice. Lovely. We tried to tell the Exxon management before it was an issue. Who had the last laugh now? We would have, but where were we supposed to relieve ourselves now?

Exxon conceded that maybe we were correct. They got some heaters and ran extension cords. They only heated five of the Honey Buckets, though. Towards the end of November and through December most of the companies were running smaller crews since most of the work being done at this time was Diver-centric. We had a full crew, our crane guys had a full crew, the guys filling the gravel bags had a full crew; everybody else was using skeleton crews. Five warm Honey Buckets were plenty. We peed in the river anyway, so we actually didn't use them much.

Overall, Exxon was really good to us – and all the other workers on the site. Every day they would send a couple secretaries, or administrative assistants – whatever you want to call them - to a nearby restaurant and get lunch for us. That way we had a warm lunch to eat, which helped keep our energy and morale up. There were a bunch of little restaurants around Laurel. A couple were locally owned mom and pop type restaurants with really good food at really good prices. Of course, it was Montana style food, and I guess the Exxon guys preferred southern style country food. There was a Cracker Barrel close by, so that is where lunch came from nine times out of ten. The food was good, but I would have liked to see Exxon support a local restaurant, like Four Bees maybe. There was a strip club, Shotgun Willies, that a lot of the guys frequented after shift and on weekends. I suppose that helped support the local economy – at least they supported the local talent in the area! Ha! Ha! I went in a couple times, the Coeur D' Alene kid went a couple times a week and sometimes took a few of the Exxon guys with him.

Exxon put us up in a really nice hotel on the westside of Billings. There were places closer to the worksite in Laurel, but Exxon wanted to keep everybody pretty much together. Coming from the south, they were still class oriented, so management stayed at one hotel and us troglodytes stayed at another. It was still very nice. They also treated us to dinner when certain milestones were reached. They always took us to the nicest steak house in Billings; the Montana Rib and

Chop House. It was always Excellent. Big Smiles and tummy rubbing.

The job lasted past Christmas. We spent Christmas in a hotel in Billings. My wife came over to celebrate Christmas with us, because we only got one day off for the holiday. We made little stockings and filled them with fun stuff for everyone on the dive crew. It was lots of fun. Duck Fart loved the stockings. He said stockings were his favorite part of Christmas. He had told me that before. He and I have worked together quite a bit in the Gulf of Mexico where he worked as a SAT Diver and I worked as a Life Support Technician or Dive Supervisor. We had spent several Christmases together.

We finished up our part of the job. We loaded all our smaller gear into the Conex. The big stuff, like compressors, generators, etc. were loaded onto a flatbed trailer. Our Conex was loaded on another. When that was all done, we were all done and we left. Exxon still had quite a bit of work to do after we left. One of the things in their contract with the City of Laurel or Yellowstone County or whoever, was that they return the park to the condition it was before the broken pipe and oil spill. I think that took them another six months at least. They refurbished the park and put in some structures that actually made it nicer than it was before the flooding and their pipe broke. Just so you know, that pipe had been there since the mid-thirties and that was the first time there had ever been an issue with it. It gave almost seventy years of service.

*   *   *

There have been quite a few oil spills throughout my time in the dive industry, but most of them never really affected my career. Sadly, most of them are not covered in the news in the U. S., so most Americans don't even know how many oil spills there are every year. The redeeming factor about this is that Crude Oil is a natural substance and the earth has ways of dealing with it. It is usually only when humans get involved that problems occur.

Well, that was a short chapter. When I came up with the title, I thought I would have more to write about. The truth is that Oil Spills, while a big deal for humans and animals, really aren't a big deal for the earth as a whole.

*   *   *

RAN INTO A CHUM WITH
A BOTTLE OF RUM
Chapter Ten

In the early spring of nineteen-ninety-six I went back to Montana to seal spill gates on the dams in Great Falls. There are five dams on the Missouri right in the Great Falls area. Black Eagle Dam is in town. Rainbow Dam is on the east side of town. Cochrane Dam is just east of Rainbow, followed by Ryan Dam and Morony Dam. Great Falls is called "The Electric City" because of all the dams. These dams were older and required a fair amount of maintenance and refurbishing so there was a lot of work for me in Montana. At that time, it was Montana Power Company who owned the dams and the power lines. They were a great company to work for. I worked for them so much they felt like family. The company wasn't that big so I always worked with the same people. I got to know them pretty well, and they got to know me. They got a kick out of the new tenders who got sent to work with me, especially if they didn't know anything. For several years some of the MPC crew knew more about setting up a dive station and how diving on a dam worked than half the guys sent to work with me. I had no problem sending guys home.

I would usually let them finish the week, but if they were no good, I asked the owner of Norwesco not to send them back to me. He would only send me one new guy at a time by now. But it seemed like I would have to get a new guy almost every week. I also worked at all the MPC dams in Montana. In fact. there is only one of their dams I haven't dived on (no commercial divers have ever dived on Cyr Dam) and one that only Kalispel and I dove on, Mystic Dam in the Beartooth Mountains. Big Smiles. Actually, I didn't dive, I was the supervisor. Kalispel dove, but this is a story for later.

Anyway, the work in the Gulf of Mexico was slowing down. That happened when there was a Democrat in office. Republicans are good for Oilfield work and Major Construction jobs. Democrats are good for Infrastructure work; especially now since they wanted to save all the fish. What this meant for me was that lots of guys who couldn't break-out in the Gulf were coming up to the northwest because they heard there was lots of work up here. There was, for us, but not enough for all the guys getting out of dive school. In the nineties, there were several dive schools. Diver's Institute of Technology in Seattle put out about thirty tenders a month for about ten months of the year. The Ocean Corporation in Houston put out about twenty tenders a month. There was a school in New Jersey run by a French guy that put out a bunch of tenders every year, I don't really know how many. There was Santa Barbara College that put out a few every year. Florida Institute of Technology put out a bunch too. Highline College, where I went, had shut down its diving program in ninety-two, I think. Still, lots of new tenders every month. It was not easy to break out either.

In the Gulf, the norm was you would tend for at least two

years before you had a chance to break out. Putting two years in didn't mean you automatically became a diver. It mostly depended on whether or not a supervisor wanted you to break out. The norm was that only about ninety percent of the people who went to dive school actually tried to get a job in the dive industry in the first place. After spending about a year in the Gulf about another fifty percent dropped out. The work was hard and the pay wasn't great. It was minimum wage. Yeah, you worked a lot of hours, like eighty to ninety, maybe a hundred hours a week. Typically, you would go offshore for a couple weeks at a time. When you weren't offshore, you could work in the shop if you got along with the shop guys. This still paid minimum wage and it was hard work. If you didn't work hard, or you didn't get along with the rest of the crew, you didn't get called out on jobs. You didn't get fired; you just didn't get called back.

Plus, there was a real caste to the dive industry. On the bottom was the Tender, referred to as "worth less than the parasite on the belly of a worm in a wheel rut." Next was a Lead Tender. This person had proven themselves, usually, to be hard-working and dependable enough that the supervisor could trust him to get the dive station set up and keep all the tenders in line. He was more or less the Foreman of the deck. Still not a lot of respect from the divers. The next step is a Diver-Tender. There is not much difference between an LT and a DT. LTs got to dive once in a while if they were lucky. DTs got to dive more often, and often the LT would be a DT. DTs weren't lucky enough to be in Dive Rotation though. Your next step is to Third Rate Diver or I mean Class Three Diver, sorry. Ha, ha! Not really.

You were no longer a Tender, but you were only a Diver if there was lots of work. See, by this stage you were making more money. Oh yeah, I should have said; when you become an LT you usually get a raise of fifty cents an hour, maybe seventy-five cents if you're lucky. By the time you make DT you are probably getting a buck-fifty over minimum wage. When I left the Gulf of Mexico in February of eighty-seven, I was a DT earning six dollars and twenty-five cents an hour. Woo Hoo! Yeah Buddy! We're livin' high on the Hog now. Right. I left because Can-Dive had another job for me. The pay was better and the conditions were way better. Don't tell the Gulf guys that though.

So, anyway, now you are a Class Three Diver and you are making Nine Dollars and Seventy-five Cents an hour! Yeehaw! That *is* something to crow about. Except now you are considerably more expensive than a DT or an LT but with really only the same experience. Suddenly you aren't working as much as you were. Unless you are a good diver or the supervisor really likes you. This is where a bunch more people leave the dive industry. Lots have had enough of the crap in the Gulf so they try inland diving. They think it's easy, but it's not. The crews are small, sometimes only two guys, so you actually have to work harder. The water is usually crappy. Lots of times you're working in mud. The pay is better on the west coast, but in the rest of the country, the pay isn't that much better than the Gulf. And, there is way less overtime on inland jobs, so actually the Gulf diver is making more money than the inland divers in a typical year.

After a year or more as a third-rate diver, you might get a raise and move up to a Class Two Diver. This means you've moved up on the call out list. You will work more and on better jobs. After a time kissing the supervisor's ass, or when a supervisor or three like the way you work, you move up to a Class One Diver. You are now on the first page of the call out list and typically work as much as you want and on the jobs you want. You are probably acting as an assistant supervisor. You probably get to become a SAT Diver too. It was typically a ten-year trip to become a SAT Diver. If you weren't interested in being a SAT Diver, you might just go right into being a Supervisor. If you did go into SAT, after a few years you might become a SAT Supervisor. Then from there you could become a Dive Superintendent. That could take fifteen to twenty years. That's the Gulf path. Or it used to be, until Hurricane Katrina hit the Gulf. I will talk about that later – in about ten years from here. Smiles.

So, when work slowed down in the Gulf of Mexico, lots of tenders and third-rate divers headed north or west to work. Some headed to the northeast and some to the Midwest, but I didn't meet those guys unless they came out west. Lots wanted to work in Alaska because Alaska Union Divers were the highest paid divers in the U.S. They made as much as the SAT Divers in the Gulf, but didn't have to go into SAT. Their union was pretty tight, though, and it was hard to get in. Also. there wasn't a whole lot of work in Alaska and only a few companies doing all the work. So, if you didn't know someone in there, you weren't getting in. Seattle's union was easy to get into though. Spokane's was too. When I joined the Spokane union, there were only three of us divers that actually worked. There might have been fifteen or so, but most of them were too out of shape to work. United Marine Divers was, really, the first real Dive Company in Spokane. There was one other, that I have mentioned previously, that used SCUBA divers and friends and didn't do any real underwater construction.

Sorry for the Tangent. Work was starting to pick up in the Northwest and we needed more divers. Sadly, most of the new guys we were getting were the rejects from the Gulf. Great. I didn't have a regular dive crew with me in Montana. They were regular guys, as close to "regular" as people in the dive industry can be anyway! I just mean I didn't have the same guys on my crew. Everybody wanted the longer jobs. In Montana, we were lucky if we spent a whole week at any one dam. We might work on two, three, or even as many as five dams in a single week. It all depended on what needed to be done. Great Falls was nice because of the five dams there. We usually spent a couple weeks to maybe a month there working on the different dams. Most of the other places only had one dam. They were fairly close together for Montana, meaning you could get to them in a day from Great Falls, but not really close together like those in Great Falls. We might work on one dam in Thompson Falls for a day or two, then drive to Ennis, Montana to work on Madison Dam. After that we might drive to Helena to work on Hauser Dam or to Wolf Creek to work on Holter Dam. I stayed pretty busy, but there was a lot of set-up and break down with a lot of driving in between. I loved it.

Montana is a beautiful state and I got to see almost all of it. This was also the reason why the regular guys didn't like it. It was a Lot of work for not a lot of diving. My crew was typically a three-man crew, the minimum by OSHA standards by this time; me as the supervisor, one of the Norwesco regulars, and some new guy. I didn't always get the best regular, but it was always someone I got along with and could work with. The new guy? Who knows what I might get? Remember, diving on dams is not the safest diving in the world. You have to watch out for leaks, intakes – which weren't always known about because these dams were built at the beginning of the twentieth century and the blue prints and plans may have gotten lost – gates not fully closed, and god knows what else. New guys had never dived on dams before. I had to teach them everything and hoped they listened to me.

I had one guy on a trash rack cleaning job that I just couldn't dive after the second day. He just wouldn't listen to me and kept going the wrong way when I tried to guide him anywhere. We were doing a trash rack cleaning at Cochrane Dam. One I had done several times before. It was a simple job and on the outside of the trash racks so no possible way you could get sucked into the dam. If the head gate was open all the way, you might get sucked up against the trash racks, but you could be freed just by having the dam operator close the gate. This was as safe a job as we did on the dams. These racks were in the shape of half of a hexagonal cylinder protecting the head gate. The bottom of the head gate was at about seventy-eight feet and the bottom of the trash racks was about ten feet below that. To get the job completely done, we would be diving down to about ninety feet. Because of the altitude, I had to add a table, meaning we would be decompressing on a hundred-foot table – twenty-five minutes of bottom time. I needed all my crew to be able to dive and do their work. The water was pretty black, I think with your light you might be able to see two feet. Usually, we let the dam operator keep the gate open about forty percent, so there was a fair amount of flow – this helped us clean the trash racks. It made for a bit of noise though. The head gates lift up, so the opening is at the bottom and there is cavitation around the bottom of the gate when it is not fully open. That adds to the noise. It's a little scary the first time, I understand that, but still, think about it. You can't get sucked into the dam.

As is my normal practice, I jump the new guy on the first day. I like to start the work with an experienced diver to give the job a little momentum and actually get some work done for the customer – the dam company – Montana Power Company in this instance. The first guy goes in and does a survey of what we need to do. I have done this for several years, so I have a good idea of what to expect. Normally the top forty feet are packed with algae mixed with silty mud and a few sticks and other small debris, and more people trash than you would hope for, but hey, Montana gets a lot of tourists who don't really respect nature as they should. The bottom half would usually have large branches, tree stumps, root balls and other larger debris pressed up against the racks. The first time I cleaned these trash racks, the pile of logs, branches and trash was piled up from the bottom to about thirty feet from the surface – a pile about sixty feet high – and it sloped out to about twenty feet upstream of the trash racks. That was a Lot of debris. It took us two weeks to get it cleaned out. We had a crane lower a dump truck bed into the water and we just filled it up by hand. That worked really well, so a crane with the dump truck bed was on site and ready for us to use if needed. For the algae we used our hands, a gravel rake with a short handle, and a pressure washer – only a twenty-five hundred psi one, not a ten-thousand psi one like we used in the Gulf of Mexico.

In goes the first guy. The algae and mud pack is pretty thick. He gets down to the bottom and tells me that there is a fair amount of bigger debris, but it only goes upstream about five feet. We should be able to clear these in the week. There are two sets of trash racks on this dam. The set we are working on that always has the most debris is the set closest to the bank. The second set is in the middle of the river and gets a lot less debris stuck up against it. We always start with the most clogged set. We decide there is enough debris to warrant use of the dump truck bed. I get that lined up. I show it to the crew, the regular has done this before, so knows what we need to do. I explain everything to the new guy. He will be diving next. He assures me that he dove a lot in the gulf. He says he is comfortable in the water and won't have any issues. He does have his own hat, so that is a good sign. I tell him we will lower the dump truck bed into the water first and put it where I think it needs to be, which is below the area he will be working. That way he can just pull the debris off the racks and let it fall into the bed. When the bed is full, we pull the diver, bring the truck bed up and dump it into a truck that will take it to a land fill. New guy tells me he understands and everything is good. Wonderful. I get the truck bed lowered into position. New guy sees where it is. We get new guy dressed in and checked out. He is good to go. He goes to the ladder and climbs down into the water.

He leaves the surface – meaning he goes under the water. The dump truck bed is off to his left at about thirty feet. He needs to locate it then climb the racks above it and start raking the debris into the bed. He gets to twenty feet and doesn't find it. I tell him it is down a little deeper. He says okay. He tells me he is okay, but I hear his breathing increase. I ask him if he's okay and he swears he is. I ask him to regulate his breathing, slow it down a little, take deeper relaxed breaths. He gets to thirty-five feet and can't find it. Okay, I tell him, move to your left and you should run right into it, I can see where he is by his bubbles coming up to the surface. He starts moving sideways, the WRONG way! I tell him "hey, you're going to the right, I need you to go to your left." He tells me yeah, yeah, okay, but he doesn't go left. He continues to go right. Hey Man! Move to your Left! He keeps going right. Then I see, by the pnuemo, that he is getting shallower. Hey Man! Stop. Stop right where you are and let me direct you to the dump truck bed. He stops. His breathing slows. I explain to him where he is and where the truck bed is and where he needs to go to reach it. Okay, he tells me. He is good to go and knows what he needs to do. Head left and down, I'll keep an eye on his depth and his bubbles.

He starts moving. Are his bubbles moving left? No. They are moving right again. Hey, where are you going. No answer. Bubbles are moving way right. He is going around to the wrong side of the racks. Hey! Where are you going? No answer again. Man, you gotta talk to me. Where are you going? Now his bubbles are up against the dam on the wrong side of the racks and he is at ten feet. He won't talk to me. I tell the other guy to pull him up. Let's get him to the surface and back on deck. We pull him up. Now he starts yelling "Hey! What are you doing? I'm trying to make my way to the truck bed!" I explain to him that, no, he is not going the right way. I tell him we are going to bring him to the surface, let him reorient himself and go back in. We get him to the surface. He takes off his helmet, looks around, and touches the crane wire. We're good to go.

This time I will have him go down the crane wire right to the truck bed. He won't be able to miss it this time. Yeah, right. I tell him he needs to respond to my questions and directions. A simple "Roger that" or "Okay" or anything, just a response so I know the comms are working both ways and you can hear me. Yeah, yeah, he says. First day on the job and he's already got an attitude. He gets his helmet back on and gets back in the water. We drag him on the surface over to the crane wire so he can't get lost. He finds the wire and descends to the truck bed. I got him at thirty-two feet when he says he is standing in the bed. Okay, good. All he needs to do is climb straight up to the top of the algae and start raking it off the racks. He starts climbing. I see the pneumo indicate that he is getting shallower. My other guy says his bubbles are moving to the right. Hey, man. Are you climbing straight up? Yeah, yeah, he assures me he is. His bubbles keep moving right. Now he is in the middle of the trash racks about forty feet away from the truck bed and at about ten feet. DUDE! What is your issue? You are way far away from where you need to be. No response. Hey! You need to move to your left and get back in position over the truck bed. No response. All I can do is bite my tongue and shake my head. I tell him again to move to his left. His bubbles keep moving right. I tell my other guy to pull him back to the crane wire. New guy says nothing, but is on the surface of the water on the right side (the wrong side) of the trash racks. I tell him we are bringing him to the surface. I ask my other guy to pull him up and out.

All this while, the MPC crew is watching with undivided attention. They have seen my dive operations many, many times. They know when a diver is good and when not. I think they are enjoying the show. I can see them smile and shake their heads. They can hear the dive radio, so they know what the communications are between the diver and me.

We get the new guy on deck and get his hat off. I look at him and ask him what the problem is. He tells me it is dark and noisy and disorienting. I say, yeah, I know it can be, but I thought you had diving experience. I know that not all the diving in the Gulf is done in crystal clear water. Usually, the new divers there get the worst dives – the experienced divers don't want or have to take the nasty dives. So, if he has done some diving, he should be familiar with black water. The noise and the water movement shouldn't be any big deal. You can see there is No Way to get sucked into the dam. He tells me he is not comfortable with the situation and needs a little time to calm down. Okay, that's fine. I never dive a person who doesn't want to get wet. I have no issues with that. If all you want to do is tend, I can work with that, just tell me up front. He reassures me that he is a diver and wants to dive. He should be ready to dive the next day. Yeah, whatever you say. He gets out of his dive gear and I get into mine. I have worked with the regular guy enough to know I can trust him to run my dive. We finish out the day with my dive of three-and-a-half hours in the water. When we are working for MPC we only do eight-hour days. They don't want to pay overtime unless they have to. Besides, it's a regular forty-hour work week for their employees. We get treated like their employees when we're there, so it is great.

That evening we have dinner at some restaurant in Great Falls. The new guy asks me if he is going to get his four hours of wet pay even though he didn't get any work done. I tell him, that yes, the way it works in the Northwest is that if you get wet and try to work, you get your four-hour minimum, even if you only spent five or ten minutes in the water. He is all smiles. Then he has the gall to ask me to sign his dive log. He has filled it out and puts "Trash rack cleaning" as the task performed with a bottom time of three hours and fifteen minutes. Really? Well, I can't argue that it was over three hours from the time he first got into the water until the time he last got out. He did get down to thirty-five feet. There are no false claims in his log other than no actual trash rack cleaning took place. What can I do? I sign his log, but he will never dive for me again. First off, he didn't listen to my instructions, and secondly, he didn't answer my queries when he was in the water. Hell, he didn't even respond in any way. I can let a bad dive go. I understand that dam diving takes a little to get used to. I will give a guy a second chance, even a third or fourth if he (or she) is a good worker. Just ask anybody, well most anybody, that has ever worked with me. I am positive they would tell you I am a good supervisor who treats his crew fairly. We went for a few beers after dinner, then back to our respective hotel rooms and called it a day.

The next day, starts off well. Everything is pretty much set up from the day before so we get a pretty good jump on the day. I dive the regular guy first. He spends about three-and-a-half hours cleaning algae off the racks. When he gets out of the water, the new guy asks if he should get dressed in. I tell him no. I will be diving next. I explain to him that I can't have a diver who doesn't respond on the radio. Communication is of vital importance on a diving job. I also need to see how he works as a tender. So far, he has not done anything worth writing home about. I tell him that I need to get a feel for him before I put him back in the water and he will be working as a tender the rest of the week. He turns in a huff and goes to help the regular guy refuel the compressor and get things ready for my dive. We finish out the day and it is pretty much a repeat of the day before. I get back to my hotel and do the paperwork for the day before going to sleep.

The next morning at breakfast – we have been eating breakfast at the restaurant in the O'Hare. It is pretty good. I like it anyway. The regular guy shows up like normal, but the new guy is not there. That's funny because the previous two days he was there before I was. I ask the waitress if she has seen him. She tells me that she has not. Funny. I go knock on his hotel room door. Sometimes these new guys drink more than they can handle and won't get up in the morning. No answer at his door. Well, maybe he is passed out from drink. I will get the room key from the front desk and go in there and pull him out of bed if I have to. It wouldn't be the first time I've had to drag a hungover diver out of bed. I go to reception and explain to them the issue. The girl behind the counter smiles, she knows what is going on from past experience. She goes to grab the key and sees a note in the box for me. I read the note. It is from the new guy. He has left. He won't be finishing out the week with us because he is a diver not a tender. If I won't dive him, he won't be working with me. Huh. Okay. That's fine with me, but now I am a man down.

I call the home office in Spokane and explain the situation. The boss gets upset. He knows me, though, and knows I am a good supervisor even though he never tells me that. He knows that I am a good judge of a dive crew member. He wants to know what I and the other guy are going to do for the day, since we can't work with a two-person crew. I tell him we are going to work. I will use one of the MPC guys as our third team member. That wouldn't be a first for me either. The boss is happy with that. He knows the MPC employees are very competent. We get another new guy. I never see the first new guy again. I did hear through the dive vine that he didn't own his own hat, he had borrowed it from a friend of his in Seattle. Lovely. Won't work, can't dive, doesn't communicate and lies when he does. Good riddance.

*　　*　　*

Okay, this looks like a new story, but it is actually a continuation of the previous week. Think of it as a new chapter in the same story, or a part two if you will. We are still working at Cochrane dam cleaning the trash screens. It is Thursday. We will work today and half of tomorrow. Friday, remember, when we are working with MPC we get done in time on Fridays so we can get back to Spokane for the weekend at a decent hour. Plus, the MPC guys like to do a Bar-B-Que for lunch on Fridays if the weather is good, which it usually is.

The regular guy is here and we have a new tender. He is fresh up from the Gulf of Mexico. Oh Joy. He doesn't have a dive hat, or any dive equipment for that matter. It was all stolen. Huh. Not the first time I had heard that either. At least he was willing to be a tender and told me as much. Okay, I can work with that. First thing we need to do is set up the dive station – attach the deck whips from the compressor to the volume tank and Dive Control box and all that stuff. He asks me for a wrench.

We have a tool box in the back of the truck. But where's your crescent wrench? It was stolen along with all his dive gear. He had nothing, no tools, no nothing. No life jacket, no hard hat, no gloves. At least he was wearing steel-toed boots and work clothes. Okay, it's his first day with me. I always carry a spare hard hat, life jacket, gloves and case of Mountain Dew. He told me he was happy to be a tender. That's a good start.

His eyes were all red and puffy. It is the morning, maybe he didn't sleep well. He smells like a distillery though. He is walking straight, sort of. Hmm. I think this guy likes to drink. That's okay. Most of us drink more than our fair share. I don't care how much you drink on your off time as long as you are up and ready to work in the morning. If we get a good crew together that enjoys each other's company, it is common practice for us to close down the bars or strip clubs every night. Don't tell our wives that!

Anyway, this guy is new, really new and he has no tools. That's okay, we'll make it work today and tomorrow. We finish out the day. The new guy does fine, no complaints. He listens to direction and does what he is asked. We go to dinner and then to the bar. I expect this new guy to drink like a fish, because of the way he smelled this morning, but he doesn't go overboard. He only has five or six like me and the regular guy. That's good.

The next morning, he is up at breakfast with us. He is not

hungover. So that's a good sign. We finish up for the week, get everything loaded into the truck and get ready to head back to Spokane. We are all in separate vehicles. The regular guy is not coming back next week. I will be getting another regular guy. The new guy asks if he is returning on Monday. I tell him sure, if the office wants to send him back next week, that is fine with me. I call the office, tell them where we are at and get confirmation of my crew for Monday. Nice, first time in a while that I know who my whole crew will be. I give the new guy a list of stuff I require my new tenders to have on a job; Crescent Wrench, Knife, roll of Electrical Tape, Hardhat, Life Jacket, Gloves, Protective Eye-ware, and Hard-toed Work Boots. He assures me he will be here ready to go first thing Monday morning. I wish him safe travels and a good weekend.

Monday morning. I got to the Rainbow office about seven-thirty in the morning. That was the norm for me. It took me about five hours to get to Great Falls from Spokane, so I would leave about two in the morning. I liked to have a little extra time, so I could stop if I had to. Or you never knew if you might hit a deer or something. Anyway, Monday morning. My regular guy shows up at a quarter to eight, kind of pushing it dude. He had spent the night in Great Falls, so he knew when he would be at the shop in the morning. Good. The new guy, have you seen him? Nobody has. Well. I did tell him Oh-Eight-Hundred. My take on getting to a job is that if you're not ten minutes early, you are ten minutes late. Five to eight and still no new guy. Hmmm. Well, I guess we'll head up to the conference room where we start the week out. Lo and behold, new guy is sitting in a chair in the conference room waiting for us. Nice. Funny (strange funny, not ha-ha funny) but nice. Okay, the week is starting out on a good note.

We get through the morning announcements, crew designations, and exercises then head to the dam. Once on the dam, we start unloading all our equipment and getting the dive station set up. The new guy doesn't have a hard hat, life jacket or any of the tools and stuff I told him he would need. He looks at me and explains that it was all stolen when he left the Gulf of Mexico. Yeah, yeah, you already told me. No, he says he hadn't told me that. He has no recollection of me telling him what he needed on the job site. In fact, it was almost like this was his first day on the job. He didn't even hook the deck whips up correctly on the dive station. I just shook my head. Oh boy, here we go again. The day actually went well. The new guy was a good worker.

That night we went to dinner and to a strip club afterwards. Mondays at this strip club were like open mike night – any girl could go up and strip, she didn't have to work there or anything. They called it "Amateur Night." It was fun. There was a two-drink minimum. I like Rum. I usually drink Meyers neat, but any decent rum will do. I like Kraken and Pyrate. The new guy liked mixed drinks, but not with pop or soda or whatever. He liked drinks like B-Fifty-Twos. I like those too. He liked Rusty Nails, Brain Hemorrhages, and things like that. His favorite, though, was the Duck Fart! Ha! That's funny. I had never even heard of a Duck Fart. We had a few. They were okay, I guess.

We finished out the week and got everything done that we had planned. Friday came around and we loaded the gear into the truck and everybody went their own way. I called the office and told them how everything went. The boss asked me how the new guy worked out and I told him he was fine. I explained his lack of dive gear, so he would be a tender, but I was good with that. The boss was happy to hear that and told me this new guy would be working with me for a while. That would be just fine with me.

I worked on lots of projects throughout the summer. Some were in Seattle, some north of Seattle, some around Spokane. On the weekends, sometimes I would go out for a game of pool and some beer. There was a great pool hall in Spokane Valley that I would go to. The tables were paid for by the hour rather than per game, and the beer was relatively inexpensive. They also served hard liquor.

One night I was in there and who walks in but the new guy who didn't have any tools. He had already been drinking and came in with a couple friends. He saw me at one of the pool tables and came over to say "Hi." I greeted him and asked him if he wanted to play a game or two. I was there with a couple of buds and we were just playing for fun and drinking beer. The new guy said no, he didn't really come to play pool. He liked one of the barmaids and the drinks were cheap and good compared to other places he frequented. That's cool. He asked if I needed a drink and I told him I was good. We had a new pitcher of beer on the table. He smiled said okay and went to the bar where he and his friends sat down.

I could see he was flirting with the bar tender and she was flirting back. Good for them. I went back to playing pool. Before we finished that game, the barmaid came by and gave me a little drink in a tall shot glass. It kind of looked like and orangish B-Fifty-Two. "This is from your friend at the bar" she said as she set the drink on our table. Really? I laughed. What is it, I asked. She told me it was a Duck Fart. Hmm. It looked different from those in Montana. I drank it. It was pretty good. It tasted the same as those in Montana. She had just mixed all the ingredients together instead of layering them. I still preferred the B-Fifty-Two. I waved to the new guy and mouthed "Thanks." I went back to playing pool with my friends. About half an hour later, the barmaid brought over another Duck Fart. I drank it and waved to the new guy again. He was all smiles, obviously feeling no pain. I kept playing pool and drinking beer.

The barmaid came by again about a half hour after the last time. She had a Duck Fart on her tray again. She set it on my table again. Okay, okay, that's fine, but I don't need anymore. I gave her money enough for a couple Duck Farts and asked her to treat the new guy. She left me and headed back to the bar. I could see her talking to him. They were all giggly and cuddly. She returned to my table after about fifteen minutes with a fourth Duck Fart and my money. She said our mutual friend didn't want any of my money and he could afford his own drinks. Alright I responded, but informed her that I really didn't want any more Duck Farts. She smiled and left me to my friends. I talked with them and we decided to finish up our pitcher and head out to another bar closer to home. I went up to the new guy, thanked him for the drinks, told him I looked forward to working with him again, and said good-bye. From now on I will refer to this guy as "Duck Fart."

*   *   *

The next kind of interesting job I did was in late summer. We, meaning Norwesco Marine, had been hired to clean the trash racks at Nine Mile Falls Dam just northeast of Spokane. An initial inspection of the job had been done earlier by Blanchard, Lewiston, and myself. We had determined that decades of sand had piled up in front of the dam and we needed to remove it. A plan was made and the job put out to bid. Norwesco won the bid. We did a lot of work for Washington Water Power at that time and really were the only game in town for Dive work. Other companies would bid the work, but with per diem and mobilization costs, they just couldn't beat Norwesco's local bid. That was the case on many jobs in eastern Washington, northern Idaho, and Western Montana. It turned out that Spokane was a pretty good location for an inland dive company to be located.

Okay, back to Nine Mile Falls Dam. Trash screens need to be cleaned so that water can pass through to the turbines and cause them to spin thereby generating electricity. What happens when the trash racks get clogged is that not enough water can get through. There ends up being a water level difference between the inside and outside of the trash racks. Inside the water level is lower, effectively lowering the head pressure which means less energy to turn the turbines. This prevents them from producing as much electricity as they should, so it is a big deal. Also, the difference in water level causes a real strain on the trash rack assembly which will cause damage over time. That is why we clean trash racks so often. Usually, it gets done in a day or two, definitely less than a week.

There was so much sand here in front of the dam, though, that we didn't have a hard-set schedule. We were to work until the sand was down to the bottom of the trash racks, whether that took a day or a month. I think we got it done in a week, or at least done enough for the customer. The material in front of the trash racks was sand; Sugar Sand to be precise. There were some branches, logs, and other debris mixed in, but it was mostly sand. Blanchard had suggested, and I agreed, that the easiest cheapest way to remove the sand was to use an airlift to get the sand loose and up into the water going through the turbines. It would be washed downstream and the Power Company wouldn't have to haul any of it away. This sounded great. It actually worked great for us also.

We set up our dive station on the west side of the dam. There was fairly easy access down the sandy, grassy bank into the forebay where we would be working. We could work without disrupting the operation of the dam. We weren't too worried about the flow of water around us, rather the water flow would help carry the sand away. That made the Power Company happy. We got everything set up and ready to start working – sucking sand – that took more than half the day. So, Blanchard made a short dive at the end of the day just to test everything out and see how it would work for us. We weren't working any overtime on this job either. The water was shallow enough – twenty-five feet at its deepest and usually less than twenty feet. That meant that we would only dive two guys each day, one in the morning and one in the afternoon. The weather was good; warm and sunny. It made for very pleasant work.

The area we were set up in was inside an eight-foot-high chain-link fence with coiled razor wire on top of it. The matching gate was locked at night when we left. The only other access was by boat, but the boat operator would have to float over a wire cable with floats strung across the river upstream of the dam. This allowed us to keep our dive station pretty much set up so we wouldn't have to break it down every night just to set it all up the next day. We pulled the radio, the dive control box, our dive hats, and other small stuff off the dive station and locked it in a Conex that was on site. Doing that we could be ready to dive in about fifteen to thirty minutes in the morning and the same for the breakdown at night. With that we could get a good seven hours of dive time in an eight-hour day.

Lewiston dove first on the second day. I never worry about dive rotation and I never really cared whether I dove first or last. Some people like to dive in the morning, right off the bat, others like to be the last diver of the day. Me? It made absolutely no difference to me. Lewiston wanted to go first, so he did. He jumped in, or rather climbed down the bank into the water, and we lowered the airlift to him. I think it was about fourteen feet, maybe sixteen when he started. He sucked sand for a good three-and-a-half hours straight. That was about our max dive time on days like these. We needed a little time to swap out divers, refuel the equipment, that kind of thing. When he got back to the surface, he explained that the sugar sand kept sliding in from behind and filling up the hole he was making. He said he couldn't tell that he had done anything. We razzed him a little about not getting anything done. But we had all worked in sugar sand before and knew this was how it was.

I jumped in next and went over to the airlift – we left it in the water so the second diver could just continue on where the first diver left off. Lewiston was right, I couldn't tell that he had moved any sand at all. I called to topside for them to make the airlift hot – that is turn the air on to it so it would start sucking. They turned it on and I stuck the mouth into the sand. The sand was sucked out of the area. I could see it flowing out the top of the airlift and into the trash racks being flushed downstream by the turbines. The pit that was forming at the mouth of the airlift filled back in almost as fast as the sand left it. It was difficult to see any progress being made. I looked upstream and saw a LOT of sand. We might be here quite a while. This dam was built in nineteen-oh-six so there was about ninety years of sand piled up behind the dam. That's okay, this was a very nice job to be on and it was basically in Spokane, so I would be home every night in time for dinner. That was great, because it meant I got to spend more time with my family.

This job was fairly easy. Once the diver was in the water and working away, there wasn't much for the topside guys to do. We had to keep an eye on the equipment, make sure nothing ran out of fuel. We had to keep an ear on the dive radio in case the diver needed anything or, god forbid, got into trouble. That left us a lot of time to kill. Blanchard was a bit of a practical joker, so he was always looking for ways to give everybody else a bad time. We all joked around with each other. As I've said before, dive crews are like family.

We work long hard hours together. Our lives depend on each other, literally. You know, if the air compressor runs out of air, what's a diver to do? Turn on his Bailout Bottle, thing is, back then, not all divers wore Bailouts. I always did, but most, especially guys coming up from the gulf didn't. They had them, because they would use them on the deeper dives. But dives at twenty feet or less? Most divers just figured the Bailout was more trouble than it was worth. Not me. I mean, yeah, you don't need a Bailout Bottle if everything goes the way it's supposed to and the crew keeps the compressor running.

I always used to say "Bailout Bottles; you don't need them, until you do." No matter what depth a diver was working at, there was a possibility of getting fouled – that is caught or snagged on something. That would mean the diver is trapped below the surface. If there wasn't an unlimited air supply, your number would come up real fast. It was up to the crew topside to jump a standby diver to assist the fouled diver. We were there to keep each other alive. Family.

We worked together. We played together. We drank together. We gave each other a hard time. On that note, Blanchard had found a dead, rotting Rainbow Trout along the bank. He brought it back to the dive station with a wicked grin on his face. I asked what he was planning on doing with that. He responded that he didn't yet know. I could see the gears in his head turning. He turned and looked at me after a bit. I was sitting at the dive station, listening to Lewiston suck sand and breathe air. I saw a gleam in Blanchard's eye as he informed me of his plan. He would place the fish body in the air intake of the air conditioning unit of Lewiston's Bronco. Mean. That's just mean. He didn't put it just in front of the intake, he took the air intake apart and stuck it inside there, making sure not to obstruct any of the air flow. That way, when Lewiston lifted the hood to look for a problem, nothing would jump out at him. Mean. Funny but mean, mean, mean. I didn't say anything to anybody. Practical jokes were between the Joker and the Jokee. I wasn't going to ruin anybody's fun. It wouldn't kill or hurt Lewiston. It would just be nasty. I, myself, am not a practical joker often. So, it wasn't often that people played jokes on me. I wasn't any good for a reaction anyway, so that kind of took the fun out of it.

Lewiston didn't use his air conditioning right away. It was a couple days later in the morning that he said something about a nasty smell he noticed when he turned on his air conditioning the evening before. It was all Blanchard could do to keep a straight face. Like Sergeant Schultz from Hogan's Heroes would say: "I. Know. Nuh-Thing!" Lewiston asked Blanchard to look and see if he could find anything that might cause the smell. Blanchard asked what it smelled like. Lewiston answered that it kind of smelled like rotten fish. Hmmm. Blanchard went over to Lewiston's rig, lifted the hood and poked around a little in the engine compartment. He wiggled some hoses, pushed on the spark plug caps and looked around. There was a slight fishy smell, but it was hard to tell where it was coming from. Blanchard just said he didn't know and maybe the smell would just go away. It didn't of course. I don't remember how it all played out in the end. I do remember that the job lasted for a bit longer.

At the end of the second week, the Power Company decided that we had removed enough sand. We broke the dive station down and loaded all our equipment into the company truck and took our equipment back to the shop. We had made a pretty good dent in the pile of sand, but by no means did we get the majority of it out. I heard later on that some of the engineers at the Power Company were concerned that all that sand going through the turbines might pit the turbine blades. That was a legitimate concern for sure. The Power Company came up with another plan to deal with all the sand. It was a solution that had been used on other dams with the same issues. They would put a large pipe, fourteen-foot in diameter, through the bottom of the dam. There would be a valve on the pipe that could be opened to flush the sand through. That would use a lot of water, but it could be utilized in the spring when they normally let water over the spillway, so they wouldn't be wasting any usable water. They installed that several years later with our help.

*　　*　　*

In the late summer, I was sent to another dam owned

by Washington Water Power. It was Long Lake Dam near Tumtum, Washington. I would be supervising the night shift and we would be cleaning trash racks. I think something else was going on during the day shift, but I can't really remember. In fact, I don't remember a whole lot about this job, other than the crew I worked with. The trash racks on Long Lake Dam are not large, nor are they very deep. There was less of a demand on electricity in the middle of the night, so we could work in front of the trash racks with a reduced flow, making our job easier.

My crew would be a typical three-man dive crew; myself as the supervisor/diver, and two diver/tenders. One of my guys would be Duck Fart and the second would be a new guy fresh up from the Gulf of Mexico. Wonderful. This again. Okay. Well hopefully he could dive, because Duck Fart still didn't have any equipment. He did, at least, have his own safety gear and tools by now though. Yay. Supposedly, the new guy had several years diving experience in the Gulf and was not just another I-Ten break-out. I really hoped so. Even though I enjoyed being in the water, I did not relish the idea of spending seven hours or so each night in the water.

Duck Fart and the new guy showed up about the same time at the downstream side of the dam, our pre-arranged meeting place. The new guy had a nice little Dodge pickup with all his gear in it. We needed to minimize the vehicles parked at the little boat launch. It wasn't a public boat launch. it was just for contractors working on the dam. There was no parking lot or anything, just a wide spot on the dirt road that turned into the boat launch itself. There was a small wooden dock that was starting to rot away there where the dirt road went into the water.

Duck Fart and I threw our gear in the back of the new guy's truck and we took it to the boat launch. I had already gone to the top of the dam and let the day crew know we were there so they could bring the skiff over to the boat launch and pick us up. We loaded about half our stuff into the skiff and motored over to the work site. The new guy and I stayed at the work site while Duck Fart and a couple of the day shift guys went back to the boat launch. They loaded the rest of our stuff into the skiff and Duck Fart brought the skiff back, leaving the day shift guys on the beach. I did my little handover with Blanchard who was running the day shift. By the time Duck Fart was back, Blanchard was ready to go. We transferred the rest of our gear to the Flexi-Float barge that we were working off of and Duck Fart took Blanchard back to the boat launch. We were ready to get to work. We would be using a pressure washer to clean the algae off the trash racks. We had a small Carry-Deck - a small hydraulic crane - on the barge to pull bigger debris off the trash racks.

The new guy had gone to the same dive school I had. Well, that's a hundred points in his favor. He graduated five or six years after I had. He had also been working for American Oilfield Divers, which was the company I worked for when I worked in the Gulf. I don't know if that's any points in his favor or not. He did know some of the guys I had worked with, and one guy from my class who he said everybody called Marshmallow due to his belly, I guess. He had been super skinny in school. Anyway, this guy was looking better all the time. He was also from Spokane and had graduated from one of the local high schools. He lived out in Vinegar Flats, which was a neighborhood on the west side of Spokane.

He had his own hat and it was obviously a working hat. He had a funny Bailout Bottle system; two little bottles side by side, like a miniature SCUBA twin set up. It didn't hold any more air than mine, but it also didn't stick out as far from his back as mine did either. That could be a good thing. He had no idea how much air was in it, though. He asked if he really had to use it in this shallow water. I told him when he was working on my jobs, he had to wear the bailout. His system was rated for three-thousand psi, typical for a dive bottle, but it only had about twelve hundred pounds in it. I always carried a fill whip with me on my jobs so we could fill our bailout bottles from one of the K-bottles of air that we used for standby air. We topped off his bailout. We went over the dive station so these two guys could see how we had it set up and how we worked from it. After we had checked all the equipment and topped off the fuel. We got the diver dressed in to dive. As per my normal operating procedure, I dove Vinegar Flats first. I figured he'd do fine, but I still wanted to make sure. I could tell by the comm checks that he knew how to run the radio and the Dive Control box. I wasn't worried about him running my dive. I just needed to know what kind of a diver he was. It turned out that he was a pretty good diver. I ended up working with him quite a bit in the future.

I don't remember all that much about that job. After thirty years, many of the jobs run together. I am sure it was just a run of the mill job with nothing bad happening. If it hadn't been, I would remember it better. The fact that I don't remember much about it means that it was nothing special and nothing special happened on it. That is a good thing. Diving is often described as "Hours and hours of boredom marked by moments of Sheer Terror." It's the "Sheer Terror" that you don't want, even if it is more memorable, because that is when something is going wrong. Equipment is getting damaged, something on the job is failing, somebody is getting hurt, or the absolute worst; somebody is dying. Luckily for me, nobody has ever died on a job I have been on. I have seen some close calls and been in a couple hairy situations myself though.

*   *   *

In June I had to head up a job at Lower Granite Dam on the Snake River. The job was to clear and clean the fish collection system that we had installed earlier. We would replace the fish counters that weren't working also. There were other jobs going on and this was a fairly low priority job as far as Norwesco was concerned. I would have a five to seven-person crew depending on what was going on each day. I would have to have at least two new tenders on my crew because many of the regulars were working on other "higher priority" jobs.

Kalispel was working with Blanchard and Boston on something else. I had Vinegar Flats on my crew and a couple other semi-regulars. I did get three new tenders for this job. It would be easy to send them home and get replacements here if they didn't work out. This job wasn't as remote as most of the jobs in Montana. The first new tender was a kid that had grown up in Spokane and gone to the same high school that Vinegar Flats went to. He was a pretty good worker, but kept telling everybody how much better he could do the job than the person in the water who was actually doing the job. I told him he needed to stop talking shit and put his money where his mouth was. I told him if he proved himself on deck, he would have a much better chance of actually getting to dive and prove his metal there.

I would have dived him, but I had four other semi-regular divers that deserved to be in rotation more than a new tender. He did have a dive suit and weight belt, so he could be a standby diver if I ran out of people to do that. We had a company band mask and bailout for the standby diver if needed, but he didn't want to use it. He had tools and all his proper personal protective gear too, so that was good. He talked so much smack about the other divers when they were in the water, that I will refer to him as "the Mouth" from here on out.

The second new guy was also from Spokane. He had gone to DIT as well. He wasn't sure he wanted to be a diver, but thought he would give it a shot. He was a good worker and had all the necessary gear a tender needed. He listened to direction and got the job done, without someone having to look over his shoulder. He had big, sad Puppy Dog eyes that the girls seemed to love when we went out to the bars.

My third new tender was a girl, a woman really, but a girl to me - she was in her early twenties. This was my first job as a supervisor where I had a female on my crew. It was only the second time I had ever had a female on my crew, other than dive school. She was newly out of dive school like the Mouth. All three had gone to DIT in Seattle, but I do not know if they were in the same class or not. DIT put out new students every month and we didn't have much work from Hallowe'en until after Memorial Day.

That meant there were about seven months of fresh grads from there for us to pick from, not to mention all the other schools putting out tenders. She was in good shape, had an athletic build, about five-foot six or so; close to the same height and build as the Mouth. Puppy Dog Eyes was a little taller; five-nine or ten maybe, with a medium build. The Girl was ready to go and had all the proper gear she needed to work with us also. She was a very good worker and put most of the guys to shame.

As tenders, these three set up the dive station, kept the equipment fueled up, helped the divers with what they needed to get dressed in. They helped the divers in and out of the water. They sent tools and whatever else the diver might need down to the diver. The other divers helped with this also, but the tenders did most of the hands on "tending" to the divers needs. One of the other divers would be the standby diver. The divers would be more involved in setting up the actual tools to be used under water and fab up anything that might need to be fabbed.

All the diving here was very shallow, twelve feet deep, because most of it was inside the fish collection system itself. Once in a while there might be a dive outside the collection system that would be deeper. Part of this job also was to replace the fish counting transponders and a few of those were down to a hundred feet. The divers loved those dives.

One day we had put in several of the transponders, so I had used up two of the divers. That meant that in the afternoon, when we went back to diving inside the fish collector, I needed one of the tenders to be the standby diver. I had the Girl do it. The Mouth got really upset about it. He thought he should be the standby diver. Puppy Dog Eyes didn't seem to care one way or the other. There was no real glory or advantage to being a standby diver. It only paid a dollar an hour more than tender and it was paid in a four-hour block, so you would hardly notice it on your paycheck. We didn't log standby dives, so I really saw no reason for him to be upset. The reason why I had her be standby, and I told him this point blank, was that she was a better worker. She was working circles around the rest of the guys, so she deserved to be standby if anybody did. I saw this upset the Mouth, but he bit his tongue and went back to work. We were there about a week to complete that job.

The owner of Norwesco asked me what I thought of the new tenders. I told him the truth, like I always did. I told him that the female was an excellent worker and I would gladly have her on my crew anytime. I also said the same thing about the Mouth and Puppy Dog Eyes. They were good workers and I would have them on my crew also. I told him that none of them had any dive experience other than dive school, so we couldn't use them together on a three-person crew in Montana. He said not to worry, they were just new workers and weren't going to be regulars on any crew until they proved themselves. He also said that some of the regulars were not happy about having a girl on the crew. I told him that didn't matter if she did a good job. Not everybody worked well with everybody else regardless of gender.

I worked with the Girl on several other jobs around Washington and Idaho. She didn't go on any jobs to Montana with me, I usually had Kalispel, Vinegar Flats, Duck Fart, or the owner's brother, Vancouver, accompany me to Montana. She always did a great job for me and I told her when she was ready, I would gladly start diving her and see how she did under the water. She got a dive hat, bailout and all the gear she needed to be a diver. I put her in the water on some easy stuff and she did great. I was happy to have her on my crew in any capacity. She worked hard, she did a good job, and she was willing to learn. She listened to what I and other experienced divers had to teach her. She was an excellent hand.

In the fall, I was loading up for a job in Montana and the boss came out to the shop from the office and wanted to have a little talk. Fine. Usually when he wanted to talk it was over some beef he had with me. We never really made small talk. He was alright, we just had different philosophies of life, I think. He liked employees who wanted to work more than anything else. I liked to smell the roses as I went along.

I also always told my employers that I liked to have a day off for every day I worked throughout the year. He didn't care for that. He also liked brown-nosers and I wasn't one of those. He liked to have his workers over a barrel too; where they needed him and the job more than he needed them. I also was never in that situation. If he didn't want to work me, I was happy to go somewhere else, or go on vacation, or whatever. He wasn't the only game in town. Well, he was, I guess, the only real dive company in Spokane, but there were lots of dive companies in western Washington and Oregon, so there was never a lack of work for a diver that wanted to work. I wondered what he wanted to talk about. I couldn't think of any issues that had come up.

He looked at me and asked how things were going. I told him everything was fine. I had my crew for Montana ready to go. We would be heading to Great Falls to work on trash racks at Rainbow dam. It looked like it was going to be a four-week job at least. I asked him if everything was okay on his end of things. He assured me it was, then said he was letting the Girl go. He wasn't going to work her anymore. I asked why not. He said she just wasn't working out. She couldn't lift a K-bottle into the back of a truck by herself. Neither could half of the other guys I replied. He said she put a hacksaw blade in backwards, so obviously doesn't know her way around tools. I just shook my head. Have you never put a blade in backwards on *any* tool?

He said one of the other supervisors didn't like having her on his crew. This guy was the bosses favorite so he got special treatment and whatever he wanted, he usually got. He was a beanpole and not a good worker, so he probably didn't like the fact that this girl outworked him and made him look bad. Anyway, if he wanted the Girl gone, the Girl was gone. I never saw her again and don't know if she ever went to work for another dive company or just gave up on the diving as a career. Sad, because she really could have made something of herself in the industry. Diving was like all construction then though, hard for women to break into it.

*   *   *

I drove over to Great Falls Sunday afternoon. I took the company flatbed because I could load everything I needed onto it without needing a trailer. We still weren't hauling a Decompression Chamber around with us on every job yet. The other two guys would drive their own vehicles and meet me there in the morning. Vinegar Flats and the Mouth were my crew. That would be fine. We were repairing and replacing trash rack screens on Rainbow Dam. It was projected to be a four-week job. The job would be to clean and burn out the sections of trash rack that were rusting away and replace them with new sections.

The new sections were to be bolted into place. The sections of trash rack that only had one or two of the bars rusted away were to be cleaned. Then we would burn out the rusted bar and weld a new bar in its place. I had done an inspection on these trash racks earlier on in the year, so MPC had a good idea of what screens needed to be replaced and which just needed some bars replaced.

We met at the Rainbow shop at eight in the morning. We went over what we were doing and who we would be working with. We were only responsible for the diving portion of this job. Another company had been contracted to do the actual job. They would have the cranes and be responsible for everything out of the water. That included supplying the new screens and repair materials and also disposing of the pieces of screens we removed. This was a little different for us, because now, instead of just answering to MPC, we also had to answer to the construction company. Normally when working on a job as a sub-contractor you only answer to the company that hires you. This construction company didn't hire us because we were the lowest bidder, they hired us because they were told to by MPC. It was one of the requirements in the bid. This caused a little tension between us and the construction company, but not much.

We set up our dive station on top of the dam above the trash racks. Rainbow Dam has a different set up than many dams. There is a channel that leads from the river to the forebay area which has trash racks on two sides. The water level was down about ten or twelve feet from normal, since this was the fall and they were in the process of lowering the pond levels for the winter. This meant we had to have a ladder down to the water level.

MPC supplied us with a section of a dock that we put in the

forebay so we could use that as a dive platform. We would tie that off to the trash racks right above where the diver was working. We had a ladder going down from the top of the dam to the dock and another from the dock into the water. That made it easier to tend the diver as well as making it easier for the diver to get up and out of the water. We could set all the tool hoses and leads on the dock and tend them at the water level. Since the dam had limited access - it was all inside locked gates - we could leave everything pretty much set up at night. That saved us lots of time every morning and every evening, giving us more time for actual diving. We were still working eight-hour days; no weekends and no overtime.

The bottom of the trash racks was at about twenty feet, so it was shallow diving. Pneumatic tools would work well on this job. The diver would be working the whole water column from the bottom to the surface. It was fairly strenuous work. We used a pneumatic peanut grinder with a wire wheel on it to clean the bars on the trash racks. It was a little awkward and lots of bubbles exited one end, so the diver had to know how to use it. It had a lot of power, so did a very good job removing the rust from the good metal. It was slow and tedious work and gave the diver a good workout. Of course, the Mouth jibber-jabbered all day long how he could do it better. I kept asking him where his hat was, and he responded that he couldn't afford one yet. They typically ran a little over four thousand dollars at this time.

The Mouth had just come off another job that Blanchard had been running on one of the dams by Wenatchee on the Columbia River. It was a fairly long job and had lots of diving to do. I asked the Mouth how he liked working with Blanchard and he told me that Blanchard was a good boss, but rather intimidating. He told me that he had been talking about how he could do a better job than most of the other divers on the job if he just had a chance to dive. Blanchard got tired of hearing it, so he offered the Mouth a deal. Blanchard would let the Mouth dive - they were drilling holes - and if the Mouth could drill as many as Blanchard did in his previous dive, he would put the Mouth into dive rotation.

If, on the other hand, the Mouth could not drill as many holes, he wouldn't be in rotation and he would have to stop talking smack about all the other divers. I asked the Mouth if he had stepped up to the challenge. He looked at the deck and told me that he had not. He didn't want to ruin his chances of getting in the water. I told him that by refusing the challenge from Blanchard, he had ruined his chances of getting into dive rotation. Blanchard liked a worker with confidence. If you at least tried and did your best, he would offer you more chances to do well. By refusing the challenge, the Mouth had told Blanchard that he wasn't confident in his abilities. If he wasn't confident in his abilities, how was Blanchard supposed to have any confidence in him as a diver? I told the mouth that he really screwed the pooch on that one. That didn't keep him from talking smack on this job though.

After about a week-and-a-half of the smack-talking both Vinegar Flats and I had had about enough of the Mouth. The MPC crew that was working alongside us thought it was funny. I decided that I would give the Mouth a shot. One morning in the middle of the third week, I told him to get dressed in because I was going to dive him. He told me he didn't have a hat. I told him that he could use my hat and bailout. I also informed him that if he didn't perform, or if he complained a lot, I wouldn't dive him again. If he did a good job, I would let him use my gear and keep him in regular rotation. He wasn't sure what to do. Vinegar Flats thought it was funny and goaded him on a little. After a bit, the Mouth said he would give it a shot. I explained to him what we were actually doing down there. I told him where the rusty bars were, he would be able to see them. He was to clean them with the peanut grinder and they had to be perfectly clean, not so much for the burning of the rotten bars, but the metal had to be shiny in order to make a decent weld for sticking the repair pieces in.

I wasn't going to let him start with an easy dive, like just bolting new rack sections in, or have fun burning out the rotten bars or rusted bolts. Burning was a really fun part of the job. No, he was going to do the worst, most physically demanding, most tedious part of the job; wire wheeling the rust off the metal with the pneumatic peanut grinder. Now you may be thinking, wire wheeling, that is no big deal. I mean we've all seen the hand grinders welders use, right? Well, we weren't using one of those little grinders. We were using what the MPC crew called a "Peanut Grinder" and it wasn't small. It was about three feet tall and weighed about forty pounds. The wire wheel it used was about ten inches in diameter. It had a powerful motor and released a lot of air through the exhaust port when being used. A lot of air means a lot of bubbles under the water. Lots of bubbles can cause many issues for the diver. The diver needed to hold the grinder in such a way that the bubbles wouldn't interfere with his work. On top of the bubble issue was the torque produced by the spinning wheel and motor parts. When you put the wire wheel to the bars, it would try to spin away too. This was not going to be an easy dive.

Like I said, our deepest depth was about twenty feet, so I could keep the diver down **ALL** eight hours of the day if I wanted. I mean, according to the USN decompression schedule we were using, a diver had unlimited time at twenty feet. That wasn't even a whole 'nother atmosphere of pressure. We needed to be at thirty-three feet for that. Of course, we didn't do that. We got paid in four-hour blocks, so one guy took the morning dive and another took the afternoon dive. Typically, because of set-up, breakdown and diver swap out, I would keep the diver down for three-and-a-half hours at depths less than forty feet. At forty feet, the tables allowed us two hundred minutes of bottom time. Two hundred minutes was three hours and twenty minutes.

We got the Mouth all prepped and dressed in. We did all the checks; air pressure, comms, bailout bottle hooked up, valves properly lined up. We were good to go and the Mouth was ready. This wasn't his first dive, he had said. He worked in the Gulf of Mexico for a while. I don't remember the company, but he said he dove for them in Louisiana. It would be his first actual work dive in the Pacific Northwest though. He knew what his task was and he was ready.

He jumped in the water and found his way to the bottom of the trash racks. I marked his Leave Surface time in the dive log and added four hours to that. That would be his Leave Bottom time. If he didn't have any issues, I planned on making him do the complete four hours. That's what he gets for talking smack all the time. Ha! Vinegar Flats lowered the peanut grinder to him. When he got it, he worked his way over to the point where he was going to start cleaning. After he informed me that he was ready to make the peanut grinder hot, I turned on the air to it and he went to work. I could hear him breathing through the radio.

I could tell when he was actually working and when he was taking a little break by his breathing, even if he kept the peanut grinder going. Some divers do that; sit on the bottom, tie the control valve open so the tool keeps working, and take a nap or just sit there and don't do anything. They don't realize that topside can tell by their breathing whether or not they are really working. By the same token, the radio operator (usually the supervisor) can tell if the diver is struggling with a task that he shouldn't have any trouble with. The Mouth was actually working.

I heard him take a little break once in a while, but when he did, he shut the valve on the grinder, so it was obvious that he was taking a little break. That's okay. You need to take little breaks every now and then. Your muscles just can't work nonstop for hours on end. Sometimes we did tie the valves open so we could relax our grip or swap hands and still keep working. So far, the Mouth was working like he should. I wouldn't know if he was doing a good job until I went down there and actually looked at the work he had accomplished.

About every twenty minutes or so, I asked him how he was doing. He always replied that he was doing just fine. Some divers talk to themselves when they are working, I am one of those, so the radio operator can usually tell how the diver is doing by his mumblings. The Mouth wasn't talking at all. He was breathing hard after the second hour, but he didn't say anything unless I asked him a question. That was fine. It was nice to have quiet time on the radio. It was about the only time the supervisor could relax a little. Some divers talked non-stop. That drove me nuts. I would always tell those guys to only talk if they had something important to tell me. Dive time was Quiet time for me. Smiles. The only sound coming over the radio on this dive was breathing and the sound of the grinder running and the wire wheel on the trash rack bars.

When the Mouth had been in the water about two-and-a-half hours, he asked me how long he had been down and how much longer he had left. I asked him if he was getting tired. He replied that no, he wasn't tired, but he did feel like he was getting a workout. I answered that he had been in just over an hour and had about two-and-a-half to three hours left. I said I was happy that he wasn't getting tired. The MPC crew asked why I had told the diver he had only been in an hour or so when he had really been in over two hours. I told them it was because that way the diver would work harder, thinking he was in the middle of his dive rather than approaching the end of it. Especially with this kind of work. When we are building things or putting things together under the water, most of us want to stay until we get it done. This kind of mundane dive, though, most of us couldn't wait until our time was up. It was a little like torture.

At about three-and-a-half hours of dive time, the Mouth again asked how long he had been down, and how much time he had left. I told him not to worry about it, I would get him off bottom before his four hours were up. He said that was fine, but still wanted to know how much time he had left. I answered that he had a little over an hour left. He would be leaving bottom soon. He huffed a little, but kept on working. He wasn't complaining at all. I was happy with that, I was just hoping that he was actually doing a good, or at least a decent, job.

I was watching his time closely now. He has been in the water three hours and fifty minutes. I would keep him down another five minutes then pull him out. That would give him five minutes to get himself composed and ready to leave bottom. Five minutes passed and I pressed the talk button on the radio to tell the Mouth that his time was up and he could leave bottom. I heard him whisper "Finally!" under his breath. He told me we could come up on the peanut grinder. I relayed the message to Vinegar Flats and he started pulling up on the CP hose. He got it on deck in about a minute. I told the Mouth that the tool was on deck and if everything else was good, he could leave bottom and get out of the water. He climbed the ladder.

When he got to the surface he flopped onto the float like a beached whale. He got up on his knees with the help of Vinegar Flats, who helped him remove the dive helmet. He let out a sigh of relief when he got the hat off. Vinegar Flats helped him remove the bailout and weight belt. Normally the diver would climb all the way up to the top of the dam with the bailout and weight belt on so we wouldn't have to raise it up later. The Mouth was too worn out to climb that ten feet with all that gear on. That was okay, we let him do that. He had just completed a four-hour physically demanding dive. I had wanted to wear him out so maybe he wouldn't talk so much smack all the time.

He was worn out. I had to help him a lot getting his suit off. He could barely lift his arms. Vinegar Flats and I were laughing a little and giving him a bit of a hard time. I was up next and I wanted to see what kind of a job he did. I made him clean my hat by rinsing it out and wiping it all down on the inside with alcohol wipes. I wanted to make sure he got all his boogers and cooties out of my hat. He did a good job cleaning my hat. So far so good for him.

I jumped in the water to inspect his work and then burn the rotten bars out and weld in good replacements. I went to the work area to see what the Mouth had done. I could hardly believe my eyes. All the places that needed to be cleaned and prepped were perfect. The steel was so shiny it reflected light like a mirror. He had cleaned All the areas that we needed prepped for the next two days. He had done an awesome job. Of course, I didn't say this over the radio. Rather, I said that everything looked good and I could work with what he had done. I finished my dive, got out of the water and we broke everything down for the night. It had been a very productive day and I was happy with my crew.

We went back to the hotel and I asked where we wanted to go for dinner. The Mouth said he was too tired and was just going to relax in his room. I told him not to do that, he should come out with us and I would by him a beer or two for a job well done. I don't remember where we had dinner, but we ended up at the strip club - the Playground. That was the club we went to the most often, they usually had the best prices on drinks. There was another strip club downtown that was open for several years, I don't recall the name of it, but it had low-priced drinks and pretty girls, just not as many as the Playground. The Playground also hosted Amateur Night which was always fun. Anyway, between Vinegar Flats and I, the Mouth didn't buy any drinks that night but got pretty drunk. We had a good time. I told the Mouth that he had done a very good job and I would put him in regular dive rotation. I also told him it was time for him to get a hat so he could be a real diver. He was pretty happy with the praise and said he would get a hat soon.

We finished up the job in another week and a half. All went

well, there were a couple little issues, but there always are on longer dive jobs. The Mouth had talked his dad into loaning him the money for a dive hat. He was in regular dive rotation on my jobs after that.

* * *

FUBYOYO
F. U. Buddy, You're On Your Own
Chapter Eleven

About this time, I was getting sick and tired of a lot of the crap I had to put up with doing this job. I was mostly pretty tired of dealing with all the crap I had to deal with working for Norwesco Marine. I was sort of looking around to get out of the commercial dive business. I still wanted to work in and around the water though. Maybe something with SCUBA diving? I was seriously looking for another company besides Norwesco to spend the majority of my time working with. There were quite a few in the Pacific Northwest and I routinely worked for two of the others, but I wasn't one of the regular dive crew members for either company.

One of the guys I worked with fairly regularly, but who wasn't a regular with Norwesco, was into certifications and training.

Several of the dive companies used him to teach classes that we needed to keep all our certifications up so we could continue working. He also was a SCUBA instructor. He and I worked out a deal where he would get me certified as a Dive Master with PADI so I could get a job as an assistant SCUBA instructor. That was one thing I was thinking of doing. Maybe I would look for work in a SCUBA tourist area like Belize, or Cozumel. Who knows?

Brazil and I had gone down to Brasil over the winter with the idea of starting a dive company there. The opportunities were wide open for an inland type dive company. Brasil had lots of dams and no dive company down there really knew what they were doing on dams. The dam companies also weren't really aware of the dangers of diving around dams and used SCUBA divers a lot. A lot of SCUBA divers died down there working on dams too; the same as up here in the U.S. before the late eighties. Things didn't work out for us in Brasil though. That is another story for another time, but not in this book.

I returned home in March. I did the typical early spring stuff for MPC that spring. I didn't work much in June. My wife had been pregnant all winter and the baby was due towards the end of June. My son was born on June twentieth. He was born caesarian which took a real toll on my wife. I stayed home for a couple weeks after that to take care of our new baby and deal with everything at the house so she could rest and recoup. A couple of her friends offered to help so I could go back to work. Somebody had to pay the bills!

Brazil returned to the states later in the spring to continue his diving career in the Pacific Northwest. We got a good job with Norwesco working in Lake Washington for the summer. It was a good job and fun. We worked out of the jet boat and the diving was shallow. It was a long job and none of the other regulars really wanted to work on it.

There was quite a bit of work that summer. We all worked for several dive companies each year. A lot of us stuck with one main company, but worked for other companies depending on the work. I got shit on a lot at Norwesco and, frankly, was tired of the way the owner treated me. I was looking for a new home in the diving industry. Global Diving and Salvage, a company that Brazil worked a lot for had lots of work, but I didn't want to work for them mostly because they weren't consistent with the way they paid their employees. Most dive companies were like that. I called out a lot of companies for not being fair about pay, so there were several companies that wouldn't work me. I was fine with that.

Most of us divers were in the diver's union. I expected union pay when I went on a job and I expected everyone on my crew to get the same. It really bothered me when one guy would get union pay and the other one or two guys didn't. The companies needed to do the right thing and take care of their employees. If they didn't, I wouldn't work for them.

Late that summer, there were rumours going around the diver's grapevine that a big job was coming up in Cozumel soon. I wanted to get on that, it sounded fun. I didn't really care what the work would be, but it would be great fun to work off the Yucatan Peninsula. Lots of divers wanted to work on that job. I started asking around seriously about the job and found out that a company in Seattle - Pirelli-Jacobson - did have a contract with a Japanese company that had a job to do in Mexico the following year.

I beat feet to their office by the Seattle Locks and talked to them about getting on the job. They liked my resumé but had no idea what kind of a worker I was. They wanted to know if I would work for them this year so they could see how I might work out. That was fair and I told them I would gladly work for them. I was looking for a new company to work for regularly anyway. I didn't know any of the divers that they used on a regular basis. I did know a couple guys who had worked with them before. Those divers told me that Pirelli-Jacobson liked to use SCUBA a lot. Hmm. That was not a good thing. I would just wait and see.

That fall Pirelli-Jacobson called me up and said they had a job laying fiber-optic cable in Puget Sound and wanted to know if I was available for work. I told them I was. The job was to lay fiber-optic cable for a local phone company. We would be laying cable from Point Roberts down to Whidbey Island and from Whidbey Island to Seattle by the ferry docks. That sounded interesting. I had never been on a cable-laying job before. I learned that Pirelli-Jacobson laid lots of cable; power cable, phone cable, etc. Fiber-optic cable was the new rage. The rumour was that fiber-optic cable would be replacing all the old phone lines. That could turn into a lot of work. I was told by Pirelli-Jacobson management that they had guaranteed work for the next five years just in Puget Sound. That sounded excellent to me, but I had heard that story before. I remained cautiously optimistic.

I started working for Pirelli-Jacobson in September. The first thing we had to do was set up cable-laying equipment on a barge. Along with that equipment, which took up a lot of space, we set up a Conex with toilets and a couple showers in it. We also set up some Conex boxes that were set up as bunk houses. They had a bedroom at each end with four bunks in them and a common area with a T.V., a fridge, a microwave and a hotplate in them. Not bad. The plan wasn't for the crew to actually spend our off-time on the work barge, that stuff was there just in case any of us got stuck on the barge overnight or for a couple days. Okay, whatever you say.

It took a fairly large crew to do an actual cable-laying job, and no divers except at the shore connections if all went well. I would be doing a lot of deck work. That was okay, I was looking for a change. They also hired a cruise ship from one of the companies in Seattle that ran cruises up the Inland Passage to Alaska. That would be our quarters while the job went on. The cruise ship would follow the barge and we would have a smaller boat or a tug ferry us between the cruise ship and the work barge. This was sounding like it might be quite fun.

The actual cable-laying part of the job didn't start until mid-October. We moved onto the cruise ship then, in Seattle. It sailed to northern Puget Sound that night. Pirelli-Jacobson had hired the cruise ship fully crewed, with the stewards, chefs and all. It was great. The food was really good. To get our laundry done, we just had to leave our dirty laundry in a bag outside our door at night and we would get it back the next day all clean and folded. That was wonderful. We were responsible for making our own beds and keeping our cabin clean, but the stewards cleaned the bathrooms. This was the best I had been treated on a job since my very first paid job in Cody, Wyoming. I felt like I was being spoiled. I was getting union tender pay to work the deck too.

The very first thing we did was send the bitter end of the fiber-optic to the beach up at Point Roberts. I was part of the beach crew. The bitter end was floated from the barge by a small boat close to the beach where we could grab it. There were about six of us in the water in drysuits to take the bitter end from the small craft and drag it up onto the beach where the shore connection would be made. On the beach, there was a tractor crew that had dug a trench and the cable was laid in the trench. A "trencher" was used to bury the cable in the mud under the water.

Trenchers are sometimes called "Jet Sleds." The trencher was normally dragged by the cable-laying barge which was moved around by a tug or two. When the trencher got close to the beach it would be hooked up to a tractor and dragged up to the beach until it joined the pre-dug trench. If that wouldn't work or wasn't allowed, divers would use airlifts or water jets to dig a trench to bury the cable in. The cables were buried a minimum of one meter (three feet). If the cable couldn't be buried, there were other ways of protecting it that I will go into later. Right now, at this point of the job, we were burying the cable in the mud.

Another thing divers might be needed for was if the trencher had troubles. We would have to dive down on it and straighten out whatever mess it had gotten into. It might have spun around and twisted the cable. It might have tipped over. The jets might have gotten clogged. The jets? Oh yeah, a trencher, or jet sled, is a sled that has a guide for the cable running through the middle of it from front to back. It also has a pump on it that sucks water from its surroundings and pumps it through a piping assembly that has jets configured to dig a trench that the cable will lay in. Some sleds have wheels, but most often they just have a pair of steel runners that slide along the bottom. The sled could get fouled on rocks or debris (like sunken boats or ships) or other stuff on the bottom.

The dives on the trenchers were usually good dives too. Most often they were fairly deep and it was easy to find your way to the site because all you had to do was follow the cable down to the trencher. The trenchers were usually set up with cameras and lights so the operator could watch the progress. That was good for the diver, because it usually meant everything was lit up well and you could see what you were doing down there.

So here we are at Point Roberts in mid-October dressed in our drysuits splashing around in Puget Sound. The water is Cold; Ice Cold. I was wearing my three-fingered, quarter-inch neoprene dive mitts and my hands were still so cold my fingers turned white. I knew this because they hurt and they were white when I finally got out of the water and removed my mitts. We got the cable up on the beach and tethered to the anchor point. For all of us splashing around in the water, this was where our shift ended.

That was great for us, because it meant we got to go back to the cruise ship and take a hot shower. We had a good hot dinner after the hot shower. After dinner we played some cards. Some guys watched T.V., other guys read. We weren't allowed any alcohol. This was somewhat like an offshore job in that regard. I am sure that some of the guys smuggled booze on board, but I wasn't one of them. I was no closet alcoholic. I liked doing my drinking in public, preferably with live music and pretty girls around. When I was working offshore, I was happy to stay sober.

This job ran around the clock. We worked two twelve-hour shifts; oh-six-hundred to eighteen-hundred and eighteen-hundred to oh-six-hundred. That is six to six for you landlubbers. My shift started at oh-six-hundred. I went to bed around ten p.m. I slept like a log. I was up around five a.m. to get dressed, have some breakfast and catch the boat to the barge at five-thirty. It was our practice to start our shift fifteen minutes before the hour so we could have a turn-over, that is so the guys coming off shift could tell the guys coming on what was going on and how everything was working. They would also tell us if there had been any issues or if there was something we should be looking out for. The diving part of this job was over for a while.

I was being trained as an LCE operator, that is a Linear Cable Engine operator. That machine had grips that pulled the cable from the spindle and pushed it to the back of the barge where it would go through guides and down to the trencher. The LCE also had brakes on it to keep the cable from going into the water too fast. When you lay cable in deep water, the cable hanging off the back of the barge weighs a lot and wants to slide off the barge as fast as gravity will take it. We can't have that because we'd end up with a messy pile of cable on the sea floor that the trencher would not be able to deal with.

Being an LCE operator was one of the nice jobs on the cable-laying barge because, for the most part, I was inside a control shack that was heated; or air conditioned if we were working in the summer heat. It had windows all the way around it so

I could see everything. The cable path was right in front of the control shack so the operator could watch the cable going through the grips. That way we could see that everything was working properly and keep an eye on the speed of the cable going off the back.

There was a gage that told you the speed, but it didn't account for the cable slipping through the grips. There are all kinds of different LCEs each with their own set up and configuration. We were using one built by Timberline out of Canada. It was pretty much a special build for this fiber-optic cable, because fiber-optic cable is glass fiber and is more fragile than copper cable. It had a minimum bend radius and other considerations to contend with. You couldn't pull on it as hard has you could pull on copper cable. Cracks in the glass fiber would interfere with the signal being passed through the cable.

The deck of the barge was about fifteen feet above the sea level. There was a ladder hanging off the side of the barge where boats would motor up to. We would step up on the gunnel of the boat, grab on to the ladder and climb on up to the deck of the barge. There was no little stage or boat landing, no stairs with rails; just a ladder welded onto the side of the barge. At least it had rails at the top to grab onto so you didn't have to lean over the deck and crawl onto it on your hands and knees. I had been on some barges in the Gulf where that was the practice! Also, this set up was better than the rope climbing net I had learned to use in the navy. Ha.

We used two transfer boats; a tug and a deck boat. The tug was the best because it would nose right up to the barge. We could just climb up the front of the tug, which had more things to grab onto, and was higher so we didn't have as many rungs to climb to get to the top of the deck of the barge. The other "water taxi" was a much smaller excursion boat, I think about thirty feet long, that could carry ten people or so in good weather. Its gunnels were quite a bit closer to the sea surface – like eight feet lower than the bow of the tug – and the little boat really bobbed around in rougher seas. The tug was much bigger and handled the rougher seas much better.

This time of year – the fall – storms would blow in from the Pacific - not so peaceful regardless of its name - Ocean. When a good - or bad depending on your point of view - storm blew into Puget Sound the waves could get pretty big and really choppy. There are a lot of islands in Puget Sound that really break-up and reflect the waves, so they can get really short and really high – very choppy. That little boat would bounce around like a cork in inclement weather making the transfers to the barge unsafe. Pirelli-Jacobson wouldn't use the little boat in bad weather because of that.

We all wore life jackets when making the transfers from boat to boat and boat to barge, not because we were planning on falling in, but just in case we did go overboard. Just because you had a life jacket on didn't mean you'd survive going overboard though. In the first place, the water was very cold reducing the time you could survive in it. In the second place, the boats and the barge would be bobbing around, bumping into each other and a person floating in the water might get squished between the boat and the barge. That would Not be a pretty way to go, plus it might attract sharks to the area – not that we normally worried about what was swimming beneath us – but you don't want hungry sharks around when you had a chance of falling in the drink.

I remember one morning in November a storm was headed our way according to the weather service. The company wanted to get the shift change done so we could keep working – time is money – and they didn't want to be slowed or stopped by weather. We were rushed through breakfast and hastily loaded onto the tug. We were told the chop was already bad enough that only the tug would be used for the transfers.

The small boat captain sailed his little excursion boat into a nearby harbor to wait out the storm. Both the cruise ship and the tug were bouncing around quite a bit and the transfer was quite exciting. It was a short but very bumpy ride to the barge. I remember a couple people saying we should not make the crew transfers and just put everybody on standby until the storm blew over. It was only supposed to be a couple days. Management thought that would be too costly and the crew shouldn't have that much trouble making the transfers. I mean, we hadn't even had any close calls yet, so no one was really too worried. I know I wasn't. I loved big storms at sea, they made me feel like a real salty dog. You know, wind blowing salt air through your hair and in your face, big waves splashing over the side of the boats and barges getting seawater all over the decks and soaking some of the crew – often times me. I always carried a change of clothes in my little backpack just for that kind of thing.

So, I'm on the tug and it is a bumpy ride to the barge. Lots of water is breaking over the bow of the tug. It is pretty cold out and the water is starting to freeze on the life lines going around the decks of both the tug and the barge. "Life lines" are what we call the wire rope fencing that goes around the outside edge of a ship, or barge, or any larger structure at sea. We are all wearing our winter gear, life jackets, and gloves. The tug gets to the barge and noses up to the ladder. The first guy climbs up on the bow of the tug and is hanging on to the rubber push bumper assembly. The Tug is going up and down, dropping about ten feet with every wave trough. Your timing has to be just right and you have to be ready, because the short chop makes the up and down motion of the tug a little less regular.

As soon as the bow of the tug reaches its peak, you have to grab the rungs of the ladder that are about shoulder level, then you jump your feet onto the ladder and quickly climb up the ladder as the bow of the tug drops out from under you. You have to climb the ladder as fast as you can to get out of the way of the tug's bow as it rises with the next crest of a wave. Who knows, it might be higher than the wave that put you on the ladder and you could get squished by the tug. While you and the rest of your crew are making these transfers, the captain of the tug is keeping a sharp eye on what is going on at the bow of his tug. He is working, or fighting as the case may be, with the seas to keep the bow of the tug up close to the barge so we can make the transfers as safe as possible. The first guy makes it, but says it was pretty hairy and not sure all the crew can make it.

I am up next. I climb onto the bow of the tug and hold on to the push bumper assembly. The captain is having a hard time keeping the bow pushed against the side of the barge. I try to get the feel of the wave motion up and down. I get ready to grab the highest rail I can comfortably reach as the bow of the tug rises. The rungs are white with frozen seawater. I'll just have to make sure and grab on a little tighter. The bow reaches its peak with the crest of the wave. I grab onto the rung just about level with my nose. I feel the tug start to drop out from under me and push with my feet to jump to the ladder. I feel my feet slip on the bow as I push off. I didn't get a good enough jump to get my feet onto the rungs of the ladder. I am hanging on for dear life as I feel my legs slam against the ladder. There is no support under my feet.

I hear people yelling. I know I need to get up and off the ladder as fast as I can in case the tug smashes against the side of the barge. I do **Not** want to get squished like a grape between the barge and the tug. I'm struggling to get my feet on a ladder rung, but I can't get my legs far enough out from the ladder to bend my knees so I can raise my feet enough to stand on a rung. The barge crew has hold of my arms and is trying to pull me up. That is not helping. I need the use of my arms so I can swing my body out away from the ladder a little, bend my knee and get my feet on a rung so I can climb up to the deck. I yell for them to let me have a little slack in my arms. They respond by letting me have some use of my arms and I get my feet on a rung. As soon as I feel the rungs beneath my feet, I scramble up the ladder. I am on the deck before the next wave crests and raises the tug to the ladder. I did not get squished and I am standing on the deck of the barge, albeit a little shaky. The crew is happy I didn't end up in the drink. I am too.

The captain of the tug backs away from the barge and makes an announcement over his loudspeaker that we will not be making anymore transfers until the seas calm down. Management, whether they like it or not, must comply with the captain's call. I and the first guy to transfer are the only two from the day shift on the barge – not enough to relieve the night shift. The tug takes the rest of the day crew back to the cruise ship. There are enough bunks in the Conex boxes for the night shift and then some. They all want to get off shift and go to bed, but management needs to decide what the plan is until the seas calm down. The weather service is saying that will be two days. The barge cannot be left floating in the rough seas tethered only to the fiber optic cable – that would destroy part of the cable and mean that a splice would have to be made. Splices took at least twenty-four hours and fifty thousand dollars to complete on top of the normal daily costs of the barge, cruise ship, and crew pay. Management did not want that.

It was decided that we, the barge crew, would dump some fiber optic cable onto the seabed. This would give enough slack that movement from the barge wouldn't damage the cable. Barge movement would be minimized by two tugs that would tend the barge with a few hawsers. Hawsers are big, thick, heavy ropes used to moor ships to docks and also what tugs used to tow barges and ships with. They are typically four inches or more in diameter. One tug was already tied to us, the tug that was towing the barge while we were laying the cable.

There was another tug standing by, just for these types of situations. As soon as we put the extra cable on the bottom, we got ourselves tied to the standby tug. The taxi tug also tied up to the barge, so we were secured at three points. That would minimize our movement and keep us from spinning around.

We all got very wet and cold doing this task. Lots of seawater was freezing onto the life lines. It was a solid four-foot-high ice wall all around the edge of the barge now. It looked like a scene out of Ice Station Zebra on the barge. Luckily, we had hot-water for the showers in the bathroom Conex box. There were only two showers, but they had electric tankless water heaters, so we had no fear of running out of hot water even though we had to wait in line for our showers. I and the other day shift guy were the last in line, but we didn't mind. The night shift was really tired and now cold and wet, so they deserved to get a hot shower and into bed as soon as they could.

We were on standby now. All the equipment had been secured. We kept a couple generators running for electricity, which ran everything on the barge, so we were in good shape. We had heat, hot water, microwaves, T.V. with video recorders. It was almost like a paid vacation. As long as you kept a positive attitude about it all. We did make hourly rounds to check all the shut-down equipment, keep the generators fueled up, and remove any ice that might cause a real problem. According to the weather service, the storm would only last a couple days and it was supposed to warm up quite a bit, so the ice would be melting away shortly after the storm abated.

Three days later, the wind was still blowing. Everybody was getting a little anxious. One or two-days break on an offshore job can be nice and a little refreshing. By the time the third day rolls around, everybody starts getting antsy. We were out there to work and make money. Work made the days go by faster and work pay was much better than standby pay. Truthfully, even though we signed a contract with a clause about standby pay in it, we never really wanted to "earn" standby pay. Management was also getting antsy. They were spending money for nothing at this point. The weather service kept saying the end of the storm was near. We could only hope. We went to sleep that third night to howling winds and flying snow. In the early morning when we woke up, though, the sun was out. There was not a cloud in the sky and the temperature was above freezing. Everything was starting to thaw out. It was supposed to get into the mid-fifties (Fahrenheit) sometime in the afternoon.

The tug with the day shift showed up promptly at oh-seven-thirty to swap out the crews. I and the other day shift guy who had gotten stranded on the barge were told we could come back with night shift and basically get the day off if we wanted. We looked at each other and responded that we had just had three days off, so we would rather work. Management was happy to hear that. Laying the rest of the cable down to Whidbey Island went well and there were no more issues. We made the shore landing and got the cable to the anchor point on the beach. Everybody concerned was happy, even the customer because we ended up being only a day behind schedule. The next leg was to be laid from Whidbey Island to downtown Seattle. I hoped it would go just as well as the first leg. We got the job done and nobody got hurt. That is a success.

*   *   *

This leg of the job went fairly quick. The leg from Whidbey Island to Seattle. The cruise ship wasn't needed, so it was released. We would be staying at hotels in the Seattle area. I wasn't needed on the barge. This leg was to take only a few days to lay. Instead, I was put on the beach crew. It was dive heavy this time, because both ends went over rip-rap. Rip-rap is the rocky cover on a waterfront that protects the beach from weather and erosion. That's good for the waterfront, but very difficult to bury cable under. In this situation, we were to put "bell housing" around the cable to protect it. Bell housing looks like miniature drain pipe that is usually made of cast iron and split in half. One end is belled out to fit over the smaller end of the previous piece which usually has a ring around it that fits into a groove in the bell to keep the pieces from sliding. The housing consists of two halves that fit together and get clamped so they don't come apart. It is a labor-intensive process. Like any other dive job though, there would be a three-man crew; one diver and two topside workers. Topside would be radio operator, log keeper, tender, tool and equipment sender, and standby diver. The two on topside would fill all of those positions pretty much evenly. Except one would be the designated standby diver so if there was an issue, it would already be worked out who was going in.

I would be working with two guys I had never worked with before. The big difference this time, was that I was the least experienced guy on the crew. Both of these guys had started their respective dive careers in the seventies. Both had worked several years for Pirelli-Jacobson, but also worked for several other companies in the Pacific Northwest. Neither had any one company that they predominately worked for. They worked out of the union and went to work for whoever had the job they most wanted to do. That is where I would like my dive career to be in the near future. One of these guys had spent several years as a SAT Diver in the North Sea. At the time I got into commercial diving, that was most everybody's dream job. It was *Huge* money and the most prestigious diving being done on the planet at the time. He'd had enough of it and wanted to spend more time with his family in Seattle. By this time, too, though, the Brits and the Norwegians kept most Americans out of the North Sea. The American government had passed some legislation referred to as "the Jones Act" which basically gave the American divers the right to sue any company they worked for. Diving could be dangerous and accidents were bound to happen. The foreign offshore dive companies were not happy with this legislation being passed. They just refused to hire American divers after that.

We had a barge with a storage area under the deck of the barge accessed through a couple manhole covers. The city of Seattle allowed us to tie off our barge to the pilings under the northern pier of the Seattle Ferry docks. The phone junction station was right there and our job was to stuff the bitter end of the cable into the station building, secure the cable to the outside anchor points, and cover the cable with the cast iron bell housing. The cable that had been laid by the cable-laying barge exited the mud and rested on top of the rip-rap at a depth of about ninety feet. That is where we would start putting on the bell housing. We would cover the cable with the bell housing all the way up to where it entered the junction station making sure that none of the cable would be left exposed once we completed the job.

Of course, I would be the last diver. These two guys wanted the deepest dives and they had a specific way of working together. They had worked together many times in the past. They knew that I had over ten years of experience in the dive industry, which qualified me as a "real diver" giving me a little credence, but I was still the new guy. We started setting up the dive station. We had two dive hoses, two dive radios, a dive compressor, standby air, etc.; all the equipment needed for a proper dive station. We got the main diver set up and they announced we were ready to dive. I told them we still needed to set up the standby diver and proceeded to get the second dive hose out of the storage space. I was told by both of them that we didn't need to set up the standby diver on such a shallow dive. I told them that I thought we *did* need to set it up and kept working on that. Neither of them helped with that task. They just started getting ready to dive. They told me they weren't going to help me set up the standby diver hose because it didn't need to be done. I told them I didn't mind. I was still going to set it up whether I did it myself or not.

I had it all set up and checked out before they got the first diver in the water anyway. This job took us about a week. We never did use the standby dive outfit, but I set it up every day anyway. Neither of them said anything to me about it after the first day. They just let me do my thing. I knew they knew it was the responsible thing to do. We all knew that if we *did* need it, we would all be happy that it was set up and ready to go. They didn't give me any crap for setting it up, they just didn't help with it. I didn't care. I never worked with the one guy again, not by choice, just because we never ended up on the same job again. The SAT Diver, though, I ended up working quite a bit with and he has been a really good friend for many years.

* * *

February rolled around and I was asked by Pirelli-Jacobson to start prepping the trencher and other equipment that would be used on the Cozumel job. I asked if that meant that I would be going on that job. They told me I had been slated to go. I was ecstatic. I figured that would be a really fun job to go on. Along with getting the equipment ready, we had to prepare the cable-laying barge to go through the Panama Canal. Management had figured it would be much less expensive to set up their barge in Seattle and sail it down the west coast of the U.S. and central America, through the canal and up to Cozumel. That was nice, because we would be able to load up all our personal dive gear into a locked Conex box to make the trip. That would save us all kinds of baggage handling when we flew down to Cozumel to start the job. The actual job would start in April.

I and one other guy were flown down a month early to check on cable anchor points. We had to check the positioning and the construction of the anchor itself. The anchors were large concrete blocks with large steel eyes in them. The concrete needed to be cured by the time we were to actually use them, so had to be built a month before being used. There were anchors constructed on both the western edge of Cozumel just south of San Miguel and the east coast of the Mexican mainland at the southern edge of Playa del Carmen.

We flew into Cancun. The company had a hotel room for us and we got to spend a couple days there before we had to be in Playa del Carmen. We did the touristy stuff and had a blast. We took a taxi down to Playa del Carmen where the company had a hotel ready for us to check out. They had booked the whole hotel on the internet. The hotel was owned by an American who had moved to Playa del Carmen. He had a pet spider monkey that went everywhere with him. He showed us our rooms where we dropped our bags. After that he gave us a tour of his hotel. It looked pretty nice. All the rooms had both fans and air conditioning. I only used fans when I went to warm places. I liked to acclimate myself to the climate. It was better for me to be able to work in the heat if I didn't use the air conditioning.

After the tour of his hotel, the owner took us to an Italian restaurant. He bought us dinner there, and we found out later that he was a good friend of the owners. He wanted us to recommend that restaurant to our management. They were looking for a restaurant that would open up early to serve breakfast for our crew and to make box lunches for the crew when they were working on the barge. The job was forecast to be eight to ten weeks of actual cable laying and burying.

The scope of the job was to lay seven new power cables from the mainland across the channel to the island. The cables only had to be buried on the beach approaches. Down the sides and across the bottom of the trench, we were allowed to let the cable lay on the surface. The Cozumel Channel is about eleven miles wide and over sixteen hundred feet deep at its bottom. We could not dive that deep and were not required to. The company rented ROVs which were used to observe the cable-laying progress down the Playa del Carmen side, across the bottom, and back up the side to the Cozumel approach. On the Playa del Carmen side, the trencher was to be utilized to bury the cables. On the island side, we were to do it by hand with small airlifts.

After I spent a couple days in Playa del Carmen, management had sent me to San Miguel del Cozumel. They had rented a three-bedroom house for me and two other divers who would be working on the shore connection on Cozumel island. The house they had rented was very expensive. They had found it on the internet. I had talked to the rental agency when they gave me the keys and showed me around the place. I spoke a mixture of Spanish and Portuguese with them. They thought I was originally from Brasil, because I spoke Spanish with a Brasilian accent. I never told them I was from Brasil. I told them I was American. They treated me really well and gave the company I was working for a better deal because I had spoken with them.

The management of the dive company had also sent me to the rental car agency. They had authorized me a budget of six hundred dollars a week to rent a vehicle. They told me I could rent whatever type of vehicle I wanted as long as it could carry four people or a dozen SCUBA bottles. I think they thought I would rent some sort of small pickup. Instead, speaking Spanish, I rented a T-top VW Bug for three hundred dollars a month – saved the management a lot of money. It was a very fun vehicle to drive too.

While the other guy from Seattle and I were waiting for the rest of the crew to show up, we had a lot of time to play around. Basically, we had two full days of work for the three weeks we spent there before the rest of the crew arrived. We were paid our full offshore day rate the whole time we were in Cozumel. It was fabulous! Cozumel was a great place to visit. It was lots of fun. We weren't treated like tourists, because we were working there. I also think it helped that I spoke Spanish with them. We did the touristy stuff. You know; glass-bottom boat rides, SCUBA for fun, rented little one-person boats, took the bus to Tulum. We ate at the restaurants off the main strip where the locals ate. They had fantastic local food that was very inexpensive and the beer was inexpensive also. We drank Sol, like the locals. We went to Señor Froggy's and Carlos 'n' Charlie's too. We got to know the locals so we got pretty good discounts at those places. It was the most fun I had ever had on any dive job.

The management had rented out a small marina just south of San Miguel that was owned by an American who kept his gigantic Catamaran stored there. We needed a place to moor the boats that we were using to dive out of when we did the trenching on the Cozumel approach. They also made a deal to have the marina manager work with us and hire a couple locals to work with us with the boat handling. I knew we would be working with locals and had bought a case of folding knives that I brought down with me. I gave one to every one of the locals that worked with us. They loved that and they were immensely helpful to me after that. I also brought down a case of shaded safety glasses and gave all of our local coworkers a pair of those too. They treated me very well. None of them SCUBA dived either, but they liked eating Conch. So, when my work day was over and Conch season was open, I went out and made a little dive to collect a bag full of Conch for them. They loved that too and made seafood ceviche for all of us. They also took some home to their families. That was great fun and good camaraderie.

Since Cozumel and its surrounding waters were a Mexican National Marine Sanctuary and Park, we were not allowed to drag the trencher across the bottom and up the beach. We were required to hand trench the cables in. The Mexican government wouldn't allow us to use hand jets either. We were allowed to use only a small airlift. We had to disturb the bottom as little as possible. We had to make sure the cables were laid around any rock piles or protrusions. We had to go around any forms of sea life that had attached itself to the bottom; sea fans, barrel sponges, things like that. It was easy to do here, because our visibility was over one-hundred-fifty feet on a bad day. The water was also a balmy eighty-four degrees. We were working in the channel between the island and the mainland. There was a constant half-knot current that ran from south to north twenty-four/seven. It made the work very easy.

The rest of the crew showed up the first week of April. Our barge was about a day out, maybe two. It depended upon the weather and the seas. Our weather on the Mexican Riviera had been excellent, and still was; sunny blue skies and cotton-puff clouds scattered about, and temperatures in the mid-eighties. It had rained six or seven times since I arrived, but always at night. By the time the sun was rising, the rain clouds evaporated away. All the grass and trees were green. We weren't going to be working at night. We would be working twelve-hour days. Management had said we would be working from six in the morning to six in the evening.

No cable had been laid yet. A cable laying ship had been sent over from Italy – Pirelli, you know, they were the manufacturers of the cable – with a completely Italian crew. They sort of spoke English and sort of spoke Spanish. It added to the fun, having several languages spoken on the job. At the same time our crew arrived, a Japanese dive inspection crew also arrived. I found out that it was actually a Japanese company which had contracted the job with the Mexican government and that company had sub-contracted our company to actually do the work. Of course, the completion of the job was the Japanese company's responsibility. They wanted to make sure the job was completed to their standards and satisfaction.

We had a crew meeting at the Italian restaurant that evening after everybody arrived. There our superintendents laid out the scope of the job for us. All the teams were there and all the foremen of the teams and the superintendents. The information was pretty much the same as what the other guy and I had already been told. There was some new information. We would start at the Playa del Carmen side. The Italian boat would lay the cable. Next, we would dive off our barge to bury the cable. There was almost a mile of trenching to do on that side of the channel. There was also about a quarter-mile by the edge of the actual trench – a depth of about seventy to eighty feet – where we couldn't trench because it was where the limestone was exposed. The cables would lay on top of the rock and the Playa del Carmen team would cover it with geo-mats. Geo-mats are ten-foot by ten-foot mats made of ten-inch by ten-inch blocks of concrete woven together with rope. A crane or davit would be used to lower the mat to the bottom and a diver would guide it into position.

My team would not be doing that. I would have three divers working with me on my regular team. At the beginning of work on the Cozumel side the working depth would be over eighty feet. I would need more divers. They would let me borrow divers from the Playa del Carmen team as I needed them. Two of my regulars were younger than I, and one was about fifteen years older. He had more tending and cable-laying experience, but way less diving experience. He thought he was running the crew, but actually I was. I made the decisions and wrote the reports. I made sure our banks of SCUBA bottles were filled every night and ready to go in the morning. I communicated with **all** the locals we worked with and hired them when I needed them. I dealt with the captain of the port and even paid him the required bribes supplied by the company. But I let the older guy think he was running the show. He set the dive rotation, which I didn't care about at all. I let him pick our dive crew and add whoever he wanted when we needed more people. That was fine with me. He had worked with most of these people for years, I hadn't.

There was a master bedroom in the house the company had rented. It had a jacuzzi tub in the bathroom as well as a separate two-person shower all glassed in. I had been in that room for three weeks by the time he arrived, and he never asked me to change rooms so he could have that one. A few times when we were at the bar and after he'd had several beers, he would make snide remarks about me having the nicest room and control of the only car we rented on the island. I don't know if he ever said anything to the management. I never heard anything about it. We had a maid and a cook at the house that the company had hired for us, and they always asked me when they needed direction. I just figured it was because I spoke Spanish. Nobody else that had been sent to this job spoke Spanish. We needed an interpreter and shore support person who spoke Spanish. They didn't use me for that because I was needed to run the Cozumel dive team and deal with the port captain and marina employees.

After a couple weeks, the company paid one of the guys' wives to take a Spanish class and hired her to be the shore support employee. I talked to my wife about it; thought she might want the job. She was Brasilian and spoke Portuguese, a little Spanish, a little Italian, and a little French. The company was going to pay almost seventeen dollars an hour for that job. I figured she'd jump on it, but she didn't. She didn't want to have anything to do with that job. I don't know why. Anyway, one of the other guys' wives got that cushy job.

My team would be working on the Playa del Carmen side to start. No point in us waiting around on the Italians to lay the cables. It would be almost a week before the Italians had reached the Cozumel side with the cables. When we started diving, the cable had already been laid and we would dig a trench right under the cables. The cable would fall into the trench as we dug it. The motion of the ocean would fill in the trench within a day or so. It was slow going. The barge had one dive station with a hose. That was what my team used to dive. They also had a high-pressure compressor used to fill their SCUBA bottles. While we were diving surface supplied, several of the other guys would dive SCUBA. I thought that was a little silly, but they had more bottom time that way. When we started diving on the Cozumel side, we did the same thing.

The barge deck was about fifteen feet off the surface of the water. The water was crystal clear, well not quite, but visibility was a hundred and fifty feet easy. We could see the bottom even when we were diving at seventy or eighty feet. It was incredible. We had a ladder welded to the side of the barge at an angle of about twenty degrees for getting out of the water. Most of us jumped off the deck of the barge into the water. That was fun. A couple of the SCUBA guys climbed down the ladder to get into the water. I thought that was fine. They had a lot of hoses and stuff hanging off their get up; pressure gage, regulator, octopus (spare regulator on a hose), suit whips if they were diving a drysuit, BC (buoyancy compensator) whip, knives on ropes, tools on ropes, and on and on. A couple of them looked like that cartoon of the OSHA approved SCUBA diver. Some of us got a giggle out of watching them get ready to dive. Commercial divers just dress differently and work differently than SCUBA divers. It's sort of like the difference between a real ranch hand and a city slicker that goes to "work" on a Dude Ranch.

The water here was so warm that I wasn't wearing any wetsuit or drysuit. My diver's dress was shorts, t-shirt, cotton socks, bib coveralls, high-top Converse tennies (Purple of course), and gloves. I wore three-pound ankle weights, my Bailout Bottle and my dive hat. That was it. It felt so nice to be able to dive in such a lightweight get up. It was nice too, because I was usually the last diver. I just wore the same clothes to work in as I did to dive in. That made for really quick dive turn-arounds. All our diving was done no-D. We didn't have a Deck Decompression Chamber on board. Instead, we had contracted with a couple locally run chambers, one on the island and one on the mainland, to serve us if the need arose. Hopefully there would be no need. Regardless, we needed to be ready for a worst-case scenario. I had made a point of talking to the Doctor who ran the one on Cozumel. I even ran a couple of table sixes for him, before the whole crew had come down to work. It was amazing how many SCUBA divers bent themselves down here. I was keeping a good eye on how the tourist side of diving worked. I was still mulling over the idea of getting out of commercial diving. Cozumel seemed like a really good place to do that.

Back to the commercial diving side of the barge. We pushed the tables down to the last minute. There were five of us commercial divers. We all used Superlite Seventeens. We all had way over ten years dive experience, so we knew our bodies well. When we dove at seventy feet we ran forty-nine minutes, at sixty feet we ran fifty-nine minutes and so on. We were just airlifting. We could see everything around us and we left the airlift on the bottom for the next diver. It was piece of cake diving. All we did when our time was up was shut the air off to the airlift and leave bottom. We dove how ever many divers we could fit into the twelve-hour day that way, but we didn't do any re-petting on this side of the channel. The shallower we got, the longer our dives became and the fewer divers we used.

After a couple weeks, the Italians had laid the cables all the way to the island and got the cables secured to the anchor points. The Italian cable laying ship had completed its task and left the jobsite. At that point in the job, my dive team moved our work back over to the island side of the channel. The company had sent the little "water taxi" excursion boat - that we had used in Puget Sound – down on the barge. That would be our dive boat. We set up a bank of four SCUBA bottles to use as our air supply. I had set up the manifold to allow us to swap out individual bottles as they were used up while still diving off another. That way the diver never lost air. I also had a single SCUBA bottle set up for the standby air. It was the same system we used when we used a rack of K-bottles as our source of air. The main difference being SCUBA bottles were much easier to handle than K-bottles. I took the empties in every evening to have them filled.

We started trenching at the underwater cliff edge which was about eighty feet deep. There were seven cables to trench in. Each cable had its own trench. There was a reason for this, but I don't know what it was. All I knew was that it made for a lot more work for us. That was okay with me, because these were the best conditions I had ever dived in for work. It was also one of the most amazing places to dive in the world. I could hardly believe I was being paid - and Seattle wages no less - to dive here! Was I in heaven? If not, it was a close second. I love Mexican food. I love Mexican Beer. I love Tequila. I love the Mexican people, at least all of them I had met on this adventure. They were friendly, fun, and generous. It didn't hurt that the girls (women really) were beautiful and friendly too. Big Smiles.

On top of the bottle rack set up for diving, we used SCUBA. Funny thing about commercial divers, though, is that we didn't like to get our heads wet. I guess that once you start diving a helmet, you prefer to keep a dry head while you are working. That's fine, because Superlite Seventeens have a regulator to breathe through. It is basically the same as a SCUBA regulator. We could hook our hats up to the SCUBA bottle and dive just fine. One guy would dive his hat surface-supplied like a normal commercial diver. Another guy would run the radio and keep the dive logs. A third guy would be on deck to tend and help swap out bottles. The fourth guy would dive SCUBA. If the Playa side could spare a diver or two – which they did almost every day when we were diving over thirty-five feet – we put two guys on SCUBA to help airlift. When we were doing that, those of us using our dive hats would make re-pet dives. We would dive one type of gear in the morning and the other type in the afternoon. When I dove SCUBA, I used my hat rather than a mask and SCUBA regulator so my head would stay dry. This ended up causing me an issue one afternoon.

It was completely my fault, but it almost killed me. I dove surface supplied in the morning. My depth had been just over fifty feet, so I dove a sixty-foot table. We had been diving here for about four weeks by this time. I was super comfortable in the water. I always am comfortable in the water, but the conditions here were so nice that I almost forgot I was diving. Breathing was so natural and everything so comfortable that I wasn't really thinking about all my equipment like I should have been. My equipment was in good shape and working properly, that wasn't the issue.

The issue was that I was so comfortable when I was on SCUBA, I didn't think about my limited supply of air. In my head, when my air ran out, I would just call to the surface and have the radio operator switch bottles. He was supposed to watch that and switch when the bottle pressure got down below five hundred psi. We were pushing it down to two or three hundred psi on a regular basis. Sometimes the radio operator would get distracted and not swap in time though. When that happened, I would just call over the radio to have him switch bottles. No biggy, all he had to do was open a valve. I could see the bottom of the boat. I could see the anchor chain. I could ditch my gear and get to the surface if I had to. I wasn't worried.

Here I am diving my re-pet dive at about fifty feet. Working, I would breathe the bottle down before I could get bent, that was the least of my worries. I was trenching along, looking at the sea life. My fins were in the way, so I took them off. I didn't usually wear fins when working, but it made it easier to get to the surface when I was on SCUBA. There was no umbilical to climb. Darn it! Ha ha. I'm trenching along, the crabs are scurrying around. Trigger fish are nipping at my ankles. I see Barracuda hanging off in the distance. There goes a sea turtle. It's just amazing down here. Bathtub warm water, excellent visibility, easy work.

It really doesn't get any better than this. I take a breath and I feel the air pressure go down to nothing. I say "Hey, topside! You need to swap bottles." I think to myself "Oh, Shit! I'm on SCUBA!" I try to take another breath and almost feel the air supply hose collapse in on itself. I stand up and see the bottom of the boat. My hat is too heavy for me to swim to the surface without my fins. I don't have them with me. I left them at the side of the trench a little while back. I turn around and see them over fifty feet away. I do not have time to go get them and swim to the surface. I see the anchor chain. It is only about thirty feet away. I can get there, I think. I don't want to ditch my hat. I still have air in the shell. Besides, then I would have to dry it out and probably have to replace the comms. I make a run for the chain. My body forces me to take a breath. I feel the neck dam suck into the helmet. Water comes into my hat when that happens. Fan-fucking-tastic! I grab the anchor chain and start climbing. My body forces another breath. This time I get a mouthful of water and start choking and coughing.

I can see the blue sky through the last ten feet of water. I am climbing as fast as I can. The boat hull is almost in reach. Another breath, I can't stop my body from forcing it. A mouthful of water again. I feel it burn as some of the salt water enters my lungs. I cough and choke some more. My hands are out of the water. I can see the radio operator's back. I bang on the back of the boat as I pull my head out of the water. Hanging on with one hand on the chain, I pop the catch on my neck dam and push my helmet to the back of my head. I take a big deep breath and cough the seawater out of my lungs. The radio operator turns around to see what is going on. He is right there. The back of the boat isn't all that big. He sees me struggling with my hat and grabs it by the handle, lifting it into the boat. I shrug off the SCUBA bottle on my back. He takes that up as well. I climb into the boat, sit down and take a sigh of relief. Shit! That was a close one. What an Idiot I was. I've got to make sure and keep an eye on my air from here on out. After I catch my breath, the radio operator and I laugh about the situation. Yeah, just a reminder that you always need to keep your mind on what you are doing when you are diving. Situational Awareness is our byword.

A couple weeks later we were working close enough to the beach that we could make the dives from the beach instead of from the boat. Our dive depths were under thirty feet by this time giving us unlimited bottom times. The Mexican government wouldn't let us run a compressor on the beach because of the noise. All my diving was done using surface-supplied from here on out. I was still using my hat, I just made sure to watch my bottle pressure better. We also got a couple more SCUBA divers from the barge. They were done burying the cable and were at a point where they were having to lay Geo-mats over the cables because the bottom was rocky and not sandy. We spent another week diving like this.

The last fifty feet or so going up the beach was rocky. We could no longer trench to bury the cable. Over here on the beach the Mexican government didn't want Geo-mats laid. Instead, we put bell housings similar to what we used in Puget Sound around the cables to protect them. They were still cast iron, just bigger because the power cables were bigger than the fiber optic had been. Each of us divers would spend about four hours in the water and the rest of the time supporting the divers from the beach. We would carry bell housing pieces out to the divers as far as we could, which was pretty far, because the beach had a fairly gentle slope.

The Japanese diver had shown up this last week of the job. He had finished inspecting the Playa del Carmen side and was ready to inspect this side. He carried a probe with him to make sure that we had indeed buried all the cables the required meter of depth. After he had inspected all the buried cables, he would hang around and watch us install the bell housings. It was a little unnerving having this guy hang around. He didn't bother us, he just hung in the water like a Barracuda. The Japanese supervisor watched us work from the beach while his diver was doing his inspecting. I saw them talking and figured the diver was giving his supervisor reports of what he saw under the water.

After a few days the Japanese supervisor came over to me and made a little small talk. He asked about our dive crew and what kind of experience we had. He was mostly curious as to why most of the divers used regular SCUBA gear and I used a hard hat and more commercial looking gear. He also asked how it was that when it was my time to dive, I just threw on my Bailout Bottle, my hat and ankle weights and jumped right in. He had timed me over several days and told me it took me an average of three minutes to get dressed and in the water. He noticed that the other SCUBA divers took closer to an hour to get dressed in and in the water. I told him it was because I just went in with my work clothes on. He asked why I didn't use a wetsuit and all the special SCUBA stuff – extra regulators, gauges, etc. I just told him I was fairly experienced and didn't need all that gear. I told him the water was really warm so there really was no need for a special dive suit. He smiled, shook my hand and thanked me for talking with him.

We completed the job. We loaded everything up on the barge and readied it for the trip back to Seattle. A lot of that had been done while my team was still diving because they had finished the Playa side before us. Most of the people were packing up and going home. This was kind of sad for me. This had been a great job and I really enjoyed being down here on the Yucatan Peninsula and the island of Cozumel. The company needed one person to remain for another week with one of the company managers to tie up all the loose ends. I got along really well with the manager that was staying and I volunteered to stay. Nobody else really wanted to stay anyway. There wasn't much to do. There were only a few hours of work to do spread over a week. It was a really nice way to finish up the job. I was still sad that it was over, but it was also nice to complete a job. After seeing how the tourists treated the locals down there, I decided that work in the tourist and hospitality industry was not for me. I would have to look for something different somewhere else.

*   *   *

No sooner had I got back home then I was on my way to another job. This time it was with the company that I had worked with up at Lake Pend Oreille several years ago. SoCal was a superintendent and dive supervisor for them. He had asked me earlier in the year if I would be available over the summer to work with his company on a job in the Gulf of Mexico out of Galveston. I told him I would be. I was expecting to work on the job. It wasn't a surprise. The surprise was how long the Cozumel job had lasted. I was there a couple weeks longer than I had originally thought. I only had a week at home before going down to Galveston. SoCal got me to Galveston on First Class flights. That was really nice. He had hired me as a supervisor and diver and told me that his company treated their employees very well.

This job was supposed to be the start of a five-year project laying fiber optic cable from the beach out to the oil rigs off the coasts of Texas and Louisiana. The project was called Fiberweb and was being put in place by MAERSK. The plan was to link all the oil rigs to each other and the beach with fiber optics to supply communications and internet service to the rigs. This first leg of the job would start in Galveston, loop out to several rigs then head back to the beach in Louisiana. Several crews would be working on different sections of the cable at the same time. I would be working with a crew out of Galveston.

We had a meeting in Galveston with all the divers, a lot of the main crew, the supervisors and the management team of MAERSK. They went over how the project was laid out and where we were to start. Management went over all the details that the divers and cable layers needed to know. The second part of the meeting was for upper management only. I was not upper management. I was just a supervisor and diver. SoCal was upper management though. The working crew was asked to leave for the second part of the meeting. That was fine with me, I wasn't much for meetings unless I was meeting a friend or two for a drink or two.

We hadn't been told where we were meeting afterwards and I didn't feel like heading down to the boat we were going to be working from. There was nothing for us to do until management laid out the plans. What were we to do? Most of the crew were younger than I and they had never been to Galveston before. I had been here a couple times before and knew of some good bars. There happened to be one just a few blocks from where the meetings were being held. Perfect. I took the crew there and bought the first round just to get everybody started. It was fairly early in the afternoon, maybe too early to start drinking, but I wasn't on a leash and I hadn't been given any direction. Where's the Rum?! Devious smiles.

About four rounds later, SoCal and his immediate supervisor came into the bar. Cell phones weren't really a thing yet. They were really expensive and the coverage wasn't great, so people like me didn't have them. We could have beepers, but I really didn't care for those either. I could be found if someone needed to find me. SoCal and his boss found me without even trying very hard. His boss told me I was easy to find because my reputation for a drink preceded me and he knew to look for the nearest bar. I smiled and told him I figured I'd be easy to find. What he found harder to believe was that all the rest of the crew was there with me.

SoCal and his boss sat down with us and had a drink. After

that he took us down to the supply boat that had been hired to serve as a dive vessel for us. There were four cabins with four bunks each in them. This is where we would be staying for the foreseeable future. Lovely. Just like the supply boats I was on when I worked for AOD at the beginning of my career. I really didn't think I would be on one of these again. They were smelly, hard to keep clean, and there was no privacy. We would be offshore for weeks at a time maybe and the only communication with the beach we would have would be through the marine radio which could access a landline phone. It was a big pain in the rear.

Happily, SoCal's management team was all about crew morale. It would take us several days to get the dive station set up on the boat. Most dive companies would have the crew stay on the boat while doing all this work. SoCal's bosses had rented a block of rooms at a nearby hotel for us to stay in. They wanted us to remain somewhat respectable. We were told that there would be no tolerance for being drunk on the job. That was the way I preferred it. I liked to drink, but I also wanted to make sure my crew was capable and ready to work every day.

SAIC/Maripro did a lot of diving for the U.S. Navy. The majority of the diving they did was on SCUBA. When they got jobs that required more commercial style diving, they would hire a bunch of commercial divers and tenders. Laying cable took a lot of non-diving hands, especially when loading the cable on the cable laying barge. It was labor intensive and the workers were only needed for a few days. For this type of work, they would hire people from the work-release programs run by the local prisons. We worked with some interesting characters at those times.

One memorable day, we were working close to the beach. The contract called for a coil of several hundred feet of fiber optic cable to be buried just off the beach to provide slack when splices needed to be done. We were to hand jet a pit about ten feet deep then coil the cable in the bottom of it and bury it.

SoCal had the greener divers do the hand jetting but he wanted a more experienced diver to do the coiling because the chances of getting tangled up were extremely good. I would do the coiling. Even though we were diving at a depth of less than thirty-five feet, there was exactly Zero visibility. There was no point in having a light on my helmet because all it did was let me see a yellow-brownish glow through my faceplate. If I put my thumb on my faceplate and spread my hand out in front, I could only see to the middle of my palm. I did not use a light. As I was coiling the cable, I would stir up the silt in the bottom of the pit.

In this silt lived a very small form of sea life called "Dinoflagellates." They were bioluminescent, meaning they flashed bright blue when disturbed. As I was working, there were blue flashes all over the place. It was a little reminiscent of the blue spots you see when you are about to pass out from carbon dioxide poisoning, which is what I thought might have been going on at first.

It is fairly easy to over breathe your hat, especially when diving deeper. Superlite Seventeens have a dial-a-breath on them so you can lighten the tension on the regulator spring making it easier to breathe. It is designed to relieve just this issue. I wasn't diving that deep, but I was working pretty hard laying this coil. I checked my dial-a-breath, it was fine. I asked topside to check my air pressure. They responded all was fine. I was feeling fine; no headache which usually accompanies carbon dioxide poisoning. I thought about it a bit and realized it must be the dinoflagellates flashing blue. I kept on working.

There were also little stinging creatures in the mud. My first dive in this pit, I was wearing my normal warm-water get up; shorts, t-shirt, bib coveralls, socks, high top tennies, and gloves. I was getting stung a lot, especially on my forearms and lower legs. It wasn't too bad and didn't really hurt. It felt more like being poked with a pin. It was more irritating than anything. The next dive I made though, I put on an eighth-inch soft-stretch full-body wetsuit. I wore my bib coveralls over that and neoprene booties. That kept me from getting stung. I would rather be as comfortable as possible when I was working.

For the past couple days, a small tourist fishing boat had been hanging within a couple hundred feet of us. A couple times we had to tell them that they needed to stay at least two-hundred-and-fifty feet away from us. We had our Diver Down and Alpha flags flying, but it was quite common for personal boat operators to ignore those. We figured our work was stirring up food that was attracting fish. I think it was. And I think those smaller fish were attracting bigger fish. The water was pitch black and we couldn't see anything, so we really had no idea what was swimming in our immediate work area.

I do remember, as I was coiling the cable and getting close to finishing, something bumped into me. At first it was just a little bump, like a nudge. Then I got bumped again. This time it knocked me over. I couldn't see anything, so I don't know what it was. I had studied biology and sea life so I knew that sharks liked to circle their prey and bump into it before they actually attacked it. I thought this might be a possibility. Sharks don't attack commercial divers though. I had never heard of a shark attacking a surface supplied working diver. SCUBA divers, sure, but those kooks provoke the sharks and put themselves in situations just asking to be attacked. My wife recently checked and discovered that there have been thirteen commercial divers killed by sharks in Australian waters between nineteen-sixty-two and two-thousand-seventeen. Huh, who knew? Scientists I guess. Ha! I wasn't worried, but I did make sure my knife was handy and I opened the free flow on my hat to let a lot of bubbles escape. I figured the noise and motion from the bubbles might scare off the shark if that's what it was. I didn't get bumped again, so maybe it worked.

At the end of this day, we went back into the port of

Galveston. As we were working this close to shore, we moored in Galveston rather than spend the nights bobbing around the Gulf. We were not working nights. Anyway, the fishing boat that had been hanging around us, followed us into the beach. We usually moored next to a bait shop that had a bar and had outdoor seating on the wharf. The little boat moored next to us and the captain jumped off his boat and came running up to ours. He was trying to catch us before we all deboarded. He had seen that we had a davit on our boat. He asked if we might use it to unload his catch of the day. He and his crew had landed a fifteen-foot Bull Shark in the afternoon while they were fishing near us. They had no way of getting that big of a fish off their boat. We unloaded it for them. They were happy enough that they bought us several rounds of beer that evening. I figured that must have been what had been bumping into me while I was coiling the cable. May I have another beer, please!

*   *   *

Later on, working on the same job – the Fiberweb project – we were somewhere out in the Gulf of Mexico. It's hard to tell from the water where you really are. We were trenching in cable that had already been laid. We were using a Norwegian trencher that had wheels. It was pulled by the supply boat. We had a little dive tender named FUBYOYO. I didn't know what that meant until I asked SoCal and he told me it stood for Fuck You Buddy, You're On Your Own. I thought that was funny. It was the Perfect name for a Dive boat too, because divers usually worked in the water all by ourselves. We had surface support sure, but the actual work was done by one guy in the water by himself. It reminded me of that Farside cartoon by Gary Larson. You know, the one where the Deep Sea Diver in

Mark V gear sees his dive boat with his air supply going down to the bottom of the sea? Funny, sort of. Don't think about it too much you wives and girlfriends.

The FUBYOYO was set up with a bank of high-pressure bottles as the main air supply for the divers. They weren't K-bottles like we normally used, instead they were some fiberglass containers, maybe Russian made(?), that held more pressure, so more air. Our working depth here was between one-hundred-thirty and one-hundred-forty feet. We were diving air and using the USN tables. The worst tables for this depth at this time. I was supervising and diving. SoCal was superintending, supervising and diving once in a while. We were not using any SCUBA divers on this part of the job. Everybody was a hard hat diver, even though a couple of them had only been navy trained. The Mouth was even in on this job. It was fun working with him down here.

We had a diver who had worked with Torch before they were bought out by Tiberon. We had another young diver, SoCal knew him from previous work, who was comfortable in the water but had Terrible umbilical sense. He got tangled up all the time. I ended up calling him "Spider" because he wove a web with his umbilical and the fiber optic cable all around the trencher. We were diving two divers at a time quite a bit on this part of the job, because a lot of the work went quite a bit faster with two hands rather than just one. Plus, we wanted diver overlap as we swapped out the divers because we didn't want to leave the trencher unattended. Spider would invariably get tangled in the second diver's hose. That second diver was usually me. I didn't have any problem untangling him. We didn't have Round Robin communications, so we couldn't talk to each other. When I needed to untangle him, I would ask topside to tell him to just relax and pretend he was a bag of potatoes. That way he wouldn't interfere with me while I was untangling us.

In reality, he probably only got tangled up three or four times, but by that point he was Spider and we all enjoyed giving him a hard time about it. I do have to say that his umbilical sense did improve dramatically over the span of that job.

*   *   *

One day we were setting everything up to dive on the job and going through all our checks on the dive system; comm checks, air supply checks and all that. We had five or six pressure gages on the air supply system from the actual tanks themselves and along the piping to the Dive Control Station. The gages were checked for accuracy every six months and labeled as such. Still gages would fail. No big deal. We had several gages measuring the same system.

Anyway, during our checks I noticed one of the gages was not reading properly. It was reading about a hundred pounds low. It was reading about seventy-two psi when all the other gauges were reading one-hundred-seventy-five. In my personal tool kit, I had a gage on a quick-disconnect for just this issue. I would plug it into the system and check the pressure. I had this gage checked for accuracy in between every job I did. I plugged my gage in and the system was pressurized to one-hundred-seventy-five pounds just like it was supposed to be. As far as I was concerned, we were ready to dive. Normally I would just put a red tag on the gage or put a couple wraps of red electrical tape over the face of the gage. That is not how things are done in the navy, though.

Our two navy divers were really upset about the gage not reading the proper pressure. They were saying that we couldn't dive until the situation was remedied by replacing the faulty gage. Okay, we'll replace it. No big deal. I went looking for a gage. We didn't have a spare. We could get one from the beach, but that would take a couple days. A boat would have to go into the beach to get one and return with it. SoCal told us that was impractical and couldn't we just dive anyway, knowing that all the other gages were working properly? I was fine with that, as were all the other divers, except for the senior navy diver.

He was adamant that we shut down dive operations until the gage was replaced. I told him that he didn't have to dive if he wasn't comfortable with the situation, but we were commercial divers and we did things differently than the U.S. Navy did. We were construction workers and big money was involved. We couldn't shut down the whole job over a little gage that didn't matter at all in the grand scheme of things. I reminded him that there were three ways to do things; the Right way, the Wrong way, and the Navy way! Ha ha! He didn't think that was very funny and put his foot down. There would be No diving until the gage was replaced.

Well, we didn't have a replacement gage, and we weren't going to send a boat on a two-day round trip just for a gage. We also weren't going to stop diving operations. What do we do? Tie a large shackle or three to this guy and throw him overboard? Just kidding! Geez! I had found a quarter-inch plug in our box of spare fittings. So, I removed the bad gage, Teflon taped the plug and inserted it into the top of the tee where the gage came from. I pressured up the system and checked for leaks; found none. I announced the situation had been remedied and we were ready to dive. The navy guy didn't believe me so I asked him to go check the system and if it didn't pass his inspection, we wouldn't dive until it did. He checked out the system and came back satisfied. We were ready to dive from his point of view also. Another crisis averted! Smug smiles and giggles. Sometimes you just gotta do whatcha gotta do.

*　　*　　*

The last week in July, basically in the middle of this Fiberweb job, was the anniversary of my second wedding. My second wife didn't really like me going away for work all the time. She did, however, enjoy the money and the time off I got. She was from Brasil. I had met her in Brasil. The time off I got from diving allowed us to make trips to Brasil fairly often. My work schedule also had me working on birthdays, holidays, and other important days families like to celebrate together, like wedding anniversaries. This would be our Seventh wedding anniversary. I think I had missed the last five, maybe six. I had also missed her birthday five times out of the past seven years we had been together. Funny thing was, I had never missed a Christmas nor had I ever missed my daughter's birthday, nor my son's birthday. I didn't plan it that way. That was just the way the work schedules had played out. I think she thought it was a devious plan of mine though.

We were in troubled waters with our relationship. I was doing what I could to keep the marriage together for the kids, but it was not looking good. Anyway, I had been given an ultimatum by her; be home for our wedding anniversary or don't bother coming home ever again, and good luck trying to see your kids ever again. I told SoCal that I really needed a few days off to spend my anniversary with my wife. He was great about it and said I could have a week if I wanted. I told him four days would be fine.

When I got home, my wife was happy about that. I had salvaged the marriage for a little while longer anyway. While I was home, though, I got news that my good friend, the Texan, had died on a job in Massachusetts. It was the Deer Island project, there is a book about it. That really tore me up. When the job was first being bid, I had been asked to go on it. So had the Greek, Blanchard, and Kalispel. We all talked about it and didn't like the way it was being set up.

One huge problem Kalispel and I had with it, was the penetration pay. It was to be a penetration of about nine miles, which we figured should pay about forty-thousand dollars just in penetration pay. Another issue was the hourly pay, which was considerably less in New England than it was here in the Pacific Northwest, like half of what we were used to. That would not work for me. The owner of the company and the contractor just laughed at that. So, of course, I was out. The other guys had their own issues with the job. I don't really know what those were.

I had talked about the job with the Texan and he agreed that he wasn't sure about the actual set up or the pay. The plan was to utilize a couple of Humvees to transport the dive gear and divers up and down the pipe. He really wanted to drive a Humvee and looked at this as a perfect opportunity to do so. Whatever, you could rent one if you really wanted to drive one. Just be careful and don't do anything stupid. Yeah, yeah.

By the time that job was being set up, I was working with Pirelli-Jacobson. I don't know much about what went on other than what the guys on the job actually told me. The Coeur D' Alene Kid went on that job along with the Texan, the Rancher, another kid from the Pacific Northwest, and Montreal, the engineer from east Canada. Norwesco Marine had made some sort of deal with a small dive company from the northeast to complete the project. A few of their guys would be on that job too. If you are really interested in that story, read the book. It is not my story to tell. I do know that if the Coeur D' Alene Kid hadn't kept his senses about him, there would be five dead instead of two. Montreal wasn't as much to blame as the book implies either. He ended up being the scapegoat though.

I called the Texan's wife to see how she was doing. She was not doing well as you can imagine. She told me she was planning a memorial for him at her house in August. I told her I would be there for sure and that if she needed anything at all from me, just to let me know. I felt horrible for her. I was very sad myself. The Texan had become a very good friend. After my four days back home and the little anniversary celebration with my wife, I returned to the Gulf of Mexico to continue working with SoCal, the Mouth and the others.

*   *   *

When I got back to the FUBYOYO, everything was the same. It was like I had never left. The weather was even the same – hot and sunny. It was a great job, because we weren't around any oilrigs. Our outfits on deck were shorts, flipflops or low-cut tennies, and gloves. When I was diving, I wore my warm water get-up. Most of the other guys wore some sort of shorty or lightweight wetsuit. The water was so warm and there wasn't any dangerous sea life around, so I just didn't see the need for a wetsuit. We were far enough out from the beach that the visibility was actually pretty good. If we didn't stir up the bottom mud too much, we could see fifty to seventy-five feet. That was fabulous. There were some fish swimming around. It was a sandy or muddy bottom with no protrusions and no oilrigs, so not much to attract life. It was like an underwater desert.

The job went well. I don't remember any other exciting or exceptional episodes taking place for the rest of the job. I met a lot of new people. I made some good friends. I worked with some good people. I got to know both SoCal and the Mouth better. Both have become good friends. The big diving part of the job was completed in August. There was still a lot of work to do on the beach to finish the project. SAIC/Maripro had their own crew who handled that work. I returned home to Spokane the last week of August to go to the Texan's memorial. I also spent a lot of time with my family.

The last weekend of August, I went to the memorial for the Texan. My wife and I went over a couple days before so we could help set up everything. The Texan's wife had decided to have it at their place in Snohomish, Washington and not in a church. I thought that was nicer and more akin to what the Texan would have wanted. The Texan's family came up from Texas too. It was nice to see them so I could give them my condolences. Lots of hugs and lots of tears were spread around. Quite a few people showed up, most of us were divers. It was a very emotional gathering. The Texan was a great guy and was a good influence on a lot of people's lives. It's been twenty-some years and I still miss him.

In mid-September I went back down to the Gulf to help SoCal finish up some river crossing work with the Fiberweb project. The Mouth was there when I got there and we worked together like we never left the project.

After that I was really ready to work for a different dive company. I really didn't like the direction that Norwesco Marine was headed. The owner had been taking more advice and direction from the Canadians and less from the people that were actually getting the work done for him. It seemed that we were getting more crews and more work, which was good in a way, but we were losing the family feeling of the work. It was becoming more like working for a regular company and most of us were treated like a number rather than a person.

*　　*　　*

The week before Christmas I got called to do an emergency job at Madison Dam in Ennis, Montana. It seems they were having the electrical panels replaced in the operator's station when one of the electricians pushed the Big Red Emergency Dam Shutdown button. That slammed the headgate down.

Madison Dam has a fourteen-foot diameter penstock that is about a mile-and-a-quarter long. The dam was operating at about eighty percent when the gate slammed shut. Water had been flowing down the penstock at around two knots. That resulted in a very large water hammer to slam back into the gate popping the head gate out of its guides. The gate could not be operated as a result of that action.

The electrician was not an employee of the dam. He had been sub-contracted to do the electrical work. This was one of the new policies of MPC. All this work would have been done by the company employees in the past. Now, however, the powers that be figured it was more cost effective to contract out all this electrical repair work. They were working on reducing their permanent workforce. That really saved them a lot of money in this instance. Sarcastic smiles.

I went to Ennis the second day after Christmas. I took Vancouver and Duck Fart with me. We were ready to dive the next day. We showed up at the dam in the morning and set up our dive station in the control shack. It was really cold outside, about ten below zero at noon. The water was really cold too. It had been measured at twenty-eight degrees Fahrenheit. The only reason it didn't freeze solid was because of the current and the turbidity of the water. We were diving drysuits. I had requested hot water, but the owner of the company had said it wasn't in the budget. It probably was, he just didn't want to put the money out for it.

It was so cold that we couldn't stay in the water any longer than forty-five minutes. Our hands would quit working so we would have to exit the water. Climbing out of the water, our gloves froze to the ladder and the regulator on our dive hats would freeze in the position they were in just as the helmet left the water. It was either free-flowing like crazy or frozen shut and no air was flowing at all. The tender would stand above the ladder and pour hot water from the coffee maker on the diver's hands and helmet as he climbed the ladder.

Every day I told the owner of the company that we could really use a hot water unit and every day he would tell me there wasn't money for it in the contract. Sure there wasn't. The dam crew kept asking why we didn't have a hot water system with us. We ended up swapping out divers so often that in an eight-hour day, we only got about five hours of actual dive time. To my way of thinking, that wasn't very cost effective, but the boss didn't want to hear it.

Vancouver and I ended up cutting through the brass nut that secured the shaft to the top of the gate. That took several dives because of the cold. Next, we rigged the gate to be pulled out with a crane. That took much longer than normal too because of the cold. This job was going really slowly because of the cold mostly, but also because of the damage to the gate and the gate guides. Those had been blown out by the force of the gate being pushed upstream. The damaged guides had to be burned out and new guides had to be drilled and bolted back in place. There was also some welding to do to them to get them back into useable condition.

MPC wanted us to work six days a week. We did that first week, which meant that we were there over New Year's. Of course, the MPC crew shut down early on the thirty-first because the Longbranch Saloon always had a special Lobster Dinner for New Year's Eve. You had to make reservations several months in advance. It was The place to go in Ennis for New Year's Dinner. We didn't have reservations, but the owners knew me so they set up a table just for me and my crew. They treated us very well. They felt bad for us that we were away from our families. The dinner was Mahvelous! We tipped them very well.

After dinner we went to the Silver Dollar Saloon. They were having a Champagne Party to celebrate New Year's Eve. That was a first-come-first-serve party. It was packed. The owners of that place knew who we were too and had heard that we were in town. They also felt bad for us and had saved a table just for us. Duck Fart loved that.

Vancouver was pissed at his brother for not letting us have hot water. He had decided that he was heading home on the first of January – a Saturday that year – and he was not coming back. The owner sent me another hand for Monday. I can't remember who it was, but by the end of the week, he had decided he wasn't coming back either. The conditions were just too cold for him too. He would not dive there without hot water.

The following week, the boss was not happy. He thought everybody was complaining about nothing. He never worked in these conditions, so he didn't have a clue. I had worked many jobs in the Montana winters and also in the northern Cascades in the winter too. I knew the conditions well. I think the deal was that I didn't kiss anybody's ass so I didn't always get the equipment I wanted to do the jobs I was supervising. The customers were always happy with the work my crews did when I was supervisor. Nobody ever got bent on the jobs I ran either.

Anyway, the boss sent Blanchard over to see what the deal was. He was hoping that Blanchard would tell him that the job was easy and the conditions were fine. Of course, when Blanchard showed up Monday morning, he couldn't believe how cold the water was. He dove a couple times and had to come out after forty-five minutes like the rest of us. His hands were white, his lips were blue and it took him a long time to warm up. I also think this was the first time the regulator on his dive hat froze up when he exited the water.

Blanchard called the boss and told him that the conditions were exactly as I had said. He also told the boss that if he wanted to get this job done in a timely manner, hot water had to be utilized. A hot water set up arrived that Wednesday. Blanchard was having fun on the job, but couldn't stay the following week. He had another job to run.

The boss sent me Kalispel for the final week. There was a fair amount of welding to do and Kalispel was a good welder. With the hot water, we could get about seven hours of dive time in an eight-hour day. With that we finished up the job that week. A job that PPLM was hoping would only take two weeks at most to complete actually took four weeks to finish. At least the engineers were happy with our work once it was completed.

*   *   *

IT'S HUMANLY IMPOSSIBLE, BUT I THINK I CAN DO IT
Chapter Twelve

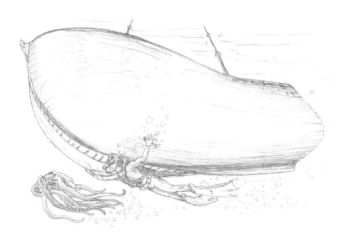

There was a fair amount of work going on this spring and quite a lot scheduled for the summer with other dive companies. I was still looking for somewhere else to work or something else to do. The problem is that I was too ingrained in the dive industry. I liked the diving. I liked the travelling. I like that each job was different from the others. I liked that I got to work outside rather than be stuck in some office somewhere. I liked that I could take time off whenever I felt like it. The pay wasn't too bad either.

I started working with a smaller company out of Bellevue, Washington by Seattle over the past year. It was a very small company run by a very intelligent man. He ran his company out of his garage and rarely had more than one crew working at a time. His main Diver and supervisor was an ex-Marine. He still looked like a Marine and really liked to yell like a Drill Sergeant when things weren't going well, or when he got excited, which was more often than you would hope.

The very first job I did with this company was in Caldwell, Idaho a couple years earlier. I had been called by a friend of mine who had gone to the same dive school as I, but had graduated the year after me. He said he needed a diver to meet him just outside of Caldwell for a dive job. He wanted to know if I would be interested. I would be paid for my travel time – six hours each way – and I would be put up in a hotel for one night – the night before the job. It would only be a one-day job so he was having a hard time finding someone to do it.

I told him I would be happy to do it. I asked what the job would entail and he told me we were just replacing a worn-out pump in an Anaerobic Settling Pond. I had no idea what that was. He said the bottom of the pond was only fourteen feet. Also, there would only be two of us who had been to dive school. His brother would join us as the tender. I was okay with that.

I drove down to Caldwell and met my friend at the hotel. The weather was great; sunny and warm. It got pretty hot actually the next day when we were working. He went over the job. It was fairly simple – just pullout the old pump and put in the new. There were eight bolts on a flange on either side of the pump and four mounting bolts that held the pump to the support frame mounted to the floor of the pond. Easy-peasy. Hah!

In the morning we got to the worksite and set up our dive station on the side of the pond. The pond was above ground so where we set up was actually the top of a giant rectangular berm that formed the pond. The stuff in the pond stank. It stunk real bad. It almost smelled like sewer water. I asked him what was in this "anaerobic digesting pond."

He told me that this was a factory where they made many potato products; chips, fries, hash browns, stuff like that. They also manufactured cottage cheese. All the waste products were sent to these digesting ponds to break down the waste into a more liquid form which would then be pumped to another part of the plant and turned into fertilizer. It was a settling pond just like in the sewer plants and it was basically the same biological process going on here as in a sewer plant settling pond. No wonder it smelled so bad. Oh well, work was work, I guess.

We had looked at the blueprints and knew where the pump was supposed to be. I would be the first diver. I would go down, find the pump, tie a downline to it and remove the old pump. My friend would be the second diver. He would guide the new pump into position secure it in place and make all the necessary connections. The customer had sent us a couple employees and a carry deck to raise and lower the pumps. Nice.

I got dressed in, made all the necessary checks and jumped into the pond. It looked like clam chowder from the surface and it felt like swimming in clam chowder when I jumped in. It was quite warm and very thick. In fact, the liquid was so thick that it didn't let my regulator work properly. I had to make the whole dive on free-flow mode. That was okay, we had a compressor with us, so I had all the air I needed.

This stuff was so thick that my regular weight belt was not enough. It brought back memories of diving int the pond at the Champion Lumber Company with Boston and Hope. Awe, the life of a diver. I smiled to myself. I had to get back to the surface and put on my friend's weight belt as well. That worked and I was on the bottom in no time.

There was absolutely no visibility. It was exactly what you would imagine diving in thick New England style clam chowder would be like. I moved in slow motion and fought every step of the way. The piping was laid out exactly like the blueprints so it was easy to find the pump. I got the downline established and removed the pump. Topside sent the rigging down the downline, so I didn't have to search for it. That was nice. I finished my tasks, guided the pump to the surface and exited the soup. My dive was done.

We took a short lunch break. The customer employees were union and had to take their designated half-hour lunch. We couldn't work without them, so we took a lunch break too. They had brought their lunches with them as we had, so we all enjoyed a nice relaxing lunch in the sun.

After lunch, my friend got dressed in and finished the job. All went well and everybody was happy. The only issue was the smell of our dive gear. It stunk. It stunk like we had soaked it in a septic tank. I was glad I had driven my truck and could just throw it in the back so I wouldn't have to deal with the smell on the drive back home. It took several weeks for that smell to wear off. I got kidded with by the other divers on the next few jobs I went on because of the smell. We always joked that the one type of diving we would Not do, was sewer system diving. Somebody had to do it though. I just never thought I would be one of them. And I wasn't; yet.

*   *   *

In the fall I got notified that there was a substantial job on a dam about an hour south of Great Falls. It was scheduled to last eight to ten weeks, or more if things didn't go well. The job was on Holter Dam just out of Wolf Creek, Montana. Montana Power Company had a house at the little community at the base of the dam that they had told us we could stay in while we worked at the dam. That would be perfect. The dam foreman and two operators lived there with their families making up the little community.

Over the summer, MPC had actually been bought out by PPL – Pittsburgh Power & Light. They were an international power company. So now, everything that used to be MPC was now PPLM – PPL of Montana. Except for the transmission of power – that became Northwestern Energy. It was a sad day for people that owned MPC stock after all the dust settled from those transactions. That didn't affect us much. PPL kept everything and all the people pretty much the same at first. It took them years to implement their changes. It was very slow in affecting our relationship with all the MPC employees and dam crews. The worst consequence for me was that some very good engineers and other employees opted for early retirement. They lost some good people.

Since we were going to be working there for so long, I moved my family over into that little house. My daughter was ready to start First Grade and Wolf Creek had a little two-room school with a gymnasium there. They taught students from kindergarten to sixth grade there. That would be great for my daughter. I had been trying to get my family to move to Montana for several years anyway. The Brasilian didn't like small towns though. She didn't like snow and cold weather either. What was I thinking?

I would be getting two guys on my crew. One was Puppy Dog Eyes and the other name the owner of the company couldn't quite remember. The name he mentioned sounded like Spider's real name. That would be good. Spider had wanted to try diving in the Pacific Northwest, but he was from Colorado and didn't know any divers from there, besides me. He didn't have much experience and he wasn't really sure he wanted to be a diver. He had been a pretty good worker on the job with SoCal. I was hoping it would be him. It wasn't.

The Friday before the start of the job, I loaded the flatbed truck up with our dive system. We still weren't towing a chamber around with us unless mandated by the client. We had a deal with the Air Force base in Great Falls to use them if we had any issues. That was an hour drive away from Holter Dam. That was still closer than a helicopter ride to Virginia Mason in Seattle. Anyway, as I started loading the truck, the owner came out and showed me the new guys resumé. As he handed it to me, he was saying "You should see this guy's resumé, it's very good and he has lots of experience relevant to what we do." I had heard that so many times before and it rarely meant the guy was a good diver.

I looked the resumé over. There were no photos of the guy himself, but he had photos of many of the jobs he had been on. He was from Illinois, had gone to a University in Montana and had spent the last few years working on the dams for the Tennessee Valley Authority. This thing was as thick as a book. Are you kidding me? I was Not looking forward to working with this guy. Oh well, I would give him a chance, work with him, and give him the benefit of the doubt. He was to meet me at the dam Monday morning.

I got to the dam site on Sunday night. The other two guys were there bright and early Monday morning. We met with the PPLM crew from Great Falls and the PPLM engineers from Butte. That was the normal protocol at the start of bigger projects. Sometimes the engineer would stay through the whole job and sometimes they would only stay until things got rolling. We all went up to the top of the dam. We were meeting with some other contractors also, who were supplying equipment for part of the job.

The scope of this job was to replace the batter boards on the spill gates. There were no head gates for the spill gates and

PPLM wanted to do the work on the spill gates in the dry. In fact, there would be no way to do the work at all without some sort of caisson or bulkhead to block the water from coming into the work area. A company from Idaho had a "Floating Bulkhead" that I had worked with before on other dams. This job would be the first time this type of bulkhead had been used on the Montana dams. The PPLM engineers had asked for our input as divers, because they knew that I had worked with similar bulkheads in the past. I had, in fact, worked with this same exact bulkhead on dams in Idaho. The PPLM's engineers idea was that if this bulkhead worked, they would have the company from Idaho design and build a special modular bulkhead that could be configured to work on several of PPLM's dams.

We met on the top of the dam and went over the scope of work. The first step was for the divers to clean the algae and any protrusions off the bullnoses and the concrete face at the bottom of the spill gate. These would be the surfaces that the bulkhead would set against. The second step was to place the bulkhead in position. The third step was to seal any leaks between the bulkhead and the sealing surfaces we would clean in the first step. The first gate would be the slowest and the one where we would try different scenarios until we found one that worked.

We set up our dive station and gear, getting ready to dive. The company from Idaho unloaded their bulkhead and placed it in the water. The engineers from PPLM watched the progress. The Rainbow crew assisted us as we needed. We also got the use of one of the dam operators from Holter dam. He was a tough little bugger. One of the last Real Cowboys left in the west. He was less than six-feet tall, but he was built like a tank. The way he was described by other workers was that a task might be "humanly impossible, but I think he can do it." We loved that statement and adopted it for ourselves.

I had Puppy Dog Eyes dive first. His task was to clean

the sealing surfaces with a pressure washer and look for any protrusions that might interfere with the bulkhead seals. The bottom of the sealing surface was at twenty-four feet. Adjusting for the altitude, I dove him on a forty-foot table. The new guy from Illinois had never worked at altitudes that required decompression schedule adjustments before. I explained to him what I was doing and showed him how the table adjustments worked. He actually paid attention to what I was teaching him. He was also a very diligent worker. He knew his way around a dive station, even though we did things a little differently than what he was used to.

Puppy Dog Eyes got the surfaces washed down in about three hours. He had discovered tie wire protruding from the concrete face along the bottom. He could cut those off with wire cutters. He also found several bolts protruding from the bullnoses. We had a Broco torch that he used to burn those off flush with the concrete face. When he had finished those tasks, we brought him back to the surface and out of the water.

By this time, the company from Idaho had prepared their bulkhead. The bulkhead had separate horizontal chambers inside. On each section were valves that they could open to fill each chamber with water and sink the bulkhead in the vertical position. The idea was to put enough water in the lower sections to sink the bulkhead to the proper level for the specific gate it would be placed in front of. The bulkhead was made of steel and needed some means of sealing the area where the steel would butt up against the concrete. Their idea, and what they brought with them, was a U-shaped tube made of Hypalon – the same material used to make white-water rafts. Their idea was to fill this tube with air and it would form a water-tight seal between the concrete and the steel. Yeah, No. Sorry guys, that will not work. Hypalon is tough material, but not that tough. In the past they had used soft rubber seals that had to be replaced every few times the bulkhead was moved. They were looking for a seal that would last longer.

I told them the tube wouldn't handle the air pressure inside the tube when they were trying to seal it. They assured me that it would, they only needed a few psi to inflate it. Sure, I told them. That is correct before you put the thing in the water. What will happen though, is that the water pressure at the bottom of the gate will pressurize the air to about ten to twelve psi. Then you have the added pressure of the bulkhead pressing against the seal. You could do a rough calculation to see what the pressure would be. I didn't know what it was, but I knew it was a lot. I am pretty sure that much pressure will pop the tube.

I was told that, yes, the pressure might be that much at the bottom of the gate, but it would only be atmospheric pressure at the top of the seal. Yes, but you have a hollow, flexible tube. Whatever pressure is exerted at the bottom will be felt at the top in a closed system. We're talking gage pressure here, not Absolute. In Absolute pressure, what the tube is actually dealing with is twenty-five psi or so – fourteen-point-seven psi plus ten to twelve psi equals twenty-four-point-seven to twenty-six-point-seven psi, plus the pressure from the bulkhead itself. Anybody want to figure that out? I don't think the Hypalon can handle that kind of pressure. I was assured that the seal would hold. Okay, we'll see.

The company from Idaho put the seal on the bulkhead then filled the bottom two sections with water to make the bulkhead float in the upright position. When the bulkhead got vertical the sealing tube held. You could see the Hypalon had a lot of pressure in it. It looked like it might pop any time. The PPLM crew had a couple small boats that they were using to push the bulkhead into position. They slowly got the bulkhead lined up where they wanted it and secured it in place with ropes. The next step was to remove a couple boards from the spill gate and start to drain the water out from the space.

As soon as the water level downstream of the bulkhead dropped about three inches, there was a very loud *Pop!* The seal had ruptured at the top on both sides. I smiled. Not because I was happy that the seal failed, rather, I knew I had been correct and now everybody else knew that too. I was asked what I thought should be used to seal the interface. I suggested hard rubber P-seal just like what most gates on dams used. It could be permanently attached to the bulkhead and would be much more durable than a Hypalon tube or the soft rubber they had used in the past.

The bulkhead was re-floated in the horizontal position so the seals could be replaced. My dive team continued cleaning the sealing surfaces. There were thirty-one spill gates to deal with. If everything went well, we might get two cleaned per day. That meant we had at least fifteen days in just cleaning. We didn't work weekends, so that was a minimum of three weeks. Along with cleaning, though, we had to seal the leaks around the bulkhead after it was set. Just that task would take us half-a-day if all went well. That just doubled our job length. We were aware of this before we took the job, so it was no surprise to us.

We had actually figured that this would be an eight to ten-week job. We had agreed to help the PPLM crew with the movement of the bulkhead and other tasks that would be easier with the use of a diver. We were told it would take two to three days to get the P-seal material. We prepped the gate slots as we could. When the P-seal arrived, we helped put it on.

Puppy Dog Eyes was married and he liked to touch bases with his wife on a daily basis. There was new technology out called the internet, I had heard about it and used it a little, but I had no idea what a powerful tool it could be or would become. Puppy Dog Eyes was more in tune with that stuff. He also wanted to do something besides diving as a career and was looking at a couple things. He found an Internet Café in Wolf Creek. I had No idea what he was talking about. He informed me that he could use the internet to communicate with his wife. He also had a digital camera (a What?!). A camera that he could take photos with, look at instantly and send to his wife over the internet. Oh, wow. That was pretty incredible.

Puppy Dog Eyes was a trusting soul. He left his camera by the dive radio when he went diving. That may not have been a wise thing to do. Especially because he would "download" all the photos he took during the day and send them to his wife over the internet without looking at them first. We didn't know that was what he did though. Hell, we didn't even know something like that was possible. Illinois and I, each having a little devil residing on our shoulders, took some photos that were **not** appropriate for mixed company. They surely were not G-rated. Remember my Kissy-Lips tattoo? Well, all I can say is that Puppy Dog Eyes' wife knows what it looks like too.

One afternoon, Illinois and I followed Puppy Dog Eyes into the internet café. They served coffee, sandwiches, soup, and soft-serve ice cream. Yumm! They also made Milkshakes and Malts using powdered malt. Oh Yeah. I knew where my first stop would be every night after shift for the rest of the job. Usually we messed around a bit, had dinner, and ended up at the Oasis – the local bar. We also drank with the Cowboy on a regular basis at his home in the little community.

The main bartender at the Oasis was married to one of the dam operators. She was a real hoot. Every time we entered the bar she would yell "Here come the Dam Divers to have a Dam Drink in the Dam Bar served by the Dam Barmaid one more Dam Time!" She put "Dam" in front of every noun she could – Dam husband, Dam job, Dam you name it. You get what I mean. I had heard this kind of thing many times in most of the little towns with a dam nearby, but she was definitely over the top. It reminded me of Hungry Horse, Montana which referred to itself as "The best little Dam Town in the West!" Fun times. I'm not sure Illinois appreciated the western humor.

Another of the bartenders was a very large woman. She was tall and well-fed. She was quite intimidating and there were never any issues in the bar while she was around. Once in a while, locals would come into the bar, have a drink or two then try to start trouble, especially when new guys were in the bar. I had worked at Holter dam several times before so I knew these people and they knew me. I was not really a local, but I was not a new guy either. If anybody even thought about giving me or anyone on my crew a bad time, this barmaid would step in and take care of business before **anything** happened. They had a pool table in there. We drank a lot of beer and played a little pool. We loved that place and they loved us, or at least the money we spent there!

This little crew became quite cohesive. We worked really well together and ended up doing quite a few projects around Montana, and sometimes the other states, together. Puppy Dog Eyes had thought he might want to be a police officer, so he was working towards that. One Monday, he showed up and told us about a ride-along he had done over the weekend. He had gone out on a domestic abuse call. He said it was the scariest thing he had ever been through. There was lots of screaming and yelling, things being thrown and someone was shooting at the officers. He decided that weekend that he didn't want to be a cop. Instead, he had applied to the University of Washington. Because of that, after this job, he didn't work with us as much as he used to.

Illinois and I got along really well and he liked Montana, so we started working together quite a bit. His personality was a little in your face, but I liked him a lot and I thought his personality was fine. If you can't take a little shit, or put up with a type-A personality, maybe you shouldn't be in the dive industry. If you can't handle somebody yelling and screaming at you, you definitely should not be in the dive industry, especially in the Gulf of Mexico. I didn't yell and scream – unless something or someone really pissed me off – but that took quite a lot. I am a pretty patient and calm individual. I have a really long, slow-burning fuse.

We finished this job before Hallowe'en. We were home for the holidays this year. I worked on a few more little jobs in Montana before Christmas and a couple in Washington state and Idaho.

*   *   *

On the first of December I got sent to do an inspection on Lower Granite Dam. Norwesco had a contract for a major job putting in a swing gate on the southern-most spill gate as part of the fish collection system. That job would start in January. I made the dive and took some measurements for the placement of a concrete pad that the swing gate would rest on when it was not in position at the spill gate.

The first Thursday in January of two-thousand-and-one, I got a call from the owner of Norwesco. He said there was an emergency job to do in Las Vegas. We would be flying out that night and work until the job was complete. We would work twelve-hour days. There would be lots of overtime. The customer was putting us up in a hotel and paying for all our food. It sounded like a really good deal. The only issue was I had to be ready to go and at the airport within a couple hours. I could do that.

I met Duck Fart and another regular from Norwesco at the airport. The other regular was the bosses favorite guy and supervisor. He and I worked together okay. Anyway, he had already dealt with the airline getting what dive gear that we were taking with us loaded. We would be diving off of K-bottles supplied by the customer. We were taking minimal equipment as it was pretty expensive to fly it down to Las Vegas for a two or three-day job. Everybody was hoping it would only be a two or three-day job except for me and Duck Fart. We were hoping it would last at least through Sunday. We wanted all the overtime we could get.

We were met at the airport by an employee of the customer. He had a rig that we could load all our dive gear into. It was late already, so we just planned on diving first thing in the morning. What was the job? Well, a new casino was being built in Las Vegas. New casinos were popping up like weeds in Las Vegas at this time.

This casino was going to be called "The Venetian" or something like that. It was going to have canals with gondolas and gondoliers and everything Italian. They were hoping for a spring opening. Really?! They hadn't even started on the main building yet! True, but construction happened fast, really fast, in Las Vegas. And Time was Money.

I still didn't know what the job was. Why did a casino need divers to help in the construction? The answer was; they didn't. Not until an employee had gotten in a rush dredging out a canal and poked a hole in the bottom of the work barge did they need divers. I didn't see the need for divers even then. I mean, you could unload the barge, get it in the dry, make the repair, put it back in the water, load it back up again, and you were ready to go.

No, no, no. That takes way too much time and if we leave the barge in the water, we can keep our crew working while you guys are making the repairs. Time is money you know. Yeah, so you keep saying. We were to jump our diver, find the leak and weld a plate on or whatever we needed to do to make a semi-permanent repair. Easy-peasy.

We got up bright and early Friday morning. We grabbed breakfast at the hotel lobby and headed to the jobsite. The supervisor dove first and found the hole. It was a horizontal slit puncture made by one of the teeth on the back hoe. He said it looked like a plate welded over the puncture would take care of it. The steel around the puncture was pretty flat and appeared to be in good shape, just rusty. We would have to clean it real well to make the welds.

I was thinking to myself that this would have been a perfect job for Kalispel. I don't know why he wasn't here. Duck Fart was a good welder too, though. Neither the supervisor nor I were real good, but we could stick two pieces of metal together. I could clean and prep steel for welding like nobody's business though. Heh, heh.

Each of us dove each day. We spent the first day-and-a-half cleaning and prepping the area for the welding. The last half of the second day, Duck Fart started welding. This was Saturday. We would definitely be working on Sunday. That made me and Duck Fart happy. I don't think the supervisor was too upset about it either.

We were working out of a little aluminum skiff. We had two K-bottles laid down on either side of the skiff. Both the main and the standby hose were in the skiff. We all wore our drysuits the whole time. There was no place for us to change and there was no room on the barge for us to set up our dive station. It was kind of a pain. But we weren't complaining. The money was too good.

The customer's crew kept working. They did a pretty good job of watching out for us and staying out of our way. We also did our best to stay out of their way. The customer did **not** want anything else to interfere with the progress of their building the casino.

We finished the job Sunday afternoon. The steel patch plate had been welded on and checked for leaks. There weren't any. The customer was happy with our work. They had already made the plane reservations for us early the next morning. We barely had time to get cleaned up and packed up before we were on a plane headed home. Talk about a Wham Bam Thank You, Ma'am! We didn't even have a chance to see anything in Vegas.

Not even any of those all you can eat buffets! Oh well. The job had been interesting and the pay was outstanding. Who was I to complain?

*   *   *

In mid-January, I started on the Lower Granite job. It was a huge job. Boston, the Rancher and a couple other regulars had been busy setting up several barges – at least three – that would be involved in different aspects of the job all going on at once. Blanchard had started working with a different dive company. He would be missed on this project. This was to be the finalization of the fish collection and guidance system on the upstream side of the dam. We had been working on this project for several years.

They needed several dive supervisors and lots of divers. They asked me to run one of the barges. I told them I would be happy to do it. The barge I was to be in charge of would be setting up and building the footing pad for a big swing gate that could flip in front of the southern-most spill gate and channel the fish over the dam, somehow increasing their survival rate. Basically, my dive crew would be responsible for building a concrete pad on the river bottom.

That sounded pretty up front and simple. The big issue was the depth. The river bottom was sloped where the pad was supposed to go. That in itself was not a huge issue. What *was* the issue was that the deepest depth was one-hundred-thirty-eight feet. Wonderful. *The* worst USN decompression schedule. We would be diving Sur-D-O2, which meant we could dive longer and the divers would do most of their decompression in a Deck Decompression Chamber breathing Oxygen. It was a little healthier and much safer than in-water decompression. There were still a few in-water decompression stops, but the majority of the decompression would be done in the dry in a tank on the surface. It was much easier to control the decompression this way.

My part of the job was to start towards the end of January and go through March and maybe into April, but hopefully not. If all went well, my crew would be done in mid to late August. When I got to the jobsite, my barge was mostly set up. Dive control was inside a Conex box. The DDC was under a wooden shack. There was another Conex where the diver's personal gear could be stored and also used as a change room for the divers. I had the proper compressor for the depth, a rack of K-bottles filled with air for standby air and another rack of K-bottles filled with Oxygen for decompression. Inside the dive shack I also had a bottle of fifty-fifty Nitrox. That would be great for my divers' in-water stops of less than seventy feet. Everything was looking good.

The only thing wrong with this job that I could tell so far was that Big Load was the Superintendent. I think Blanchard might have left because our boss was using Big Load more and more. There had been several incidents on jobs that he ran, and some of us didn't like working with him. At least he would be on the dam or in the office mostly. Hopefully I wouldn't have to deal with him much. Yeah, hmm.

I got everything set up on the barge the way I liked it. Kalispel would be helping me out like an assistant supervisor. He would run the dives and fill out the dive logs when I was diving and decompressing in the chamber. On this project we were diving to one-hundred-thirty-eight feet. Add three feet for the safety factor and we were at one-hundred-forty-one feet. That puts us on a hundred-and-fifty-foot decompression schedule. I didn't like to Zee my divers out.

The USN decompression schedule uses letter designations to determine where a diver is gas-load wise for re-pet dives after completing a dive. "Gas load" is how much extra Nitrogen is in the blood and body tissues of a diver under pressure. The next designation after Zee is "Extreme Exposure." That was back then, now a Zee diver is considered extreme exposure. I liked my divers to be an "O" when they left bottom. You know, O for Optimum. Smiles.

For this project, I planned the dives on the bottom to be run on the hundred-and-fifty-foot schedule. To leave bottom as an O diver, I could let them have a fifty-minute bottom time. Subtract my five-minute safety margin and that left a bottom time of forty-five minutes. The first water stop would be at fifty feet, followed by stops at forty and thirty feet. The total in-water decompression with travel time would be just over seventeen minutes. I would have them on the fifty-fifty nitrox while they were doing their in-water deco to help them off-gas better. All that, I did, to reduce the chances of my divers getting bent. I explained all this to Kalispel so he would understand what I was doing and why. There was more to being a good supervisor than just reading numbers out of a book and putting them on paper.

As always, the boss didn't want to pay overtime. I would be going through a lot of divers. Like on the job I had done at Wanapum, he had my divers start at different times. For this job, we would be working ten hours a day, six days a week. Supervisors, like me, and select crew, like Kalispel would get to work the full hours. It was really good money for us. We got both depth pay *and* overtime pay. Some of the divers referred to my barge as the "Lotto Barge." Ha! On the other hand, the run-of-the-mill divers that had been hired to fill in as needed only worked eight-hour days and only worked on Saturdays if more than the regulars were needed. It was a scheduling head-ache.

We guided a clam bucket on a crane to remove the soft mud

and debris from the pad site. We laid out the edge of the concrete platform with marking posts and rope. We guided in buckets of gravel that we used to level the bottom. We guided a big tamper that pounded down the gravel before pouring the concrete to help reduce the settling. We built and set up the concrete forms. We guided the tremie hose used to pump the concrete into the form. All this was done without any hyperbaric issues on my barge.

I think we were three or four weeks into the job when I saw a lot of frantic activity on the barge up against the dam. I'm not sure exactly what the scope of their job was. It had something to do with attaching the actual swing gate to the dam. They were using hydraulic and pneumatic tools. What I saw was the Mouth drag a guy out of the Dive Control Conex and stuff him into the DDC. This guy was about twice as big as the Mouth, but the Mouth was moving him around like nothing. Lots of the other hands were running all over the deck like a bunch of ants that had just had their ant hill disturbed.

I kept an eye on them and an ear on the radio in case they needed anything. I heard over the radio that the big guy had just completed his dive and was running the radio for this dive when he started having trouble breathing. The Mouth saw he was in distress and put him in the DDC to recompress him and minimize the problem. Normally you would press a diver in this situation to the point of relief -usually around fifty or sixty feet.

Above sixty feet was always optimal because you could treat the distressed diver with pure oxygen. Below sixty feet, oxygen becomes toxic to the human body. Big Load told the Mouth to press the patient down to one-hundred-sixty-five feet. I thought that was the wrong thing to do, because first of all no one knew what the issue was. Secondly, this diver was working at a hundred feet. He didn't need to be pressed below that for relief. The deeper you press a diver, the longer and more difficult it is to decompress them.

A doctor had to be called to check this guy out. He needed to be a Hyperbaric doctor, and the closest ones I knew of worked at Virginia Mason Hospital in Seattle – three hundred miles away. It would take at least five hours to drive. Hopefully they could helicopter him in or something. I don't know where the doctor actually came from, but he was not prepared to get into a DDC. He had all the equipment he needed to do the initial assessment, but he did *not* want to get pressed in. I saw them arguing about it from my vantage point and heard little tidbits over the radio.

Finally, the doctor went in. The big guy was diagnosed with a Pneumothorax – a tear in the lung tissue resulting in a gas bubble in his pleural cavity – that is the space between his lungs and his ribs. What had happened was that the bubble went up to his neck and had started choking him as it expanded. That was a horrible situation and I was glad it didn't happen on my barge.

I talked to the supervisor on that barge about how they were running their dives. I was informed that they were Zee-ing their divers out every time. I told them what I thought of that and was told that is what Big Load had told them to do. Stupid.

The big guy was decompressed on a Table Six – one of the longest decompression schedules used. He was told he couldn't dive for at least two weeks. His lung would heal faster – it is one of the fastest healing tissues in the body – but it was normal practice for a diver to take a two week break after any type of hyperbaric incident. If I were him, I would have seriously considered getting out of diving. He didn't really have the physique for it anyway.

That incident was kind of a wake-up call for the divers and supervisors. It should have been for Big Load too, but I don't think he really cared about the well-being of the crew. He was all about numbers and profits and stuff like that.

Anyway, that barge got another diver and things on the job

went back to normal. All my guys were happy that we weren't having any issues on our barge. Several weeks later, Big Load called me into the job shack. He called Kalispel in along with me. I had no idea what it was about. We were making good progress; right on schedule, maybe even a little ahead of it. Nobody was getting hurt or had any issues that I knew of. What could it be?

Kalispel and I went up to the job shack and walked in. He was waiting for us. Right off the bat he asked what I wanted another bottle of fifty-fifty Nitrox for. Oh, yeah, I had just asked for another bottle.

The one I had been using was getting low and I needed a refill. I explained that to him. He glared at me and said that fifty-fifty was for emergencies only. Emergencies? What was he talking about? Emergencies like what had happened with the big guy? Nitrox would not have helped him at all after the fact. He probably should have been doing his in-water stops on it in the first place. Maybe he wouldn't have had the issue if that had been the practice.

Next, Big Load handed me a stack of dive logs. I looked at them and they were all from my barge. He asked if I saw any issues with any of them. I looked them over and responded that, no, everything looked fine.

"Fine?!" He yelled, "What do you mean 'Fine'? Your bottom times are *way* short! You have been under diving *all* your divers and now I find out you've been wasting Nitrox during the decompression of your divers!"

I looked at Kalispel and back at Big Load. I explained to him how I ran my dives and why. I looked to Kalispel for back-up. He looked gob-smacked and didn't say anything one way or the other. I thought he would at least back me up, but he didn't. If he had disagreed with me before, he could have let me know and we could have talked about it. As far as I knew, Kalispel liked how I ran the dives. He had been saying how much better he felt after decompressing on my schedule versus how he had felt when Big Load ran his dives. He didn't say any of that here in the job shack.

Big Load told me I needed to change the way I was running the decompression. He also told me that my deepest depth had been one-hundred-thirty-eight feet, so I should have run that on a one-forty table rather than the one-fifty that I had used. He said he would get me another bottle of Nitrox, but I was expressly forbidden to use it. Are you *Kidding* me?! Why have the Nitrox at all if I can't use it?

I explained again to Big Load why I ran the dive times like I did. I also pointed out that there had been zero hyperbaric issues on my barge. No one was complaining of aches and pains and nobody was getting sick. I thought my record spoke for itself. Kalispel just stood in the corner not saying anything. Big Load just ignored him more or less.

Big Load shook his head. He was angry. He told me I had been costing the company too much money. I was going through divers too fast, using Nitrox, and god knows what else. Things had to change he said. If I wanted to continue working on this job, I would have to run the dive times like he did. I replied that Zee-ing out the divers was not the proper thing to do. He reiterated that it was in the USN dive manual like that and there were no express dangers of running the table out to the end. If it wasn't meant to be done that way, the navy wouldn't have published the tables with those numbers in them.

I shook my head more. Those numbers and schedules were written like that to help you out and give you more information in case you ran into problems. They were not there so you could "run them out to the end." He looked at me and gave me an ultimatum. "Run the dives my way, or hit the highway."

I told him I would continue to run the dives like I had in the past. I was not about to endanger my divers to save him and the company a buck or two. How much did that little incident with the big guy end up costing? None of my business? I'm sure it was considerably more than a bottle of Nitrox and five minutes of dive time shaved off each dive. Whatever. I couldn't get through to this guy. That was one of the main reasons I didn't like working with him in the first place. He never listened to reason or to any other diver's input. Or maybe he did, just not mine.

He told me that if I wasn't going to change the way I ran the dives, then I didn't need to come into work the next day. This was a Saturday, so I told him tomorrow was Sunday and nobody was coming into work. He snarled and said don't bother coming back on Monday. He told me he already had another supervisor to take my place. Excellent, I replied. I hoped no other divers would get hurt on this job. Not for his sake but for the sake of the divers.

I walked out of the job shack and back to my barge. When I got there, I packed up all my gear and loaded it into one of the skiffs. I had one of the tenders drive me to the beach and I moved everything from the boat to my truck. The divers on my barge asked what was going on. I told them that Big Load and I didn't see eye to eye and he was removing me from the job. He didn't even want me to finish out the day. Too much overtime, I guess. Hah! If I had thought about it more, I might have shown Big Load the Kissy-Lips on my ass, but I didn't.

When I got home, my wife said the boss had called and he wanted me to call him back. It was late and I didn't want to talk to him. I told her I would call the office on Monday morning. Sunday morning I got up and went for a Motorcycle ride. It was the first weekend in March, so it was a brisk ride, but it still felt good. That was my spiritual renewal and release. I really needed to clear my head. I don't think I will work for that company any more. The Texan's wife didn't want me to anyway. The only reason I did was because the money was good and I didn't get enough work from the other companies yet. I could afford to take six months off if I wanted to, though. Maybe I should go back down to Brasil for a while.

Sunday afternoon the owner of Norwesco called me and said I was needed for work in Montana; Great Falls to be exact. The spring work there was starting and he needed someone to run some jobs over there. I told him I would get down to the shop and get the truck. He told me it was already loaded up and ready to go. All I needed to do was pick it up and drive it to Great Falls. Okay, I told him I would be at the shop as soon as I could get there.

I spent a few weeks doing that stuff in Montana. I worked with Puppy Dog Eyes and Hope for those couple of weeks. The work was fun and I enjoyed the crew I was working with. I was really tired of working with Norwesco though. In fact, this was the last time I would work for them. I think they changed their name over the summer. Norwesco had a bad mark on their safety record after the Deer Island incident. A name change would give them a clean safety record. I know that is a rotten deal, but that's how it works. I never worked for them after the name change. I heard that Big Load and his wife now had controlling interest in the "new company" and the *last* thing in the world I wanted to do was work for him. I would move on up to bigger and better things.

*   *   *

The rest of the summer I worked for a couple other dive companies. The company I worked for the most was the one owned by the guy in Bellevue who ran the company out of his garage. I worked mostly with the Marine and Duck Fart on those projects. We worked all around Puget Sound and western Washington. Some of my favorite jobs we did were in the San Juan Islands. Visibility on those jobs was usually very good. We could see all kinds of sea life when we were working in the north sound. The very large purple and orange Sea Urchins were all over the place. Lots of little Green Sea Urchins were crawling all over too. We saw all different kinds of Sea Stars and Brittle Stars. There were Nudibranchs, Sea Cucumbers and even the occasional Octopus. Of course there were lots of huge white and orange Sea Anemones and Sea Pens . It was almost more like diving in a giant aquarium than work sometimes. I loved it and every day I was reminded why I had gotten into diving in the first place.

People go into Commercial Diving for all sorts of reasons. A lot of them used to get weeded out right off the bat in dive school. That doesn't happen so much anymore. Money – perceived salary no matter how inaccurate, is a big draw initially. Travel is a huge draw and one of the main reasons I got into it. Diving seems dangerous and adventurous which attracts a lot of adrenalin junkies – I am probably one of those too. The desire to work outdoors rather than in an office is a big draw also. Even just being around the oceans – a lot of people are attracted to that; I know I was.

Once we get into the industry and discover what it all entails, many people may wonder "What the Fuck did I get myself into?" and those people usually quit after a little while and go into something else. Others of us – like me – think "Oh My Gawd! This is amazing!" for the most part. Sure there are times when it is not so great, but for those of us who choose to make a career out of it the work is nothing short of fantastic most of the time. We wouldn't stay in it if we didn't think so. Overall I know I made the right decision from the first moment I went underwater with a SCUBA bottle on my back many years ago. I couldn't imagine doing anything else with my life – except, perhaps finding a way to get paid to ride my Motorcycle all over the world. Big Smiles.

*　　*　　*

The End

Or is it?

ACKNOWLEGEMENTS

I would like to thank my parents for bringing me into this world. Without them, obviously, I wouldn't be here. Hey Pop I'm sorry for all the shit I put you through.

I would like to thank Walt Disney, Jacques Cousteau, and **ALL** the people involved in their productions for television and the movies that turned me on to life under the sea.

I would like to thank Rachel Carson for her books (The Sea Around Us, et al) on marine biology and oceanography that helped me understand the ocean systems and how they affect the planet earth.

I would like to thank Terry Walker, my SCUBA instructor from 1978, for introducing me to the wonderful wet world under the waves.

I would like to thank Maurice P. Talbot for teaching me how to get started in the Commercial Dive industry. Also, thanks to his wife for the delicious meals she prepared and let me share with her and Maurice while I was enrolled at Highline Community College.

I would like to thank Marty Fortney for all his help with the editing of this book.

I would like to thank my good friend Joel for his illustrations.

I would like to thank my wife, Cindy Lou, for putting up with me and my diving career – among other things – and supporting me the whole way. She has been instrumental in the help she has provided that allows me to write and publish my stories.

ABOUT THE AUTHOR

Sam Humphrey

Sam lives in Helena, Montana with his lovely and hard-working wife, Cindy, and their two cats, Spook and Boo. He still loves Motorcycles and hopes to get back in the Wind. He spends his time reading, writing, doing craft projects and puzzles. He enjoys a good game of Backgammon or Chess when he can find someone who wants to play.

Sam first became interested in writing when he was in fifth grade, but didn't write much until his sixth grade English teacher introduced her class to Creative Writing. In eighth grade he took a class in Creative Writing with a very supportive teacher and the seed was planted. He also took a Creative Writing class at Highline Community College his first year there while he was waiting to get into the Underseas Technology program. His writing was constantly corrected and censored by his mother and both his grandmothers who were all English teachers. He kept on writing despite their editorial influences on his efforts.

ABOUT THE ILLUSTRATOR

Joel P Rabe

Joel is a self-taught artist who developed the basics of art through the public school system with additional education at the college level in Commercial Art. Growing up in the Pacific Northwest and Alaska has inspired him to capture the outdoor lifestyle through his artistic endeavors. Expressing himself through humor has always been in his nature. He tends to lean toward cartooning, but realism is a close second in his artistic style. His preferred mediums are Pen & Ink, Pencil & Water Color, and Carving; although he works in many other mediums as well. Joel's artwork has been featured in **The Spokesman Review** and **Liberty Lake Splash** newspapers and featured on the cover of the **Spokane Coeur D' Alene Living** magazine. He has also been featured on television. He ran a successful art business – Davinci Painting – from 2002 to 2016; working in both residential and commercial sectors. His work included, but was not limited to, design, faux finishes, murals, sculpting and carving. He believes "We should use our creative gifts to make a difference. Art should evoke positive emotion."

WET PAY

Stories and more stories from my career as a Commercial Diver. I travelled all over the globe to work underwater and work on tunneling projects.

Wet Pay

Stories from my career as a Commercial Diver. I travelled all over the western United States to work underwater.

Drying Out

More stories from my Career as a Commercial Diver. I travelled all over the globe to work underwater and work on tunneling projects

BOOKS BY THIS AUTHOR

What The Hell Happened To Me?!

Look for
WET PAY Volume Two
coming soon!

Including Chapters such as:

Travelling Man

Fish Out of Water

Back in the Water

Hurricanes
Good for Divers, Bad for Everyone Else

Dessication

and More!

Travelling Man
Chapter One

I spent the early part of the following summer (two-thousand-and-one) working on a month-long job repairing pilings under the Seattle ferry docks with the company based out of the Bellevue guys garage. Duck Fart joined me on that job. The Marine was the main Supervisor and I was the assistant supervisor. We had another tender that worked with us rounding out a four-man crew. There was a lot of diving to do, so we needed three strong divers. Duck Fart had turned into a really good diver and worker.

I made a practice of carrying around a set of Dive Safety Manuals and Emergency Procedures. We were doing a lot of jobs for government

Printed in Great Britain
by Amazon

48200952R00219